PRAISE FOR

MUSALAHEEN

"*Musalaheen* is the kind of book that needs to be in every civics class to waken Americans who have mistaken the news for knowledge, and in every mental health center that tries to help veterans recover from what they have been through. Seemingly quiet in approach, it possesses intense gravity, the brutality of truth, and even beauty in the urgency of its howl. I felt the need to read."

—David S. Atkinson, author of
Apocalypse All the Time and *Not Quite So Stories*

"Arment's unyielding cadence is candid and addictive. *Musalaheen* illuminates the human costs of endless war recounted by an important, rising literary voice—and everyone should read it."

—Dorothy Bendel,
Managing Editor of *Atticus Review*

"Narrated with raw and unwavering grit, *Musalaheen* blurs the distinction between the heroes and the terrorists, the innocent and the condemned, the 'us' and the 'them.' Jason Arment is a masterful storyteller whose stunning debut memoir will haunt you eternally."

—Melissa Grunow, author of
Realizing River City and *I Don't Belong Here*

"In words that are simple yet lyrical, *Musalaheen* deftly captures a Marine grunt's experiences in American-occupied Iràq and concludes with their heartbreaking aftermath in America's heartland. Author Jason Arment spares no one in the interlocking episodes of this shocking war memoir— least of all himself. *Musalaheen* should be required reading for any president who contemplates committing idealistic young Americans to another 'war of choice.'"

—Paul Guernsey, author of *American Ghost*

"*Musalaheen* is not an easy read on a visceral level but definitely a damning and graceful firsthand account on a subject I'm ignorant of besides what I've read in the media and from ex-soldiers putting themselves out there as patriotic heroes; which is always hard for me to swallow with good conscious. Arment destroys the American war hero archetype in his memoir through candid reflection, which is why I love it."

—Jay Halsey

"*Musalaheen* is that rare book I found so compelling I looked forward to the next time I could read more. An absorbing, relatable, and very human look at war, military service, and how peril and tedium work together to pull a person apart. This isn't a tale of some super-man, but of a guy looking for his place in the world, and how he found himself after he found it. Thoroughly recommended."

—David W Jones, government employee

"[The chapter entitled 'White Whale'] manages the feat of conveying the odd blend of fear and extreme tedium that characterizes much of the war experience but does so within the context of a highly compelling narrative, packed with sharply observed, surreal details and a gift for capturing the in-the-moment fears, hopes, and daydreams of the average Marine."

—Phil Klay, author of *Redeployment*

"Jason Arment taught himself to shave with a straight razor, enduring weeks of bloody cheeks before perfecting that skill set. In this age of oversimplification and acronyms, he's long been dedicated to an extremely demanding form of calligraphy, requiring extreme attention to the manual aspects of penmanship. Deliberately following the course of most challenges, ever-mindful of the laziness of taking the easy way out, is a part of his constitution on life's battlefield. Accordingly, with this book, Arment has made the horrible experience of war, and its sick psychological aftermath, powerfully relevant to all his readers' lives, in the voice of a charred songbird. This writing is so good it hurts."

—Zack Kopp, Managing Editor of *Doggerel*,
Founding Editor of Magic Trash Press

"Each time I heard pieces from *Musalaheen* read aloud and read pieces published in various journals, I remain in a haunted state from each image snapshot conveyed. Arment has an ability to ambush his reader and catch them off guard with the brutal, often mundane life of living overseas during wartime. He attacks with a vulnerability that doesn't easily slip through the tough exterior of metal and camouflage. This is what makes Arment's writing a brutal soft spot we all believe we can run to for cover. The softness of secrets and strangers from a land far away are brought to their breaking point, showing Arment's experiences not from a cruel, desolate land, but a place of vulnerability. His words remain too powerful to come across as anything but striking and not easily forgotten."

—**Hillary Leftwich, author of**
Ghosts are Just Strangers Who Know How to Knock

"Jason Arment stands as the foundation of a house divided, a microcosm of modern America. His body is theirs: cleaved, marked, manipulated by a yearning to approach the definitions that have been beyond reproach. He's a peaceful man of violence, a patriot felled by fists of other patriots, an island of great patience and of none. In Arment, to borrow from George Bernard Shaw, is an authentic example of that troubled, hopeful nation."

—**Mathew Mackie,**
Editor-in-Chief of *The Big Smoke Australia*

"The scale is epic, but the flow is intimate and radically honest, untainted by jingoism or sentimentality. Arment's limber, propulsive prose works covert magic, making a hefty memoir march forward in a flash. The plot unfolds like a series of re-awakenings—a lucid dream that lands the civilian reader in a new country of understanding."

—**Melanie McGee Bianchi, Planet Zeus Media**

"Jason Arment's memoir is a book of confounded expectations and a vivid, detailed account of one Marine's tour of Iraq. Trained to engage in combat, a young machine gunner is deployed into the day-to-day grind of occupation in a bleak landscape where empathy can get a soldier killed. *Musalaheen* is a page-turner that will leave the reader with a lump in their throat. It's also a reminder that the war in Iraq hasn't ended but inhabits in every veteran who returns stateside. It manifests itself in ways that the civilian population will never understand."

—Daniel McGinn, author of
The Moon, My Lover, My Mother & the Dog

"With beautiful, careful language, and in painful detail, Jason Arment describes his first tour of duty in Iraq—the stultifying sameness, the explosive moments of startling violence, the rage and the pity, the steady hardening of a young soul. In the tradition of the warrior as witness, Arment writes down things we don't want to know. We cannot bear to see. We cannot look away. Read this memoir and vote."

—Jacquelyn Mitchard, author of
The Deep End of the Ocean

MUSALAHEEN

MUSALAHEEN

JASON ARMENT

A WAR MEMOIR

HELL PRESS
UNIVERSITY OF HELL PRESS

This book is published by University of Hell Press
www.universityofhellpress.com

© 2018 Jason Arment

Interior Design by Olivia M. Croom
oliviacroomdesign.com

Cover Design by Vince Norris
www.norrisportfolio.com

Cover and Title Page Illustration by Jon McKenzie
https://www.instagram.com/jonmckenzie/

Published in the United States of America
ISBN 978-1-938753-30-5

Dedicated to Austin Tice

CONTENTS

EVERY MAN A FORTRESS

I STOOD STIFF, HEELS TOUCHING, FEET SPREAD apart forty-five degrees, eyes straight ahead, hands clenched at my sides with thumbs pointing parallel to my inseam at the Position of Attention (POA). The second-story squad bay was filled with two parallel lines of sixty recruits. Mine mirrored the line opposite. All one hundred twenty of us had been standing at the POA for more than an hour waiting for our Drill Instructors (DIs) to show up with the Captain for an inspection.

I'd been sure to claim a rack of bunk beds in the middle of my line. I'd heard recruits in the middle received less attention than those on the ends, so when one hundred sixty recruits had flooded the squad bay the day before I'd headed for the center. The forty recruits who hadn't the initiative or courage to claim and hold a rack had been formed up, rank and file, at the front of the squad bay and marched back to those bays where recruits waited until training spots opened. No one had tried to take my rack from me.

Recruit Schnieder had come to both have a rack and be my rack mate when, walking with his face downcast, he looked at me with hopeful eyes and asked, "Can I share a rack with you?" I'd said "yes" and had to reiterate my choice of rack and rack mate to half a dozen larger recruits who'd tried to push Schnieder's short, fat, newly bald, and probably always pasty white body out of the way. We traded snippets about ourselves when the chaos allowed and found we'd both joined the Corps to make something of ourselves, serve our country, and shoot things. Schnieder wanted to be a Rifleman while I was already slated to be a Machine Gunner.

Before enlisting, Schnieder had been a degenerate living in his parents' basement. I'd enlisted eight months prior at seventeen and had just graduated from high school before shipping out. I told Schnieder how the Army Recruiter had blown off my appointment and when the Navy Recruiter asked me why I wanted to join I'd told him "to shoot things," so I'd been sent across the hall to the Marines. We were scared but determined. Neither of us had any intention of washing out. When we watched the rackless recruits being marched away he said thank you and meant it.

I slowly rocked my weight to the balls of my feet and then back onto my heels again to alleviate the pain in my lower back. When the Drill Instructors had left after putting the platoon at POA, they laughed and joked about how they'd come back to find a squad bay of recruits passed out face first on the concrete floor. Recruits swayed as if drunk on their feet. When knees lock, they cut off circulation, but when a recruit stood at the POA he needed to "lock his body." As new recruits, we hadn't figured out how to almost lock our knees or rhythmically tense and relax them to keep blood flowing.

Heads bobbed and weaved as things started to gray out. I relaxed my knees, not realizing I'd tensed them, hoping it wasn't too late to recover before passing out. If I fell, no one would move to help me. The DIs had been clear that if a recruit went down, no one was to help him up. They said not to help others throughout boot camp, to destroy our expectation of assistance. "Seek nothing outside of yourself," the well-built Korean DI said. Once every man became a fortress, we would be Marines.

The florescent tubes hummed overhead. Light became dizzy staccato flashes. I tried to motivate myself by thinking back to why I joined the Corps. My memory of that morning blurred into a kaleidoscope of images. The initial scene of a single smoking tower seared into my mind. I could still see a 747 glide into the second tower and erupt out the other side, a shotgun blast of fire, twisted rebar, and broken glass. Smoke pouring out of the first tower and wreathing the second. The way flailing figures spun as they plunged to the street, their descent tracked frantically by cameras. People running, screaming, as tidal waves of ash and debris flooded the surrounding avenues. They just fell, one after the other. First the bodies, then the towers.

I wondered if there had been trumpets that morning, as my teacher sat panicked and dumbfounded. From the doom on his face, my stomach had knotted in fear. My classmates and I stared at the television screens with blank expressions. The cyclical nature of the newscasts, hashing out and then rehashing what had happened with never-ending repetition. Images of first responders digging through rubble were replaced by the towers standing, just in time to watch them get slammed into by 747s and come tumbling down again. The narrative stopped being linear and became a jumble of destruction on screens I had to watch. The humming of fluorescent lights took the place of sirens and screaming as my teacher switched on subtitles. The same sound filling that day buzzed above me now, and the same scared looks and blank stares.

Silently, the door opened and Stahl stepped through. Silently, it closed again. "Look to your left and right," Stahl said.

The platoon looked.

"Some of the men to your right and left won't be here a year from now. Hell, some of them won't even be alive six months from now," Stahl said.

Staff Sergeant Stahl paced the length of the squad bay, his flashing Coraframs *click-clacking, click-clack* as he drove his heels into the floor. He told us about himself, how he was going to run the platoon with an iron fist while the First Hat was away bucking for promotion. Stahl was a "been there, done that" Marine. He came from the Old Corps, from when things had been much harder. He had also served in Iraq, leading a Mortar Section in combat operations and earning several decorations for their performance. Stahl had taken lives, rifled through dead insurgents' pockets for cigarettes and food. He had seen teenagers, their hair already gray, break down, shaking and sobbing as they begged not to be the first through the door this time. He had watched his men die, blood bubbling out of their nostrils as they screamed for their mothers. Stahl knew something we couldn't imagine—we weren't all going to make it.

4

"And some of you shouldn't be here!" Stahl shouted. "Take a look around and you'll see who they are. Schnieder wouldn't even have a rack if it wasn't for his rack mate telling a bunch of recruits twice his size to fuck off. You know what kind of recruits can't seize and hold a rack? Non-hackers."

Stahl explained that "non-hacker," like almost all military jargon, was not counterintuitive. Later in our careers as Marines, we would learn idioms and rhymes that seemed childish: "red means dead" to remind us if we could see the red dot below a pistol's safety then the safety was disengaged; "brass to the grass" to remind us to load ammunition into machine guns *always* with the shiny side of the brass rounds down and the black connecting links on top; "tap, rack, bang" to remind us of the correct immediate action of tapping the magazine, racking the bolt, and trying to fire again when our rifle misfired; "treat, never, keep, keep" to reduce the four weapons safety rules to something small and manageable. "Treat every weapon as if it were loaded. Never point your weapon at anything you do not intend to shoot, keep your weapon on safe until you intend to fire, and keep your finger safe and off the trigger until you are ready to fire," was easily remembered as "treat, never, keep, keep." Non-hacker was the first in a long list and the most self-explanatory.

Stahl explained it anyway.

"A non-hacker is someone who can't fucking hack it, good to go?" Stahl asked. He didn't look up to see if there were any questions. The platoon couldn't move or speak when at the POA.

"Recruiters, they don't go to combat and watch men die. They sit stateside and don't do shit, like the fleet dodgers they are. All they care about is numbers. So, some of you were recruited by men who knew you don't have what it takes."

Stahl's head whipped like he'd heard a sound. He stalked over to a short, fat recruit with freckles, a red nose, and red stubble on his head. The recruit looked straight ahead while Stahl stared at him, inches from his face.

"Your Recruiter was slumming when he picked you up," Stahl bellowed. "What the fuck did you do in the civilian world?"

The recruit didn't answer for a second, then spoke in a quavering voice.

"I—" the recruit started.

"This recruit!" Stahl screamed, his spittle speckling the recruit's face. "You no longer say 'I' do you understand? You will only say 'this recruit' when referring to yourself."

"This recruit—" he started again, voice cracking, "used to roller blade and hang out with his friends."

Stahl took off the hat DIs wore, the same kind worn by Smokey the Bear. Holding his hat in one hand, he ran the other down his face. When his hand fell, it revealed a mask of hate where Stahl's face had been. The sudden transformation could have been comical in the civilian world, only because it would have been safe to assume it jest. Stahl wasn't joking though. His face turned purple with rage, a hue I hadn't realized brown-skinned people could achieve. His right hand knotted into a fist, pointer finger extended at the second knuckle, which he slammed into the recruit's cheek.

"And you didn't think it might be important to lose some fucking weight for Marine Corps boot camp?"

Stahl asked, returning the hat to his head. "What did your friends say when you told them that you were going to join the Marine Corps?"

The recruit looked ready to shit himself.

"They told me not to," he said. "They told me I wouldn't make it."

"They were right! You are *disgusting*!" Stahl's body made a retching motion; his head swung down to slam the brim of his hat into the recruit's face.

The recruit started to cry.

"What did your dad say?" Stahl asked.

"My father killed himself when I was young—" the recruit started to explain, slipping back into the first person.

"Oh, you don't have a dad?" Stahl said, interrupting. "Well it makes sense he killed himself, doesn't it? I wouldn't want to be your dad either!"

The recruit wept openly. Stahl turned away in disgust and spat on the floor. His muscles bulged as he stalked between the two lines of recruits. His head swung back and forth, looking for certain ones. When he found them he'd stick his hand in their face, all his fingers and thumb pointing forward in what the Corps called a "knife hand," and asked them if they had a father. Every time the answer was no. Every time Stahl leaned back and brayed at the top of his lungs about what degenerates the recruits were, how no man would claim them as their children. When the recruit's race allowed, Stahl would say their father "ran back across the border," or "got lost, drunk on the reservation," or "their momma couldn't pick which one because it was dark." He broke them down, left them struggling against their sobs.

I was terrified. Stahl could pick out the bastard children. That wasn't in our Service Record Books which had transported our basic information—height, weight, hair color, religious preference—to boot camp. Stahl had only been able to observe the platoon for a few hours that day before the inspection. I wondered what kind of predatory instinct allowed him to feel out weakness. I realized I was dealing with someone very good at his profession, what he grimly referred to as "making Marines." But Stahl offered a lot of clichés and the next was something about "needing to break a few recruits to make an omelet." Stahl offered to fight any man in the platoon, said he'd take his rank off. He walked up to the largest recruit, a six-and-a-half-foot tall, three-hundred pound Texan with the last name Payne.

"What about you, corn-fed white boy?" Stahl asked, his voice a hoarse croak from smoking.

Payne stared ahead, "No, sir!"

"Had to think about it," Stahl said, stepping in close so his face stared up into Payne's. "You sure? Maybe it'll be like wrestling a steer?"

"Sir, no sir!" Payne's voice shook.

Stahl walked away and addressed the platoon, his heels *clacking*.

"That's goddamn right you don't!" he said, jabbing his finger in the air. "Gentlemen, welcome to boot camp. I make the rules here!"

Stahl had a group of "problem children" recruits; they weren't just pet projects, little toys he'd play with on the quarterdeck until he got bored or they broke. No, the problem children represented the fault lines in the platoon's granite foundation—the people who would

8

crack under pressure, who made mistakes not out of laziness, but ineptitude. Recruits who couldn't figure out how to get dressed quickly enough when the platoon woke, couldn't remember to use "Sir" at the start and finish of everything they said, who didn't understand making the entire platoon wait on them several times a day couldn't be justified with an excuse. Stahl hated them for it. Veins bulged in his neck and forehead as he screamed at them. Stahl barked diatribes-turned-psychoanalysis that probed the depths of the mind. Stahl examined recruits' foibles with the steady rhythm of an oncoming train, divining the gruesome future from their pupils.

Oou was one of them and so was Schnieder. Schnieder's carelessness struck early in the morning when he wanted to move slowly. He'd forget how his shower towel hung folded from his rack, or to shave. The more Schnieder messed up, the more Stahl rode him. The more mistakes he made, the more attention he got—to the point where I shared in the punishments because I shared a rack with him. Stahl told me that's how it went, that I needed to make up for the shortcomings of my brothers, and that I was failing not only the platoon, but Recruit Schnieder and myself.

"I'm sorry I've been fucking up a lot lately," Schnieder whispered to me after a particularly bad hazing session. "I'll do better, I promise. Just don't hate me. Stahl is trying to get everyone to hate me."

"You've got to get better," I replied.

Schnieder eventually stopped making incessant mistakes and life got easier for us. After he'd kept it up for a few days, he apologized to the whole platoon when we got turned to hygiene (released to shower). From then on, the platoon widely accepted him. Schnieder proved he could hack it. He'd walked through the fire; maybe not well, but well enough. Stahl even gave him a few kind words in passing. I could tell Schnieder's heart swelled with pride that he'd turned things around. When other recruits turned into problem children, Schnieder didn't hate them but accepted it as part of the process. But there was one problem child that tested all our patience collectively, even Schnieder's. I felt bad for Oou at first, because he was a nice enough guy.

"Things aren't so bad, guys, right?" Oou would say. "Pretty soon we'll graduate and boot camp will be over."

Oou didn't realize that after boot camp there would be war. No matter how many times Stahl showed him the dead in the papers and explained the similarities the dead Marines and Oou had in common, he didn't understand. Oou had a look of perpetual astonishment on his face. Always. No matter how many times he made the same mistake and the entire platoon got hazed for it, Oou was surprised. Stahl knew how to fix him. Before lights out, the platoon stood online in front of the bunks locked at attention. While we were waiting for taps to play over the loudspeakers, Stahl called Oou front and center. Stahl made him drink one canteen of water, then two. He had Oou refill the canteens and come back out in front of the platoon.

"No one gives a fuck about you, Oou," Stahl said. "Because you're weak, a non-hacker I couldn't wash out. I failed you, Oou. You shouldn't be here. And it's going to get you and the men around you killed."

Stahl turned to us, grin spilling across his dark face like milk.

"What do you think, 3111?" Stahl asked, addressing the platoon by its number. "If the rod should be spared, speak out."

My jaw set. I wasn't going to stick my neck out for Oou who had been fucking up at every opportunity. I'd been sucked into the mind games, made to hate him for his shortcomings when I should have tried to help him. I thought about how Oou kept letting us down, how push-ups bruised my palms. How he sat there looking like a child while the rest of us paid for hours. I knew Stahl would stop the punishment if someone spoke out, but I kept my mouth shut.

"Drink the other two," Stahl said. "While you jump up and down."

Oou made it halfway through the third canteen before he threw up— once, and then twice. Stahl made him keep drinking and jumping until the third canteen was empty and Oou bent over retching long tendrils of bile that hung from his lips.

"Should I have him roll in it?" Stahl asked. He looked at the platoon for a reaction.

The platoon didn't need to say anything. Stahl already knew the answer.

"3111, always too soft," Stahl said. "Well, Oou, I guess everyone likes paying for your mistakes."

BEFORE BEING SENT out into the world as full-fledged Marines, we'd had the boot camp version of a battalion meeting. The entire purpose of this meeting was to instill the idea in Marines that they should not do drugs on leave or get arrested. But especially no drugs. Several DIs took the stage in an auditorium and pleaded with everyone to "piss clean" at the School of Infantry (SOI). When we checked in to SOI it was explained that as many as half of us would be randomly selected to take a urinary analysis. The Marine Corps' zero tolerance policy toward illicit drug use made passing the test an imperative. If a Marine failed the test, he would be separated from the Corps.

* * *

THE FIRST THING I heard out of a Marine's mouth after leave was, "If I have to piss, it's going to be dirty."

"What did you smoke?" I asked. "And when?"

Schnieder had a sickly pallor and looked like he hadn't slept all leave. As a short, overweight, balding guy with the first signs of meth-mouth, he usually looked pretty bad—but now he looked terrible. I had no doubt he would be picked for a urine screening and so did he.

"I smoked meth last night," Schnieder said.

Sure enough, when the Marines formed up outside of the barracks, the first thing that happened was roll call for urinary analysis. My name was one of the first called and Schnieder's one of the last. We stood in line together, cups in hand, waiting our turn. I learned an important lesson that day: Marines were frequently men of extremes. Maybe the Corps owning Marines drove men to excess of drinking, drugs, and women, or maybe the kind of person who seeks out the profession of United States Marine is predisposed to immoderation. Schnieder had decided to go on a ten-day meth bender knowing that he was going to be tested and that if he failed it would ruin his life. This lesson didn't stop with our piss test.

I saw him in line later at the Post Exchange (PX) buying a pack of smokes and a cheesy lighter. I tried to get his attention. I wanted to ask him what he was going to do about the piss test, if there was any way to fight it. While we were waiting in line, cups of piss in hand, I'd had the idea that maybe he could blame it on an over-the-counter medication causing a false positive. Explaining away the results was a long shot, but I wanted Schnieder to make it. He had become a part of my Marine Corps experience and I was having a hard time imagining it without him.

Like a lot of guys trying to claw their way out of the gutter, Schnieder never imagined he'd be a Marine. He came from a life of meth and video games in his parents' basement. When Stahl had got me down, Schnieder cheered me up with his lopsided grin and easy humor. The first time hunger drove me to dumpster diving, Schnieder stood watch and I'd split it with him. When the San Diego skyline exploded with fireworks, we'd stand and watch from the squad bay; it made us feel better to know that the whole world wasn't boot camp. Something changed, though, and he started thinking about using again—talked about it with other junkies. When I waved to him from across the PX, he just looked at the ground and shuffled out the front door.

BETWEEN THE WEST BANK AND THE SEA

KNOWING WHERE YOU ARE IS SOMEHOW VERY important a long way from home. I'd never left for parts unknown before so when one of the senior Marines asked me to find a landmark in the dark I thought it was a fool's errand.

"Can you see the Eiffel Tower?"

I peered out the plane's window. "I can't tell," I answered.

"What do you mean you can't tell?" Sergeant Wood asked, his voice sharp.

I stepped back from the window and shrugged my shoulders at him. "It's nighttime, raining, and we're high off the ground," I said. "That's how."

The flight to Israel had been close to thirty hours with all the waiting around in airports. Echo Company, 2/24 Battalion was on its way to Israel to go through the Israeli Defense Force's (IDF) Counter Terrorism School and

14

play war games in the desert. The next four weeks would be my first Active Training (AT) period with the Marine Corps Reserves (MCR) and I was excited, as were the rest of the Marines. A brooding mood fell over Echo when the Company First Sergeant kicked off AT with a speech about how this needed to be taken deadly seriously, that we needed to study and take to heart every instruction given to us by the IDF Instructors because Echo had another deployment slated within the next eighteen months.

The veteran Marines of Echo shook their heads—how fleeting time seemed since they'd come off three months' leave after the last deployment—only six months ago. Most of them were "short timers" with contracts that expired shortly after returning to the United States once AT finished at the end of July 2006. A deployment slated within eighteen months made this AT the last chance for junior Marines to use senior Marines as mentors. The Sergeants in MachineGuns took this responsibility seriously—Woods, Johnson, Smith, Harris, Schaffer—men all in their late twenties or early thirties. But relations had strained between the junior enlisted and the senior men. I'd had plenty of time to think about it during the long journey across the Atlantic and Mediterranean. Trying to keep things civil, I smiled thin-lipped at Sergeant Woods. Neither of us wanted to start off the AT with bad attitudes. Ducking my head, I moved toward my seat across the aisle.

"I'm sorry," Woods said. He took a deep breath and let it out slowly. "I just wanted to see it is all. I don't want to be shitty this early in the AT."

I didn't respond. The veterans' tempers flashed like Stahl's had, but without his smile to distort seething rage.

I didn't want to risk Wood playing the Sergeant card and freaking out on a 747. He sat staring at his GPS as its alarm went off telling him that we flew over Paris just a few miles away from the Eiffel Tower. I knew more bothered him than not seeing a tower though. Nostalgia for careers gone by hovered near the edges of the veterans' thoughts. Back at Fort Des Moines, I'd heard Woods say he considered going to Iraq the coolest thing he'd ever done; meanwhile, a Marine who'd survived being shot in the head during their deployment tottered by, barely able to keep his balance, in the process of being medically separated from the Corps. When he couldn't look me in the eyes it was because he saw his own youthful reflection before war had burned naïveté out of him and the desert wizened his features, etching deep lines into his forehead, around his eyes, and at the corners of his frown. Woods wanted to get out of the Corps, but he didn't want to leave young men like me behind. He no longer wanted the burden but hesitated to shrug it off to the new joins, unsure of how well we'd bear it.

I sunk low in my seat. The six months since getting out of SOI had flown by. The fiery baptism spoken of at check-in never came to fruition. The units getting pounded on the front lines had instead used active-duty Marines to fill the spots left by the dead. Boot camp and SOI had made me late to the party; I enrolled last minute in classes at the local community college and found myself surrounded by barely post-pubescent eighteen- and nineteen-year-olds who wanted a college experience that was far more involved in drinking, drugs, and sex than learning.

My peers bored me. Unlike the Marines I'd lived and served with in boot camp and SOI, none of the community college kids cut in the lunch line, much less had the courage needed to take a hill under enemy fire. They scheduled their own classes, complained about waking up early, then slipped into absenteeism. Around campus I would see students in Reserve Officer Training Corps (ROTC) and other delayed-entry programs proudly walking around. I wondered how they could consider themselves part of something when they hadn't earned the title.

My perspective still carried with it the sheen of a newly minted Marine and I didn't stop to challenge my own visions. I saw combat as a grandiose proving ground, knowing nothing about what it really took to fight an attrition war with guerrilla forces. I hadn't yet broken up the war into two parts in my mind: the invasion and the occupation. To me it was all the same thing. The years, deserts, and violence blended together into a single mosaic spoken of vaguely in the Koran and Bible. I thought jihad was a religious struggle that bound Muslims in holy war forever with all those in opposition to Islam. My own intentions were equal parts war tourist, mercenary, and civic duty.

We disdained our civilian life because of its boredom while nurturing our sophomoric views of war—another reason Sergeant Woods couldn't bring himself to look at me or any other new Marine. Woods knew the Corps bred this in us, that the fearlessness of young military men came from stoic self-sacrifice for ideas not yet fully understood.

The plane touched down in Tel Aviv as the sun rose. Marines loaded onto buses. IDF troops escorted us to a secret base within sight of towns flying Palestinian flags in the West Bank.

* * *

HEAT CAME OFF the asphalt in waves, distorting the air. When we left the United States, I'd thought myself ready for the desert but had no idea. The southern California desert seemed like a trip to the pool compared to the kiln-like conditions in Israel. I stood in line waiting my turn to run another drill while the three Counter Terrorism Instructors watched. Uday, Gal, and Thom took turns policing the drill in which Marines practiced sprinting to a downed enemy combatant and shooting them in the head. The IDF Standard Operating Procedure dictated that any and all terrorist threats must be neutralized immediately. A wounded enemy could still call out locations of friendlies, operate their weapon system, or detonate a suicide vest. The IDF's Counter Terrorism Instructors insisted that all enemy threats or possible enemy threats be terminated without regard for their medical condition.

"Who will tell the parents of dead Marines that you were just looking out for an injured enemy?" Thom asked as he watched Marines run the drill again and again.

Thom, at twenty, was the youngest and most junior in rank of the three instructors. He never seemed to need a break, always moving to correct a Marine's stance or posture, sandy blond hair bleached by the sun. The second in command, Gal, seemed to be two people: an easygoing, short, wiry man with a genuine smile when he wasn't instructing and an ultra-professional special forces trainer with laser-like intensity whenever he stepped in front of the group. Uday had shorter hair than most of the IDF, looking more mature than his age of twenty-two due to a receding hairline and white bristles in his beard. He headed the Counter Terrorism Unit and led instruction at the Counter Terrorism School (CTS). All of them had beards, the norm in the Israeli military because of their religion, which stood in stark contrast to our clean-shaven faces.

Although everyone in the IDF was close to my age, their eyes glinted with a mettle that made mine look soft like a child's. The constant threat of violence from the ongoing conflict with the Palestinians put them under immense pressure. The women in the IDF challenged my conceptions of what it meant to be a warrior. Most of them served as snipers, a highly technical job requiring great endurance. In all arms of the U.S. Military, women weren't allowed to fill combat roles, dogma deeming them too physically and emotionally weak. Not only were the Israeli women in very direct combat roles, their beauty struck me dumb. At nineteen, I hadn't the life experience to smile and chat easily with them like some of the senior enlisted Marines.

"You want to sleep because it's hot?" Thom screamed.

I looked up from daydreaming about IDF women to see Thom in front of me instead of the next person in line. It was my turn to run the drill and I'd dropped the ball. Without waiting for an answer, Thom stepped forward and booted me in the chest as hard as he could. The armor plate in the front of my flak jacket absorbed the blow and I hopped back a few feet instead of crumpling to the deck. I recovered and pantomimed shooting a silhouette target set up twenty meters away, then rushed forward to plant the butt of my rifle in what would have been its gut and pretended to shoot it in the head when it hit the ground.

"Faster! Faster! Faster!" Thom screamed.

The drill wasn't tactical, only meant to build aggression and confidence. Since arriving, Echo had spent every waking moment running drills on the ranges under the watchful eyes of IDF instructors. When Marines had arrived at the camp and dismounted the buses, Uday had been waiting for us.

"Who among you has fought in Iraq?" Uday asked.

Three-fourths of Echo Company's Marines raised their hands.

"I am honored," Uday said and it sounded like he meant it. "But it will be important for you to listen to the instructors. Our war is constant. When the instructors leave here they take their weapons. They're never off duty. The enemy could strike at any moment. We must always be ready because war is part of our everyday life. We struggle to survive."

The instructors bore down on us from the beginning. Twelve hours at the range on the sweltering gun line firing thousands of rounds, working our rifles as if searching for their weaknesses. Our style of gun slinging differed from theirs in that the Marine maxim "slow is smooth, smooth is fast" made us measure our steps and slow our breathing before aiming controlled bursts of fire. The IDF wanted a hailstorm of bullets, as much fire as our fingers could muster so that the enemy never had a chance to peek around the corner. Marines teach Close Quarters Battle techniques as a kind of knock-down, drag-out fight that goes house-to-house, street-to-street. The IDF wanted us to think of it as a battle with our eyes instead of bare-knuckle boxing. Whoever saw the other first in a gunfight could shoot first. Not all of their doctrine was so readily accepted.

"When you are firing around a corner and need to reload, don't duck back," Thom said. "Bring your weapon up in your line of sight so you can see the reload while watching the enemy."

"What if you take fire?" Prockop asked. "The bullets that hit the wall will spray shrapnel in your face."

"What if? What if?" Thom pointed at Prockop. "If you want one hundred percent, you sit at home on the couch. In combat, there is no one hundred percent!"

Prockop moved to the back of the group of Marines running drills. Sergeant Woods followed him. I watched, not caring if I got caught eavesdropping. Prockop had deployed with the unit but came back still a Lance Corporal. A few other Marines in Weapons Platoon had come back Lances because of poor physical training scores, failure to complete Marine Corps Institute (MCI) study programs, or just plain old bad attitudes. The senior enlisted in the platoon favored Prockop due to bonds made during the deployment, but not Woods.

"Prockop, could you try to learn from these guys? They know what they're talking about," Woods said. "And has it ever occurred to you that you'll lead the section someday, so you might want to learn as much as possible?"

The second question caught Prockop off guard. The veterans rarely talked about the coming deployment in terms of who would be in leadership positions, because it wouldn't be them and they'd yet to work through their feelings of guilt. I realized either Prockop or Decker would lead the squad in Iraq as the two most Senior Lance Corporals, and most likely Prockop because Decker's weight issues held him back—the Corps looked down on fat bodies. Unlike Decker's short, plump frame,

Prockop stood tall with a square jaw. He often talked of becoming a "mustang," a Noncommissioned Officer (NCO) who goes to Officer Candidate School (OCS), but to do that he'd first have to pick up a rank of Corporal.

"Well?" Woods said, in Prockop's face now. "Answer me, Marine."

Prockop looked like he didn't have an answer. Woods took Prockop a stone's throw away from the training area and started halfheartedly hazing him with push-ups and jumping jacks. At first Uday pretended not to notice. But when Woods made it serious and Prockop started to wheeze for air in the searing desert heat, Uday trotted over and whispered in Woods' ear. Woods nodded and barked at Prockop to get back in line and to take things seriously. Prockop stood in line stunned, as if the thought of being in charge had lodged in his mind. He looked pensive, his gaze inward, brow furrowed. I tried to give him some encouraging words but he wouldn't have it.

"Shut the fuck up," Prockop said before turning his back on me.

Uday called for us to make a U, the Israeli version of the Marine Corps "school circle," when everyone formed around the instructing Marine like a football team listening to their coach.

"We've been training hard," Uday said. "And now we are going to start doing more complex drills with multiple targets. It is not enough to shoot first and well. You have to be able to distinguish between a terrorist and a civilian instantly."

The huddle of Marines broke and started walking back to the small tent city to turn in for the night as the sun set behind them. I watched the blazing orb dip below the mountains on the horizon and marveled at the bleakness of the Israeli landscape—rocks everywhere. Unlike California desert with lots of sand and shrubbery, Israeli desert was almost all rock. Sand dunes resembled a moonscape. Just over the crest of a crag in the distance, a Palestinian flag snapped in the wind. It baffled me to think that people killed each other every day for the very ground that I stood on, that the flag resided in the infamous West Bank.

I'd heard the instructors talk about some of their missions, how some of them had an "X"—a confirmed kill. Uday's mentioning civilians before he dismissed us made me wonder what the instructors thought about going to war in Palestinian neighborhoods. I looked around for Uday, knowing his friendly attitude would hold through a difficult conversation about war, but he had already started walking back to the tent city after he dismissed everyone. Thom and Gal remained behind though, cleaning and locking up.

"How do you feel about fighting Palestinians?" I asked Thom.

Mundell and Rose stood nearby talking about the training that day, their tall figures towering over Thom and Gal. They looked at me like I was playing in a minefield. Thom didn't even blink before he answered.

"I hate Palestinians," Thom said. "When one of them dies, I am happy. They are enemy who attack my people. Sometimes they blow up schools and malls, the Muslim dogs!"

I listened, unflinching.

"When we have a night range, shoot at the blinking lights over that village," he said, pointing at the

Palestinian village. "It's their minaret. Maybe you kill a Palestinian?" Thom sneered in contempt, then laughed raucously. Over his shoulder, I saw Gal watching our exchange. When he finished guffawing, Thom excused himself to eat in the IDF facilities.

"Maybe you should come back with me and Rose to the tent city," Mundell said. "Instead of asking these kinds of questions."

"I'll catch up with you," I said. "I'm going to talk to Gal."

"Be careful, Big Head," Rose said, using my call sign.

Gal smiled at me as I approached him, leaving Rose and Mundell to walk back on their own to the tent city and evening chow. Gal looked me up and down. I figured he was trying to remember my name but couldn't since we'd only been briefly introduced at the start of training. Unlike the Israelis whose facial hair made them distinguishable from each other, Marines in their flak jacket and helmet all looked the same.

"What do your friends call you?" Gal asked.

"Big Head," I said. "It's my call sign. You know, for over the radio since we don't use real names over comm. Big Head, because I've got a big head."

Gal covered his mouth and laughed.

"You Marines," he said. "I like you. You joke as you fight."

"Speaking of fighting," I said in a respectful but friendly tone of voice, "I saw you listening to me and Thom talking. Do you agree with him? Are you happy when Palestinians die?"

"No, they're my brothers," Gal said. "We are turned against each other by terrible circumstance. I do not want to fight but I must protect my people."

Gal told me he couldn't undo history, that it was forever. He said he could seek to do things to right the past,
but the future required survival. What Gal said made me
believe in him, in Israel. For me, it was enough to hear
the articulation of what I could only wish my motives
were. I didn't lie to myself or anyone else about my much
more ham-fisted desire for justice—I wanted to go to
Iraq and stomp it into a mud hole.

I wanted to be Gal, the battle-proven veteran with
a tight-lipped smile, but I was much more like Thom.
They both knew this even if I was barely cognizant of the
similarities and it made Gal sad and Thom like me. He
called them "Muslim dogs" to my face when he hadn't
to the larger group of Marines. Even though I didn't
say it back or smile and laugh, I didn't correct him. He
knew I wouldn't before he'd said it, they both had. After
I thanked Gal for talking to me and walked back to the
tent city alone, I wondered how they'd both known. I
also wondered about the conflict they had such different
attitudes about.

My understanding of the conflict amounted to the
vague idea that the Palestinians actively sought to destroy the state of Israel and its people over a land feud.
I knew little more than that, save for the predominant
detail that applied most to my current situation—Israel
was our ally. That meant my allegiance was pledged to
them unwaveringly until I was told otherwise.

I kicked rocks as I walked back to the tent city. As the
sun set, the minaret's chant echoed thinly and the sound
of cooing doves filled the air. Before coming over, I'd
had no idea that Israel had so many doves, so many they
almost seemed like a more dignified pigeon. I watched

them fly gracefully from bush to shrub and stunted trees. The sky was a clear, cold blue that reminded me how close the Mediterranean ebbed and flowed. I stopped and turned to better hear the chant from the minaret. The Palestinian flag over the village barely fluttered now in the evening dusk. I wondered if the IDF or its special forces ever executed operations in small towns like that one, seemingly long since removed from current events. I heard the Arabic from the loudspeaker, barely discernible, and wondered at what seemed like gargling broken by sudden syllables. Listening to the alien tongue lead its people in worship made me want to walk among them, to watch them put down their rugs and press their foreheads to the ground. I turned away from the sound of chant and the distant flag, resuming my uphill trek to the tent city.

MOJAVE VIPER

THE FLOODLIGHT'S WHITE FLUORESCENCE LIT THE parking lot of Echo's mock Forward Operating Base (FOB). I sat underneath it, trying to balance a well-worn book on my shivering knees, my hands jammed deep in my pockets. The night's chill had already driven most of the Marines of Echo Company to their sleeping systems hours ago. I stayed up to read under the floodlight because there was nothing else to do. The mock FOB with its guard towers and razor wire fence—the last step in Echo's three-month workup before going to Iraq. Israel seemed like a lifetime ago even though it had only been a year and a half. Since then, Echo's "stand to" had increased as more new recruits cycled into the unit, swelling the ranks even as many veterans of the first deployment got out.

"Holy shit," said a Sergeant from one of the rifle platoons as he walked by. "What the fuck are you doing out here in the cold?"

"Reading," I said. My voice quavered as my jaw shook. "This is the only light in the camp."

"This fucking sucks, doesn't it?" the Sergeant said, pulling out a notebook to read under the light. "The active duty unit I pumped with the first time didn't do any dumb shit, like live in the Mojave for months during the winter."

The Mojave taught me much about the desert. When Echo spent nearly a month straight out in the sands, I learned the desert's blistering heat during the day and frigid cold at night. Waking up early, I'd stand and watch the sun rise, feeling the warm gush of heat break over the mountain crags that rimmed the Mojave's horizon. The amount of training I'd been through was unparalleled: Arabic language and culture classes, combined arms ranges where machine guns fired over the riflemen's heads as they assaulted hills in the distance, Humvee rollover courses making the world spin through the windows, fake towns rigged with special effects explosions populated by Arab actors hired as extras, screaming amputees, covered in blood, waving their stumps in the air, fake rocket-propelled grenades (RPGs) and improvised explosive devices (IEDs) signaling my mistakes with small explosions and sand showers, and kill houses run against déjà vu-inspiring Israeli instructors with Simunition paintball rounds shot from our weapons. The climax of all the expensive hyperrealistic training was a three-week operation that included every company in the battalion. The training operation took place in a mock Arab city just a few thousand meters from the gate of Echo's mock FOB.

At first it had been fun, two and a half weeks before, when the training exercise just started. Now, I felt my stomach twist with hunger. Echo stopped having hot chow brought to the FOB soon after occupying it. The higher-ups claimed it was a "logistical nightmare" that wasn't worth the effort. The MREs (Meal, Ready-to-Eat) were filled with instant food which felt like mud in my mouth. I found it hard to choke anything down throughout our days of running around the fake ville or standing posts at the FOB. Morale had hit a low watermark a few days before when the Commanding Officer (CO) announced again that there were no plans to have hot chow brought to the FOB. My book fell off my lap and into the fine powder of the parking lot. I scooped it up, dusted it off, and headed to the portable toilets at the other end of the FOB, spitting tendrils of chew and vehemently kicking at rats as I went.

I was sick of fake imams and phony sheikhs, shooting blanks in the general direction of Marines and setting off notional IEDs that always killed everyone in the blast area. I thought that if the operation were real, Marines would just wipe everyone out. Some of the veterans were having flashbacks because of the realistic training. But it didn't seem realistic to me that we knew who the bad guys were but didn't kill them on sight—how little I understood of fighting an insurgency.

When I got to the porta-john, I sat down and lit up a smoke. Suddenly, I didn't have to go to the bathroom anymore. Constipation was the most obvious side effect of eating a steady diet of MREs. My frustration mounted as I thought about it; I hadn't shit in days. There was no way that positively affected my health. What could I do, though? I wanted to start punching the porta-shitter walls until I'd broken it to pieces, but I knew that would only make me look like a crazy person. One of the problems with the Marine Corps, I realized, was that although everyone felt the same way about some of the problems, only a few were intelligent enough to articulate them. This same intelligence that lent itself to articulation also kept Marines from doing so, knowing they would be punished for dissenting. If I complained about not getting hot chow or about the frustrations of training with a notional enemy that refused to admit when it had been bested, I would be labeled a complainer and everything I said would be marginalized or discarded. I would start being assigned the worst duties and I'd be passed over for promotion. I remembered the words of an old Doc about how Marines ate their wounded, something that was beyond my understanding then, but made perfect sense to me now.

I stared straight ahead at the porta-shitter door and then it hit me. I knew a way I could voice my feelings and get away with it unpunished. The idea illuminated my mind like a pop-up flare, the kind Marines shot up in the air that slowly floated to the ground dangling from a cloth parachute. My mouth twisted into a sneer. I'd show the old men that ran the Company. I felt around my breast pocket for the felt pen I carried with me to write on the inside of porta-johns, something many Marines did. I pulled it out of my pocket as if drawing a sword, uncapped the pen, and looked at its felt tip. I'd bought the pen from the PX because of how easy felt pens wrote on the plastic walls of the portable bathrooms. Regular ballpoint pens had a difficult time leaving their ink on the hard-plastic surface.

For a moment, I looked at the walls, wondered where I should leave my mark. I shook my head. I was being silly. The best place to leave a message for the higher-ups would be head-level, right in front of me. Eventually one of them would see it; there were only six bathrooms for the whole company to use. That left pretty good odds that at some point in the next few days one of the people in charge would have a seat to relieve themselves and come face-to-face with what I thought. I took the sleeve of my cammie blouse and rubbed the dust off the door. When I was sure it was clean, I didn't hesitate.

Echo Co. 2/24 Deployment 8-2
"Logistical Nightmare"

I leaned back to admire my words, read them out loud. I jumped at the sound of my own voice bouncing off the walls of the porta-john, then laughed. Once I righted myself on my perch, I couldn't help but smile. The words left no doubt that whoever wrote them came from Echo and what they referred to; I'd even included the deployment number. Satisfied with my work, I headed back toward the other side of the FOB to read under the floodlight.

Halfway back, I saw the silhouette of a Marine headed in my direction. I wondered if it was the Sergeant who'd spoken to me under the floodlight. He'd find what I'd written funny and the whole idea hilarious. As the Marine got closer, I noticed he had a pistol in a shoulder holster. Only the Company First Sergeant carried a pistol in a shoulder holster.

I tried not to panic, tried not to feel like I'd made a huge mistake in my scribblings. I looked over my shoulder to see if I could tell which porta-john I'd scrawled in, thinking maybe I could run back like I had diarrhea and sit in it until this First Sergeant finished and walked back. I couldn't remember which one it had been. When I looked back in front of me, I nearly ran into my First Sergeant.

"Oorah, Devil Dog," he said.

"Rah," I replied, as I turned my head to hide my face. I hurried back to my tent and tiptoed over to my rack, sitting down so I faced the door. Rose sat up on his cot, sleep in his eyes.

"What did you do?" Rose asked.

"Nothing," I said. "Shut up! I didn't do anything!"

Before Rose could make a scene, I left the tent and looked toward the porta-johns just in time to see First Sergeant disappear into one of them. Was it the one? I took a deep breath and steadied my nerves. Of course, he hadn't chosen the one I'd just defaced. I chided myself for being so easily rattled. Not wanting to go back into the tent and have to explain things to Rose, I made my way to the floodlight to read.

The Sergeant nowhere to be found, I settled my body on an empty crate and pulled my book back out. I found the words on the page harder to make out now. The floodlight dimly flickered. I swore. The words on the page blurred—I squinted, my eyes straining to adjust to the dim glow. I heard a porta-john door slam hard. My pulse rose to my throat and I could hear the *thump-thump, thump-thump* of my heart. It couldn't be the First Sergeant, furious after reading my message. I needed to stop being so skittish. So much for having nerves of steel.

I rubbed my eyes, blinked hard, and continued reading. Ayn Rand invited me into an ode to capitalism filled with such grandeur that I struggled to find the story in the lofty ideals. I wondered what Rand would have thought about my current predicament—whether she would have scorned me like she did the rest of western military as a construct of imperialism or if she would have sympathized with a young man trying to find his role in the hard and unforgiving world of the USMC infantry. My ruminations dissipated as yelling floated across the still, chilled air of the FOB. A commotion rippled through the two rows of tents where everyone slept on cots. I held my breath for a moment, trying to pick out what voices punctuated the night. Had the First Sergeant walked into the tents in his fury and demanded someone come forward to take responsibility for such a message?

No, I decided, one of the riflemen platoon's Corporals bucking for Sergeant must be peacocking his leadership abilities by throwing a tantrum over some minor infraction: a Marine leaving their rifle on their cot instead of carrying it to the porta-johns with them, or maybe a junior Marine had acted out and now found himself on the receiving end of an ass chewing. I listened and filled with dread—there were too many voices and too much commotion for it to be an isolated thing. The air jammed with the sound of jackboots pounding the ground, at first just a few, then hundreds as the entire company emptied out of the tents. I couldn't see them yet though, as the tent openings were on the opposite side from me. I sat, book forgotten, eyes locked on the end of the rows of tents.

The First Sergeant stormed around the corner. For a moment, his boot falls fell in time with all the others.

I hopped off the crate, eyes wide. He saw me below the flickering floodlight and motioned for me to join the company as it formed a circle around him. I met the company head on as they came around the tents, most of them looking like they'd just woken from whatever broken sleep they could manage, with the sputtering of the generator in the background. The Marines enveloped me and I drifted toward where MachineGuns stood in a cluster.

"Gentlemen," the First Sergeant began. "If you decided to scrawl something on the porta-shitter wall, don't put your unit and battalion designation by it. You don't want people knowing who wrote it, good to go?!"

The crowd of Marines shifted from foot to foot uneasily. Some stamped in an effort to keep warm. After a few long seconds of silence, Marines raised their eyes from the dirt in front of them to see if the First Sergeant had anything else to say. I heard agitation in his voice and knew that he hadn't woken up the entire company to leave the matter alone. The First Sergeant's glasses flashed underneath the floodlight as he looked from face to face.

"Who thinks that Echo Company is a 'logistical nightmare'?" he asked.

The question hung heavy in the air. The First Sergeant was angry and wanted someone to roger up for what had been written. Prockop and Decker looked at me. They knew and waited for me to take responsibility if he decided to punish the group. I could lose rank if he wanted to slap me with destroying government property or some other trumped-up charge to show that he was the boss and Marines didn't get to write their displeasures where the world could read them. The question went unanswered and I listened to wristwatches tick. Anxiety boiled in me as I tried to work the courage up to raise my hand and sound off.

"Yu-ut!" the Marine Corps yell rang through the night.

Silence covered the crowd again, so that boots could be heard scraping against the desert floor, then more voices rose in a clamor to agree with the first. Marines ecstatically screamed, "Oorah, First Sergeant!" and "Things are fucked up, First Sergeant!" along with other yelps and grunts of approval. The Marines of Echo Company were fed up with the desert war games turned cold weather training with no hot meals of real food. The tumult of bellows rose to hysteria, then diminished to silence. The First Sergeant stood in the center, slowly shaking his head in disgust.

"Who was it that sounded off first?" First Sergeant barked. "Was that you, Straight? And you all agree with him? Well good. When I check the porta-shitters tomorrow, they better be cleaned of all the graffiti in them. You will all pay if I see anything else about Echo Company being a logistical nightmare. Marines, we are about to experience the rigors and hardships of war. You had better harden the fuck up!"

First Sergeant stormed out of the circle of light. The company started talking and laughing as they joked about what had just happened. The flickering floodlight became hazy as hundreds of Marines lit up cigarettes. My body sagged with relief; I hadn't had to out myself and no one had gotten in trouble. I couldn't have asked for a better end. The First Sergeant had woken up the entire Company to read it to them. Wade Straight, the Marine who'd rogered up with a night-splitting cry, smiled and laughed as he smoked. I knew no one was going to chide him. Wade had been one of the few Marines to kill someone during Echo's first deployment and that carried a lot of clout. Not only had he gotten a confirmed kill, he'd done it in front of his squad in broad daylight, firing his Squad Automatic Weapon at a truck charging his patrol. Wade saved lives that day, and although his reputation as someone who liked to joke around kept him from picking up a promotion to Corporal, Wade was the kind of Marine people wanted to have with them on patrol. So, if the company First Sergeant asked if anyone thought Echo was a logistical nightmare and Wade wanted to agree, he could do so without reproach.

I lit a cigarette and took a long drag; the cherry glowed red. My knees felt wobbly and my head light. When I took the cigarette away from my mouth and exhaled, I saw Prockop and Decker standing in front of me. Prockop had his arms crossed. Decker was shaking his head slightly, smirk on his face.

"I was the one who wrote it," I said.

"Well, no shit," Prockop said.

"You made it kind of obvious when you ran in the tent," Decker said.

"I'll clean it up right now," I said.

"Goddamn it," Prockop said. "Your fucking around is going to get me in trouble someday. You didn't think that the First Sergeant would see whatever you wrote?"

I didn't say anything. If I told them the truth, that I had written the message so the First Sergeant or one of the higher-ups would see it, they would both be furious.

As it now stood, Decker didn't care except to laugh at the spectacle and Prockop was playing the weary squad leader beleaguered by the troubles of leading young Marines. They both seemed to be enjoying themselves, so I left them to it and went to erase my message. When I was done, I hit the rack. Only a few days stood between me and the end of training, then ten days of leave before the company would board planes to head overseas.

As I lay on my cot in my sleeping bag, trying not to shiver, I wondered what Iraq would be like. The Sergeant who'd talked to me below the floodlight liked to tell stories about his first deployment, to what he called "never-never land." His lips would curl and his voice came alive as he'd recall doing lines of cocaine off Humvee hoods before shooting rockets into houses from the huge TOW (Tube-launched, Optically tracked, Wire-guided) operating system that took up the entire turret. He was a nice guy and he was even slated to pick up Staff Sergeant in the near future, but it was obvious after hearing some of his stories that he'd done things which still affected him deeply.

Just when I'd gotten warm enough to slip into a restless sleep, the FOB's sirens went off and a voice over the loudspeakers shouted about incoming mortars. The Marines around me groaned. The night would prove to be full of sprints from our racks to bunkers.

IRON HEART

HOW MANY FLIGHTS DID IT TAKE TO GET TO IRAQ from America's heartland? I couldn't remember. The C-130 engines throbbed, then whined as the aircraft dropped altitude and banked sharply. The cargo bay of the plane trembled, packed with seats rank and file. The black, plastic seats all came from the same cookie-cutter mold and were bolted to brackets that secured them to the cargo bay floor. I'd been uneasy when I boarded; the seats, rivets, and brackets all looked hard and unyielding. If the plane jolted during the descent to Al Taqaddum Air Base, my knees would slam forward the half-inch to the seat in front of me; my face would snap forward to meet my pack in my lap. That's exactly what happened when the plane dropped altitude. When it banked, Marines' helmets knocked together as heads bobbled side to side.

One of the crewmen unbuckled and sprinted to the front of the hold, deftly steadying himself on helmeted heads and packs. He climbed a ladder to the cockpit.

Before takeoff, one of the crew members had given Echo a safety briefing: don't touch anything; no matter what happens, don't panic; if you throw up, do it in your pack; anticipate evasive maneuvers. The crew had made it sound as if we didn't need to worry about the maneuvers, but all I could do was worry as the twin engines screamed like circular saws moving through knotted oak. I leaned my head back and stuck my nose up as far as I could, helmet against my seat, and smelled for smoke. I didn't detect anything burning; the cold air tinged my throat with the odor of oil.

Again, the plane banked. My head whipped against the helmet of the Marine next to me. The force of the blow made my teeth hurt and head dizzy. I clenched my jaw, willing the pain away. I tucked my chin and hunched my shoulders like a football player expecting contact.

Marines hooted and hollered as the plane dropped lower out of the sky, snaking to the ground. Some men squeezed their eyes shut and whispered prayers. One guy held a picture of his family, cradled in his hands. Music, with guitars that squealed and heavy bass, blasted from a small stereo in front of me. It was the first of many times a Marine would produce a stereo seemingly from nowhere and crank the volume to accent danger with a musical score. Motes flashed in beams of light. The hold wasn't sealed. The flight crew had explained it all back on the ground in Saudi Arabia, a talk I hadn't paid attention to then when Iraq had seemed like a looming idea in front of me instead of unforgiving ground beneath me. I tried to stay calm. What had they said?

The flight would be short. They didn't expect us to take fire, but it also wouldn't surprise them. The C-130 would hug the desert, giving anyone on the ground with a Surface-to-Air Missile (SAM) minimal time to fire. Without the smell of sulfur burning from chaff, flares, or any other countermeasure, the plane wove serpentine to avoid small arms fire from the ground. The relative size of ground weaponry referred to as "small" is .50 caliber and below and includes even the lowly AK-47 that punches fist-sized holes through cinder blocks. C-130s were the airborne equivalent of buses—slow-moving, big, easy targets.

If the plane crashed and Echo turned to crispy critters in the resulting inferno, we'd all die in platoon order, right down to squad and fireteam, just as we'd boarded. Behind me, someone puked in his pack and a groan went up from the surrounding Marines. I gripped my rifle by the handle and pressed the butt to my shoulder, pinning the foregrips between my thigh and pack. Having my weapon ready wouldn't help me if the plane went down, but it made me feel better; I was ready to fight back even if there was no enemy to engage. The plane evened out its descent and for a moment I felt completely weightless. Then wheels touched down on the runway, screeching. The smell of burning rubber and smoke washed over me.

Al Taqaddum Air Base sprawled, between the landing strips, PX, McDonald's, basketball courts, call centers, living quarters, and bulletin boards advertising dances and intramural sporting events between units. The accommodations at Al Taqaddum made me think of different Marine Corps desert bases where I'd trained:

months of winter cold at Twentynine Palms and the notorious Camp Wilson, weeks living in plasterboard kennels in Kuwait. The recent excitement blurred the boring memories like a hand swept over a chalk drawing.

"What do you think?" Prockop asked me. "The Fobbits have it better in Taq than we had it in training."

I didn't know what to say. Prockop's experience in his first deployment had taken the luster out of war and the surprises. My shrug made Prockop roll his eyes. I'd never been to an FOB and didn't know that Al Taqaddum was one of the two mega bases around our Area of Operation (AO), the other being Camp Fallujah just northeast of its namesake.

Echo stood in a parking lot near the base's north gate, opposite of our landing on the strip at the south side. Seven-Ton trucks rolled into the lot kicking up clouds of fine dust like talcum powder which coated all the roads in a film, sometimes smattered with patches of gravel. All of the trucks I'd seen so far, from Humvees to the larger troop-carrying MRAPs (Mine Resistant Ambush Protected), sparkled with the gleaming edges of armor plates and bristled with machine gun barrels. The unit that manned the trucks were about to ferry us to Camp Habbaniyah on the other side of a bridge spanning an interstate—or what the military called a Main Supply Route (MSR). I didn't know yet that war destroyed bridges, leaving only a precious few maintained. I was entering a world of thoroughfares peppered with points where people would be checked and movement would be intentionally choked. Coalition Forces controlled every major bridge left standing within a five-hour drive and even lay claim to all the bridges they had felled with explosives.

The transports grumbled up the bridge. I stood as the truck crossed over the apex and spread my arms, so the wind rushing through the truck's bed cooled me. The MSR stretched out in front of me, eventually meeting Fallujah on the horizon. The big trucks carrying things on their long beds were different from the semis back home, unfamiliar brands of unusual design. The small cars coughed and sputtered as they rushed atop the broken and cracked cement. My gaze swept north. I squinted against the sun. Scattered in front of Camp Habbaniyah, at the west end of the decommissioned airstrip left by British occupation, stood strange structures. Large concrete bunkers with enormous green tetrahedron tops, scaled with armor. The buildings were uniform, towering at least forty-five stories over everything else on the landscape. Saddam had them built in an effort to erect bunkers that could withstand the world's most powerful bombs. Decades passed and technology made the fortifications obsolete. When the United States dropped two-thousand-pound smart bombs, or Joint Direct Attack Munitions (JDAMs), on the bunkers' armored green tops, the results had been devastating. The tetrahedrons had been torn open to the core of the structures, now gaping like cavities in weak teeth.

The sun's rays plunged down into the surreal horizon of broken tetrahedrons like lances. The busted bunkers silhouetted against a skyline of buildings, palms trees, and smoke in the distance. Men led donkeys on a trail running parallel with a small canal in front of the base. Children ran barefoot, laughing and playing. The southern part of Habbaniyah was visible for a moment; then the trucks descended the bridge. A winding road led up to a grim looking gate of scaffolding three stories high with .50-caliber machine guns and a Mark 19 grenade launcher pointed at the access road. On the gate's second level, a duty hut had been constructed out of ballistic glass and steel plates. Behind the glass, I could barely make out two Marines keeping watch. The brief vision of Habbaniyah, which I would soon come to call Hob, stayed etched in my mind.

"Where are the bad guys?" I asked.

I turned to Prockop and patted my M-16 as if I was ready to wipe out the whole town. It was the kind of gung-ho, phony tough guy bullshit I'd grown used to in the Marine Corps.

"I wonder when your big head will get it?" Prockop replied.

Our small convoy rolled up to the gate and paused briefly, so the lead vehicle (vic) could give the Corporal of the Guard a head count. I sat back down with a thud. Prockop seemed to be in a mood and maybe he'd earned the right to brood after touching down in Iraq to start his second deployment. Still, it made more sense to try to teach the men he would be working with and leading in the next eight months than to put us down with vague criticisms. I knew better than to pursue the question, though. There wouldn't be any wisdom from the other side of the rift that had separated us when Prockop became section leader. I didn't yet realize how absolute the authority of Sergeants was over their squads in a combat zone.

Echo's AO lay about three kilometers northeast, over the Euphrates. The slow current of the river, our only obstacle, carved a deep bed through sand. The river's myriad bends and turns came closest to touching the Tigris just southeast of Fallujah, meandering through the land as if a blue ribbon. I'd studied maps and read about the Iraqi population, research spurred by what media outlets dubbed the "triangle of death" or the "Sunni triangle." This concentrated population of Sunnis in the middle of Iraq was shaped like a triangle with tines jutting outward to envelop the three major cities in the area. Tikrit, the prong to the far north, was the only city of the triangle to fall outside of the Al Anbar Province; Ramadi and Baghdad were the western and eastern prongs respectively, with Habbaniyah and Fallujah between them.

The difference between the Sunni and Shia sects was their understanding of Allah: one envisioned a benevolent Allah, while the other believed in an Allah as unforgiving and vengeful as the Judeo-Christian God conception. Often, tribal leaders would use bloodlettings and murder to stoke violence between them. Politics in Iraq might have been the only thing more treacherous than shifting dunes during a sandstorm. While my understanding of the political landscape seemed as fuzzy as heat waves off the cracked floor of the desert, I found myself much more knowledgeable than other Marines.

Fleming, a junior Machine Gunner, had shown me the thing I'd found most disturbing. When Echo had been assigned an AO several weeks prior, Fleming had jumped on his computer and loaded up Google Earth. Zooming in on the center of Iraq, near a sharp bend in the Euphrates between Hob and Fallujah, he found Saqlawiyah. He panned around the map, zooming in and out, getting a good look at the rural town we would be taking charge of shortly.

"Well, I don't like the name of the lake by the FOB," Fleming said.

I leaned over his shoulder to get a better look at the computer screen.

"Why not?" I asked. "What's it named?"

"The Lake of Tears," Fleming said. "Or, literally translated, Lake Eye Salty."

Fleming had zoomed in close on the MSR that stretched east and west just north of the FOB. After messing with the settings for a minute, he got Google Maps to show us the landscape as if it had been captured from space with a satellite camera. Right by the FOB, on the MSR, there appeared to be a white plume on the side of the road.

"What's that right there?" I asked, pointing.

Fleming zoomed in as close as Google allowed.

"It would appear to be some kind of explosion," Fleming said.

Just then, Prockop had walked into the room behind us; it was the few days between leave and deployment when everyone felt relaxed because the future seemed inevitable and, for a time, relations between Prockop and the squad were less strained.

"Yeah, it's an IED going off," Prockop said.

He poured snack food straight from the bag into his mouth, talking between chomping.

"The Battalion Newsletter to our families released where our AO would be yesterday in an email," Prockop said. "Turns out a lot of moms know how to use Google Maps just like you guys are doing right now."

He poured more food in his mouth, snorted, chewed, swallowed, then continued talking.

"I guess a bunch of them saw the same thing and called the CO about it," Prockop said, before turning and walking out of the room without saying anything else. Like no further explanation could possibly be needed.

There was the FOB, there was the Lake of Tears, there was the IED blast, big enough to be caught in a satellite's picture from space blossoming like a roadside flower. How close to the FOB? A longer distance than a stone's throw, but not much farther than a few long baseball throws. In military speak "danger close," because of the possibility that a chunk of shrapnel would hurt someone or damage equipment. Fleming and I looked at each other as the door closed behind Prockop.

"He didn't seem too worried about that," Fleming said. "You know, not like, say, someone who was in direct charge of the well-being of you and myself might care about things like IEDs."

Fleming had worked for years in a meat packing plant in the wastes of southwestern Illinois and joined the military to be somebody. A recruiter had told him about the Reserves—"One weekend a month, two weeks in the summer, and maybe a deployment," the smiling Staff Sergeant had said—and Fleming thought it sounded like an easy way to get college paid for and see the world. The recruiter hadn't mentioned bomb blasts so big space stations picked them up.

"Have you noticed Prockop acting funny?" I asked.

Fleming looked at the door and back at me.

"He's been hanging out with Blaker a lot and the 11s," Fleming said, using a Marine Corps colloquialism referring to riflemen by their Military Occupational Specialty (MOS), 0311. "Mostly the 11s in Second Platoon."

In a few of the purgatory-like days between the Company's Christmas leave and deployment, Prockop had often wandered room to room in the barracks in some kind of daze. He'd made a habit out of imitating videos off the internet steeped in "college humor." Prockop would pantomime the actors while shouting their lines with gusto usually reserved for the bar. A few of the other Marines were members of college fraternities back home and they rallied around Prockop, talking insistently about working out, fucking girls, and the videos. The repetition had gotten to the point where I'd just walk away from the group, mostly Second Platoon veterans except for Blaker, the movie-star-gorgeous Texan. The clique seemed harmless enough, besides turning Prockop into a raving zombie who only cared about protein shakes and pussy.

That all seemed worlds away now. Prockop stared sullenly out of the Seven-Ton as we sped down the streets of Hob. The same fine powder that had covered the roads at Taq (Al Taqaddum) billowed up in a cloud behind us. Often, swaths of palm trees, shrubs, and other desert foliage lining the roads were sickly-yellow and wilted. Whatever was in the dirt made the plants sick and could not be good for humans to breathe. I thought of my gas mask in my pack between my legs, wondered if there might be times Marines wore them in sandstorms to keep their lungs clear of debris.

The old British architecture of Camp Hob looked like a movie set, as if Lawrence of Arabia would appear on horseback. While doing research on our future AO, I'd learned that the camp had once been used by the British to try to control the region through air superiority in the fifties. Allied forces were certainly going to make use of it now, although not in the same way the British had. Taq, across the MSR, was much more secure due to being on a sudden rise in the terrain away from the city of Hob itself, with a large part of its perimeter either being lakefront or cliff face. My concern didn't extend past the very immediate present—getting off the trucks and stowing my gear and machine gun somewhere. The truck's brakes squealed. The Seven-Tons lurched to a stop in front of two Iraqi buildings we were told had been converted into barracks. Before everyone dismounted, we were told that these would be our barracks away from home at Hob for the duration of the deployment and to accordingly treat doors, stairs, handrails, and racks like things made precious by war's scarcity.

All of Weapons Platoon—MachineGuns, Mortars, and Assault—were packed into a small upstairs room that would later be used to house only Echo's few H&S staff (Headquarters & Service), as opposed to the close to fifty men now setting up cots and shoving their packs underneath. Space was at a premium with only a foot's worth of room between cots and about fifteen inches of space down the middle of the cots lining the walls. There was nothing for us to do, the entire unit ordered to stand by for transport to FOB Riviera just north of Saq (Saqlawiyah). When this transport would take place never got passed. When I asked, the Company Gunny told me the information was on a need-to-know basis and he couldn't imagine a reason why a Lance Corporal in the MachineGuns section needed to know anything more than who to shoot. All of the junior guys new to country feigned disappointment at the lack of immediate action, secretly glad to have some downtime to acclimate to the blistering, barren environment, while the more salty veterans cursed the time spent idle.

"It's not good to sit around doing nothing," Schleur said.

Schleur was an NCO from Mortars squad with short-cropped red hair and a lazy eye. I'd met Schleur when I first joined the unit and overlooked his intelligence because of his quiet demeanor; it had been easier then to forget I'd be deploying with some of the men who were veterans, while those I'd paid attention to like Woods, who brooded, wouldn't be around for the hard times ahead. Schleur had learned a lot from the Corps during his career. He'd learned not to stand out, or "skyline" himself, and that every lull was followed by a storm. When I expressed that I thought he should be happy that we had some downtime, he looked at me with the eyes of someone who weighs a man on scales in his mind, wanting to believe the person in front of them has what it takes while knowing they are untested.

"We'll pay for it," Schleur said. "You'll see, Devil Pup."

Schleur used the derivative of Devil Dog that transformed the Marine from fierce, battle-hardened warrior to young man wanting to wage war. Schleur was one of the Salty Dogs—the veterans who'd been there for the first deployment, who'd seen headless corpses, bodies turned to bits and peppered on roads. One of the first things Echo had seen, rolling into their last deployment, was a hand lying on top of a burning car that had just exploded. Woods had made it sound like the opening to the movie *Yojimbo* when the ronin rides into town, sees a man's hand on the ground and knows trouble lies in the shadows. Schleur, like a lot of the veterans, didn't talk too much about the disturbing parts of their deployment.

"You'll see," Schleur said again, shifting in his rack to catch some shuteye with his back to me. "The first month is always the worst. We'll work fifteen-hour days, maybe more." He looked over his shoulder to see my reaction before pulling his watch cap down over his eyes. His body relaxed for sleep.

Relaxation didn't come so easily for many Marines, although veterans seemed to be able to turn on and off like a switch. I felt an eagerness to get things underway, a tension that manifested in exploring parts of the camp. McShane from Mortars wanted to find some action, and although we couldn't leave the wire yet, we quickly noticed that our superiors had far too much going on to keep track of two Lance Corporals. We discussed it under our breath over lunch and decided it would be best not to invite anyone else until after we scouted the camp ourselves; two Marines walking about would go unnoticed, whereas three or more might be questioned.

McShane and I, along with Rose, Hawkins, Mundell, and Lowery, were Senior Lance Corporals. As such, expectations existed for our behavior, because we knew the right thing to do in most situations, either garrison or combat—although we were all new to Iraq. A Senior Lance Corporal was expected to take the initiative and be a problem solver, especially if they wanted to make the jump from nonrate to NCO with a promotion to Corporal. The rank of Lance Corporal represented the backbone of the Marine Corps, but it also represented a refuge for all the washouts, non-hackers, and fuck-ups that couldn't maintain enough professionalism to get promoted—terminal Lance Corporals.

The terminal Lances existed in the Marine Corps because they had signed contracts and had to wait for them to expire before they could go back to the civilian world. In the Lance Corporal ranks, the number of men that were terminal Lances far outweighed those with enough sense to stay promotable, thus creating what was commonly referred to as "the Lance Corporal underground," or the syndicate of those who filled the general population squad bays who had only enough intelligence and skill to take orders and pull triggers, an underground that time and again got blamed for the spread of false rumors or the leak of sensitive information.

McShane and I decided that if we were to ask anyone to join us it would be Marines like Rose or Hawkins, who didn't mind breaking rules in the spirit of exploring. Even though we hadn't been told not to roam the camp, if higher-ranking Marines from another unit caught us, punishment could range from hazing to losing a stripe. Both McShane and I talked fast and well on our feet, usually able to confuse higher-ranking members from other units or amuse the higher-ups in our own unit. Smiling at each other, we guzzled sweet tea as we finished our meals and headed toward the door.

"Don't get caught," Schleur said dryly as we passed his table on the way out.

McShane just laughed his deep guffaw and I stuck a cigarette behind my ear, our strides never faltering. I led the way out toward the middle of the base, overgrown with weeds, where the buildings stood dilapidated and falling in on themselves. We wanted to see the parts of the old British base that had stood rotting for decades. A boyish delight filled us when we discovered a row of small buildings across the street from a factory, all of which held special promise in their absolute desertion. We quieted our talk as we approached, in case there was anyone around who would tell us to leave, but it wasn't just worry that made us soften our boot falls. McShane looked at the ground as he followed me; we moved like green shadows through the tall brush in the ditches and yards of the buildings. The overgrown tangles of desert brambles and twisted weeds stopped short of the first small building by about twenty feet. I surveyed the road and listened for approaching vehicles, then quickly bounded across the space with McShane following right behind me.

Moving with forceful confidence, hands on our weapons, I took a few steps into the building and turned right just as McShane turned left and moved forward behind me—our room clearing so hammered into us it became part of our nature without the need of thought or speech. Our dynamic entry didn't allow us the time necessary to process the scattered tiles, the chalkboards, the desks piled up and flipped over. We stood very still and toed at what surrounded us with our boots.

"Books," McShane said. He bent over and picked one up. "This must have been a school before the war," he said. The deep bass of his voice held a slight tremor at its core.

Beams of light streaked through the building—some through dusty air like spokes on a wheel, but others were larger and more erratic. Bullet holes speckled the walls. We tore the place apart as if looking for answers.

McShane went through all the drawers and cabinets while I dumped the trash, checked in desks, and inspected dozens of books on the floor. They were all textbooks: twenty or so on algebra, forty on history, others on subjects I couldn't recognize because the text was in Arabic. McShane went through the contents of what would have been the teacher's desk at the front of the classroom. The blackboard had Arabic scrawled on it from years ago, the last bits of thought to materialize there before the school was abandoned.

"I can't find anything," McShane said.

Neither of us were certain what we were looking for, but we both wanted to know as much as was possible to gather.

"Why are the books on the floor?" I asked him, holding one up. "I don't understand. Wouldn't they want to give these to the Iraqi kids?"

McShane shut all the desk drawers, one by one. "I guess saving the schools wasn't high on the priority list," he said.

The next building had a broken Xerox machine, a broken printer, more desks, and thousands of papers scattered all over the floor. I picked up one of the papers and stared at it for several minutes before I realized I held a report card. I dropped it and picked up other papers. I wished I could read Arabic. I wanted to know the names of the children on the cards, figure out what grades they got. I cursed my ignorance of the language, unable to decipher anything out of what appeared as ornate scribbles and strange glyphs.

What had happened when the bombs rained down on Iraq, when JDAMs plunged from the sky to blow the enormous bunkers outside of Hob to pieces, sundering the idea that huge amounts of concrete and steel were protection from the might of the United States Air Force? These children must have thought it the end of everything.

Or had the bombs started falling while class was in session, like watching 9/11 had been for me? Did the teacher stand in front of the class without words or had they explained? But how could they have explained to children why another country, far away and across a wide ocean, had sent aircraft carriers to fly jets over their desert town by the Euphrates and drop munitions with laser-like accuracy on bunkers outside of town by the airstrip. In those moments, whether they passed during the dark of night or in a day-lit classroom, the futures of those children derailed. Their lives would not have been lavish and many of them would have toiled in the fields of their fathers for decades, living a simple, rural life growing alfalfa and herding goats. But before the bombs fell, they had the vestiges of progress like schools, hospitals, and universities.

"Some of the report cards have dates," he said.

Speech seemed like an irreverence, as if the empty schools were tombs. McShane wouldn't meet my eyes when he spoke. McShane seemed determined not to be emotionally moved. He looked like a Boy Scout in over his head, long rifle strapped to him, pained expression on his face like he couldn't remember the way. I left the building without speaking and looked back. McShane walked out, his rifle hung forgotten across him, pointed back and down to the ground. He struck a forlorn figure in front of the decrepit school, hands on his hips. McShane spit a long tendril of chew on the dead grass. When he looked up at me, there was a moment his eyes crossed a great gulf to meet mine, his thoughts receded inward in reflection.

No one ever told us we'd see shot-up schools with the books dumped on the floor and report cards scattered everywhere. Nobody ever talked about firefights where places like schools or hospitals got sprayed with bursts of machine gun fire. Our conception of violence had excluded its impact on civilians. McShane and I didn't talk anymore after leaving the school. Neither of us knew what to say.

The factory was worse. Oil pooled on the sagging floors. In an office, records lay scattered around the room, the cabinet long ago ransacked. Looters had left heavy marks of sledgehammers and pry bars where equipment had been stolen and copper pulled out of the walls. Large pipes had been cracked and now seeped a black stain onto the wall and floor. Neither of us felt an attempt to penetrate the inner workings of the large building would be safe—jagged edges covered with rust, strange chemicals seeping from unmarked pipes, a sagging floor and ceiling. We stayed on the periphery. Soon, the noxious fumes made us dizzy and drove us away, toward the last place we'd talked about exploring.

A very large building of fine stonework with huge, elegant columns and large glass windows faced the road. Official and important-looking, I wanted to explore it as soon as I'd seen it in the distance while walking to chow. I'd discussed it with a few people, wondered what it could be and what was left inside of it. What we discovered was an abandoned theater with a stage faced by hundreds of broken seats. A mosaic, showing what appeared to be a Persian conquest of the region along with other scenes of planting and reaping, stretched across the two great walls on each side of the stage. Several curtains hung over the stage in tatters. Pigeons and bats flew around the large open space as we climbed ladders to the second story balcony seating, then up into a room with two large projectors. Antiques now, the British had used them to keep men entertained back in the fifties. After marveling at how large the rolls of film used to be, we descended a set of stairs and exited a side door which led outside to a smaller, stadium-style theater that had a great white wall instead of a curtain as a backdrop for its stage.

I was having a hard time believing my eyes. I felt like I was floundering in deep water as I tried to process the abandoned school and my mind strained with the juxtaposition of the theater. The theater had long been abandoned, for about fifty years, but the school and factories had only seen about half a decade of disrepair. Because of the hot, arid climate, the ephemera left on the schoolhouse floors had been well preserved. I had no idea what kind of environmental impact the leaking oil, chemicals, and other industrial waste would have. I took off my "eight point cover" the Marine Corps uniform used as hats, dooming us to carry the silhouettes of Police Officers as crowns, and rubbed my head.

"McShane," I called. "I just had one of those moments when you realize how fucked you are."

McShane walked over to me, kicking sand and crushing a desert flower on his way. We stood in front of the outside auditorium's white wall.

"I was thinking we should tell someone about the chemicals from the factory leaking into the water table," I said. "But then I realized that this is Iraq—a combat zone."

McShane laughed. "Earlier I was going to say that we should tell someone about the books, so they could come and get them," he said.

We headed back to the barracks, our shadows long before us. The white-hot sun started its descent into a colorless opaline sky seared with light. Neither of us spoke of what we'd found to anyone, not just because if our squad leaders heard we'd be chided for wandering off on our own, but because reservations and shock would be mocked as naïve, maybe even called sympathizing. As a Marine, I had to be stoic and brave with an iron heart. Fearing that I had somehow turned into a non-hacker, I tempered my heart in preparation for the move to FOB Riviera, where my courage could not fail. That night, I lay awake in my rack long after the platoon had gone to sleep around me. When my breathing fell into the rhythm of the pack, images of that day troubled my dreams.

SUFFER THE CHILDREN

BOOTS ON THE DECK: A SLOGAN DRILLED INTO US like cadence. We were the Marines of the second troop surge, but this surge would be different from the last. We would win or lose the war. Our Reserve unit activated as part of a thirty-thousand-troop muster to be flung at the enemy—we had been told as much.

I wanted to believe I was part of something that secured victory, but as the trucks rolled through Fallujah I wondered if the war had spared anything for triumph's embrace. While troops rotated from stateside to the Middle East and Iraqis fled or fought, the buildings stood silent sentinels and they bore the marks of violence. When the armored troop transports rose to the zenith of the bridge into Fallujah, I'd been excited to get my first glimpse of the infamous city where so much fighting had happened. Across the Euphrates, the building to the left of the road seemed like a strong point where the enemy could easily rake the length of the bridge with machine gun fire. But as the transports crossed the bridge, the building's front proved to be a facade of smashed plaster, broken cement, and holes. The structure had once boasted a large open-air patio overlooking the Euphrates, but now, so thoroughly perforated, it looked like a person with smallpox or measles.

The house stood, a grim totem of what could be found at every choke point and elevated position along the MSR that wound through the city. I sat in the back of the armored truck, watching the blocks decimated by battles. I worried about snipers, about explosions. I stood, peering down side streets to see if the city returned to normal just a few blocks away. The damage was the same in every direction. The totality continued until we made it deeper into the center of the city where things weren't yet as badly tore to pieces. I saw children with their parents, waiting to file through checkpoints, backdropped by habitable dwellings and palm trees, still uncharred.

By the time the trucks bearing Echo made it to FOB Riviera, I'd taken in the whole of Fallujah, from southwestern bridge entrance to northeastern on-ramp exit. When I saw the packs of barefoot children roaming the streets, I shook my head and rubbed my eyes. Children barely old enough to walk scampered and weaved through the traffic and crowds of Saq, where in the big city of Fallujah they would have been trodden underfoot. I wondered where their parents were, but then thought back on what I'd seen and kept the question to myself. The time for glib comments was over and I didn't want to come off as immature and disrespectful to the men around me, taking in the same scenes with funeral parlor quiet. As the truck's engines growled and whined, Marines listened to the wind hiss and pop in their ears. The FOB looked small from street level, the perimeter fence encircling maybe half a football field of desert sand and rock, butted up against a lake with a militarized dormitory in the center. As darkness approached, we unpacked Echo's equipment and got it into the FOB in a hurry.

"Weapons Platoon, gear up and head to the trucks staged in front of the gate," Gunny bellowed from the FOB's entrance.

Weapons Platoon donned our body armor and slung our rifles which we'd left rank and file. The Marines from the unit we'd come to replace had staged two MRAPs and a Humvee in front of the gate. Crawford, a Squad Leader in Weapons and veteran of the first deployment, spoke in an evangelical tenor. Everyone who wanted to head outside the wire on a patrol could load onto the trucks, NCOs and Senior Lance Corporals were being "voluntold" to go, and everyone else who didn't get on board would help the Company load gear into the FOB.

I wanted to get in the war, so I volunteered to drive the MRAP on point, the first position in the column. Unlike the patrols that would follow during the rest of deployment, this one was a mix of Weapons Platoon personnel; future patrols would be undertaken primarily as squad efforts. After Marines piled into the trucks, Crawford got a head count and took up station in the central vehicle to be acting patrol leader. I wondered if I heard the voices of our Captain and Staff Sergeant as well, but didn't have time to think for long. Over the hood of the hulking MRAP lay Iraq's night and my first time leaving friendly lines.

My chest tightened as I eyed the scant controls of the MRAP. I'd never driven one before. I'd driven a few Humvees for short periods of time, but never anything larger than that. Echo hadn't officially designated drivers until the days before we left stateside and it wasn't until after we'd touched down in Taq that some of us found out we'd be drivers. As I gently worked the gas and steering, the MRAP glided out of the gate and down the short access road to the street. The other two vehicles pulled onto the road behind me and the patrol headed toward the roundabout at the center of Saq with its towering minaret a white stripe in my headlights. A radio crackled from the back of the MRAP.

"Big Head, step on it." The voice belonged to Crawford. *"Driving this slow is going to get us blown up. You're going about seven miles an hour, take it up to twenty-five."*

I hammered my boot down on the accelerator and the six-ton, heavily armored vehicle lurched forward, engine straining. Corporal Lowery, beside me in the vehicle commander's seat, reached forward with his left hand and flipped a switch for the floodlights that pointed outboard from on top of the MRAP. The buildings on either side of the road were transformed from black blocks to rundown apartments and closed-up shops. He hadn't said anything since loading in; Lowery had been tasked out to take eight bodies from the swollen Machine Gun section and run Personal Security Detail (PSD) for the Company's CO. Taking a second from staring at the road in front of the MRAP, I glanced out my side window and scanned the structures for signs of small arms fire.

"I can't see shit," I said, "and my window has pockmarks from shrapnel."

"Yeah, the unit we're replacing got hit a few times," Lowery said. "While you guys were unloading equipment, I talked to a few of their squad leaders."

I looked over at him.

"What did they say?" I asked.

"Watch the road!"

In front of the MRAP loomed the minaret in the middle of the roundabout. Steering an MRAP wasn't as I'd imagined. Instead of handling like a solid beast of steel, diesel, and smoke, the leaf spring suspension made the MRAP's carriage bounce and jerk, bobbling around every turn. Dead spots in the steering made it hard to judge exactly how much to turn and when. I raced east out of Saq. A Marine told me from the rear of the vehicle that there was a curfew, so I didn't need to worry about hitting anyone.

My anxiety increased as we transitioned from the city streets of Saq to the rural back roads. The narrow strip of powder, white in the moonlight, was claustrophobic between the stunted trees and homes so primitive they seemed like mud huts as my headlights passed over them. I lit up a cigarette as I drove, MRAP jerking back and forth as I hit every pothole and rut in the road. The roads were terrible, some of them so run down I feared the ground would give out underneath our heavy trucks. I just kept steady pressure on the gas pedal and hoped for the best.

"Hey, there are nonsmokers back here," Corporal May, a Mortarman, said from the back.

I took a long drag, the cherry briefly lighting my reflection in the windshield.

"We're in Iraq now," I said.

"Put that cigarette out. Now," May said.

"Shut up, May," Lowery said from beside me as he lit up a cigarette.

"Goddamn it. I thought I'd got away from you smokers after last tour." May said. He shook his head and let out a long sigh. "And now I have to do another one."

"Doesn't it seem like just yesterday we were getting back from the last pump?" someone said.

I lost the conversation in the engine. Lowery had been guiding me while staring at a map and simultaneously listening to commands through the radio while the veterans in the back who were looking at their own maps sometimes offered their thoughts on what route to take. The patrol had zigzagged its way east and north until coming to the southern edge of the small borough that jutted off from Saq like a backwards baseball hat; it contained the city's marketplace, a mosque, and housing for the refugees from the Battle of Fallujah and other, smaller skirmishes that had driven people out into the desert.

After stopping to take a static position in the middle of a cluster of crumbling cinder block homes, so Marines could stretch their legs and feel the night's chill, the patrol turned around and headed back to the FOB. Instead of taking the most direct route, Crawford wanted to trace back over the route we'd forged through the country roads. At some point, it became apparent that Crawford had gotten turned around and the patrol was lost; I'd long since lost track of where we were in the dark. Every road looked vaguely familiar now, but none seemed right. When the patrol made another wrong turn, sending it east, Crawford called for an immediate one-eighty. I pulled onto a dirt path that looped through a cluster of shanties. Getting back on the road the other direction, I saw the third vehicle's brake lights flare red in the darkness.

"Look at this telephone pole," Lowery said. "How many power lines are coming off of it."

Both of us had missed it when we passed by the first time. The telephone pole had electric wires and cables fastened to it with twisted pieces of concertina wire—a wire that, unlike razor wire, was meant to tangle personnel instead of shredding. I still hadn't grown used to how much concertina wire coalition forces used to line every checkpoint, road block, and fence; stray bits of which were now used by Iraqis to fence in gardens, tie wires to telephone poles, or even strung out and used as fences for their fields. I looked up at the pole sticking out of the ground by the side of the road with so many wires attached it seemed like the center of some kind of nest.

"Think I can take it out?" I asked Lowery.

He glanced in the rearview mirror to see if the second MRAP had caught up or if it was around the bend waiting for the Humvee. I figured Crawford would wait for the third vehicle whose driver rode the brake.

"Hit it," Lowery said.

My boot slammed down on the accelerator and the MRAP jumped forward. I waited until the front right wheel was abreast of the pole, then cranked the steering so the truck's armor plate met the pole's wood with enough force to cave in the side of a house. It tore in half near the base with a splintering crunch and bloomed into an explosion of sparks. The charred and smoking transformer disappeared into the ditch. I cranked the wheel back to the left and straightened the vehicle on the road. The Marine in the turret hooted as the last of the sparks dimmed on the MRAP's windshield.

"You're an asshole," May said.

We all laughed. I looked out the window, trying to find houses with lights or television flickering, wanting to see the effects of my impulsive destruction. I didn't think for a second that what I had done was wrong, nor did I think May was actually upset. It was all in good fun. The Iraqis would figure out another way to string up their wires. The laughter hadn't been malicious but merely the same brutal ignorance children show each other on the playground. The people that filled the houses seemed more like an idea than a reality. I never gave thought to how not being able to use electricity for lights, stoves, or running water would affect families. All through training, the Iraqis had been paid actors, often white—although we were assured that sometimes blond-haired, blue-eyed mercenaries from Serbia fought for the insurgency. Knocking over a pole with dozens of jerry-rigged wires seemed insignificant after everything else we'd seen that day.

When the laughter died, I drove back toward the FOB in silence until May spoke again. "I guess you'll get to see how mad people are tomorrow when MachineGuns goes on a foot patrol to Shadyville."

Our Platoon Sergeant was a Captain, and along with our Staff Sergeant who followed him around like a puppy dog, gave higher-ups an immediate physical manifestation. Although the two men would go out on a handful of patrols with us, they faded into the background of life operating as a Marine in Iraq. When I would ask some of the salty vets what our two representations of higher did with their time, the usual answer was either "sleep" or "fuck each other," but closer to the truth was that the Captain was wrapped up in administrative and strategic duties. I'm not sure what the Staff Sergeant did most of the time, except stay in the Captain's ear. So, if May heard one of them say that MachineGuns was headed out into the ville tomorrow, I believed it—still green, I didn't know that much of the "gouge" that Marines passed from one to the other became so badly distorted it was useless.

The rest of the ride to the FOB went quickly, as all manner of third world living blurred past, lit for a split second by the harsh white of my headlights. Stray dogs were everywhere, something the vets told us we'd get used to. May talked about how last deployment they killed canines at will, for any reason they wanted, sometimes just because they felt like it. I thought about how it had felt when I killed my first deer, before I'd learned not to walk up on them while they died so you couldn't see the look in their eyes. *I could kill a dog no problem*, I thought, *especially the wild ones that ran in packs around the FOB, covered in mange. Killing one of them would be more like shooting a pig than anything else.* I wondered what extinguishing a human life would take, if I had it in me. As the MRAP's diesel engine roared past rural homes, I thought about what would happen to an orphaned child in a land as broken as Iraq. I almost asked May if there was enough infrastructure left of the Iraqi government that orphaned children would be looked after, but then didn't.

We finally caught sight of the FOB's silhouette—the camouflage shroud strung between the posts on top of the building made the stars behind wink in and out as it fluttered in the night's breeze. Gravel crunched underneath tires as the three-vehicle patrol rolled down the access road, stopping in front of the FOB. Marines piled out, while Crawford's tenor came over the radio. Drivers were to top off the gas tanks at the refueling station on the side of the FOB before parking them. The refuel station turned out to be a big elevated drum of JP-8, a diesel fuel replacement, with a hose and nozzle that relied on gravity to run fuel to the idling trucks. After I'd replaced the nozzle, splashing fuel all over my uniform, I noticed my cigarette still dangled from my lips. I climbed up the steep steps of the MRAP and hopped into the driver's seat in a hurry, so the vehicle behind me didn't have to wait long. I pulled into one of the three open parking spaces marked with leaked oil, killed the engine, grabbed my rifle, made sure my pistol still hung at my hip, and descended back to the ground.

I started walking toward the front of the dorm, in the center of the razor-wired walls that defined FOB Riviera. Now that I was inside the wire, I thought of the upcoming months of confinement. I surveyed the parking lot and the narrow strips of ground on either side of the dorm that led to the back of the FOB. Even if I jogged slowly, I would constantly be turning. I didn't think I'd be getting much privacy but knew there would eventually be downtime.

Walking through the FOB's front doors, I expected the interior of the building to be something out of a movie, full of bustle and noise. The reality was a dusty dormitory, seized by U.S. forces after the invasion years before. Sergeant Seals, from First Platoon, sat behind a desk to the left of a winding cement staircase. The desk was labeled Sergeant of the Guard (SOG) in bright yellow-on-red lettering. I opened my mouth to ask him where I should be, but Seals was a locked-on Sergeant and was way ahead of me.

"You need to get your ass in the rack. MachineGuns is headed back out the door at sun up in a few hours, to do a foot patrol. Your wing is on the fourth deck, to the right."

My boots pounded the steps as I launched myself up, taking them two at a time. I was exhausted but exhilarated. I'd just been outside the wire for the first time, on my first patrol of Iraq. Even though the impromptu night patrol hadn't run into insurgent resistance, it still made me feel like maybe things wouldn't be so terrible for the next eight months.

THE NEXT DAY, back outside the wire, we headed to the main street in front of the FOB connecting Saq to the MSR which ran east and west just to our north. This patrol was different from the haphazard night patrol just a few hours prior. The mood wasn't as lighthearted; instead of being cowboys gallivanting through the country in trucks like fortresses, we trudged over asphalt and through fields to get to Shadyville. The Corps had a special interest in Shadyville. During the patrol brief, Prockop said many of its inhabitants were refugees. For a second, I thought of them like any refugee, a person pushed out of their home by some catastrophe, but a Staff Sergeant explained that some of the refugees were insurgents who'd been wounded so badly they couldn't fight anymore.

Now I saw scars webbed on faces, arms grooved deeply by bullets, arms and legs gone, and the occasional missing eye. Faces watching us coldly. I'd never had people look at me with such bitter resentment before. As our patrol wound its way through alleys filled with garbage and over streams of sewage, I watched many inhabitants who saw us approaching run into their homes and lock the door, except one group of young men about my age. As the squad bunched up to maneuver through a street lined with rubble, one of them called out to me in perfect English.

"You guys are new," a young man said. "When did you get to Iraq?"

The patrol slowed to a standstill in the close confines of the street's bottleneck; we tried to keep about twenty-five meters of dispersion between Marines, but still bunched up. Instead of just standing and waiting my turn to move forward, I walked over to the young Iraqi man.

"How do you speak English?" I asked.

"I learned in school," he said. "Why do you talk to me, but none of the others come over when I call?"

"They're probably afraid you are going to blow yourself up when they get close," I said.

"And you aren't?" he asked.

I saw Prockop looking back over his shoulder at me from down the street. I started to walk away, and the young man stopped me as if he had something urgent to say.

"Shoot a dog," he said. He pointed at one of the sick mutts, lapping at a brackish puddle in the ditch across the street.

"No, I'm not shooting a dog."

"If you are a good shot you will shoot one," he said. "Otherwise you are a chicken."

"Why are you watching the patrol?" I asked.

The young Iraqi man looked back at one of his friends and spoke rapidly. When he turned back to me, he spoke in Arabic and waved both his hands in front of him. I realized he would no longer speak with me. I chided myself for being naïve and trying to talk to people like it was some kind of game, as if we were back in training when we'd been encouraged to be friendly with the actors, returning their broken phrases with our own. The young Iraqi men looked angry and brooding. When I turned to give them a parting glance, they had already melted back into the city. The street was empty except for a few children without shoes, running from house to house.

"Why did you talk to them?" Prockop asked.

I was startled, then looked sheepishly at him. He'd been waiting for me on the side of the road around the corner, inspecting the two columns of Marines as they patrolled on each side of the street.

"They were watching the patrol," I said. "One of them was fluent in English."

"One knew English?" Prockop asked. "Where did they go?"

I looked back at where they had been standing, then back at Prockop, and shrugged my shoulders.

"I don't know, they were standing right there," I said.

Prockop shook his head, jaw muscles flexing behind the chew in his front lip.

"You can't walk off by yourself, not even just for a second to talk to someone. There isn't anything to talk about. If they spoke English, they were probably no-shit terrorists."

I just stood looking at him, squinting into the sun through my thick ballistic glasses.

"Stay in formation," he said. "I don't want to have to talk to you again."

He spat a long tendril of chew into the sewage water in the ditch next to us, then turned and stalked back to the front third of the two columns. I put my head down and route marched faster, to make up the ground I'd lost while talking to Prockop. Over my shoulder, the last four in the patrol hurried to catch up. Prockop was right. I shouldn't have stopped to talk with the locals. We hadn't even brought an interpreter, so what was the point?

During the next two weeks, my squad spent much of its time doing presence patrols on foot through Saq and Shadyville, learning the lay of the land and familiarizing ourselves with the people. At first, we took sweets from the chow hall out with us to give to the grasping hands and chapped lips that screamed for food. As soon as they saw treats, children swarmed. They were ferocious in their appetites, often fistfighting over honey cinnamon rolls we threw in their midst. When I first saw the children ravenously tear off plastic wrappers, I wondered if they were excited to get American junk food. But soon I realized hunger drove them when they turned on each other. Larger boys would throw smaller children to the ground and kick toddlers over to get food. It wasn't just food—some Marines gave them cigarettes and watched in wonder as they smoked like adults. The first time one tried to steal from one of us, we laughed.

But that was early on, before the packs of dogs and children running in sewage and dodging through concertina wire all started to look the same. It happened quickly; I don't know if it was the first two-week patrol cycle or the second or the third. I can't remember when exactly. I was exhausted, staggering through the ruins of Shadyville. Dizzy with heat, I took deep pulls from the rubber tube of my Camelbak, the water gushing hot in my mouth. The sun warmed my helmet, making my gear warm to the touch. I focused on the Marine in front of me, Ulrich, and tried to keep my dispersion with him a constant. The squad was getting better at patrolling; we'd realized long ago it wasn't just walking around. Now our eyes looked sharp beneath the brims of our helmets. What little we spoke to the locals was never in English anymore, only Arabic, and only the phrases for *stop*, *turn around*, and *go away*. Usually, when a Marine wanted an Iraqi to stop or obey commands without wasting time talking, we pointed our rifles at them. If anyone tried to get in my face, I'd pull my pistol out.

Iraqis freaked out at the sight of a pistol because Saddam Hussein, their newly deposed dictator, had terrorized the populace with public executions of anyone he suspected of sedition via pistol. That was during the decades before the invasion. Saddam had swung on a rope a few years ago, his corpse torn down while people cheered. The children weren't scared of pistols though; they hadn't seen how easily someone could be dragged into the middle of the street, put on their knees, and shot in the back of the head.

I trudged through Shadyville following Ulrich, head spinning. This time when the children rushed us screaming for food, they wouldn't fall back when we pointed our weapons. Ulrich swore and swatted at one who jumped away, quicker than Ulrich's squat form with all its heavy gear. Three small boys, between the ages of four and eight, rushed me and tore at my gear. Their hands hovered like snakeheads, ready to strike into my pockets or pouches and grab gear. I followed unit Standard Operating Procedure (SOP) when it came to carrying my Night Vision Goggles (NVGs) in my utility pouch, attached to the side plate of my body armor. It was harder to keep their hands away from the clasp that held the pouch closed and I could sense one child trying to distract me while the other ran around my backside to tear something off me.

I hit the child quick with the six-inch barrel of my M-16, swinging so it caught the side of his head on the upward arc. I didn't use my full strength because I didn't want to hurt the child more than I had to. The blow sent him skittering in a stutter-step away from me, but he wheeled and gave me a defiant look. He was the oldest and biggest of the three and the only one still standing there while the other two ran. I stepped forward and twisted my hips with a measured amount of torque like a farmer moving a scythe through grain and struck the child again on the side of the head, more to the top and front this time. As soon as I felt the rifle make contact with the child's skull, I eased the torque in my hips and loosened my grip on the butt, letting the barrel glance upward. The child's head turned with the force of the blow, chin first, then seemed to drag the rest of his body behind it as he crumpled to the ground.

The child's body lifted a fine dust from the ground which colored the air. For a moment, he seemed to disappear. Then it cleared and I saw his face corrupted by hate. He wanted to fight but his strength fled him, though his courage held. On wobbly feet, he staggered like a just-born calf and made his way toward the short cement homes near us. I took a step after him, but a voice stopped me.

"Big Head," Mundell called. "What are you doing?"

Mundell was up ahead, the man in front of Ulrich. I locked eyes with him and shrugged, both of my palms to the sky. He let out a sad laugh and shook his head, ran his forearm over his face and grimaced. When I looked back at the children, they were in full flight, one weaving badly.

What was I doing?

I never answered the question. Instead, I trudged onward. Time blurred in cycles of weeks of patrolling and standing FOB security. Life went on and I didn't worry about any lines I crossed, lines I didn't know existed before I'd come to Iraq. Before I struck the child, there had been no hesitation. I'd just acted. The child represented a threat and I responded with the force that I thought was necessary. Had I even thought anything? Or had I simply lashed out? I knew that if it came between me having to hit a kid and keep my NVGs, I had a duty to ensure that the NVGs weren't stolen and turned against other Marines.

I pushed the memory deep into my mind and didn't think about it again for many years. It hadn't been uncommon for Marines to hit children and when I tried to remember who the first Marine was I'd ever seen strike a child, I couldn't. I did remember a time when Doc Bance went out with us and the patrol stopped at an affluent-looking house to talk to the owner and see if he would give us something to eat and drink.

The neighborhood was poor though and a few of its bolder children thought Bance an easy target because of his smile.

I watched Bance bringing plastic-knuckled fists down on children's heads, over and over, with a dull *thwack, thwack, thwack*. And then I remembered Fremil pulling out an ASP (telescoping baton) to swing at an Iraqi kid's head and miss. And then I remembered Mundell looking at me—"What are you doing"—not really asking it but saying it. And then I saw the older one fall, stumbling away from my second blow. I saw his face when he looked up at me, like an animal that would fight until killed. I wondered what kind of person beat on children with the barrel of his rifle.

We were early in our deployment and I thought a part of stoicism was a rejection of doubts, especially when the doubt concerned the mission itself. The problem I wasn't willing to face then was that I hadn't done the wrong thing, but the wrong thing had been done. How could that be? Clearly, hitting a child in the head with my rifle, a little one of the very people I was here to protect from insurgents and win the hearts and minds of, was morally incorrect. But at the same time, securing gear, especially gear with military purposes like NVGs that could easily be turned against Marines, took priority over whether or not a six-year-old got a headache or even his head split open. Where were his parents?

A big part of me blamed them somehow, for allowing their children to run wild through the streets like animals. I didn't wonder if their parents had been killed, crippled, or maimed and couldn't take care of their children anymore. I didn't think that maybe the superpower that had stomped this country into a mud hole should clean up the mess, should provide services to the orphans and the refugees. I fostered an illusion that there would be some relief for these people.

That first month at the FOB felt like forever. I had a hard time remembering life before deployment and parts of me didn't want to—it seemed so infinitesimal. Now I knew hardship, the poor and driven out. When I squeezed my eyes closed, rubbed my head, and tried to remember life stateside, I couldn't. All I could conjure up was a few static images, snippets of nightlife as if from movies, everything fading, everyone a caricature.

POST FOUR

IRAQ'S WINTER CHILL BIT ESPECIALLY HARD AT night, on post. I stared across the few palms that dotted the north side of Saq's fields of poorly irrigated crops. Rose, a tall man of twenty-three with a good-humored laugh and a friendly face, stood on a cooler in the back of the post so he could get his face level with the heater. It started with just a few tracers ripping across the streets of Shadyville. One gun, then another in return.

"Hey, Rose, come check this out," I said, my voice muffled as I breathed into my hands.

"I'm not moving. It's cold," Rose said.

For a few minutes, I didn't press the issue, because it wasn't uncommon in Iraq for people to shoot guns. Each house was allowed a fully automatic AK-47 and two magazines holding thirty rounds. After a few minutes passed, two machine guns opened up, spitting tracers like roman candles. For every tracer there are five rounds, but I wasn't counting them as they appeared in the inky blackness of Shadyville. Machine

Gunners were often asked to shoot a certain amount of rounds each burst; I'd learned early in my career how to count them accurately as I heard each individual report. Both guns opened up with no breaks in their cyclic rate of fire for a few seconds, the staccato sound of rifles set on single shot in the peripheries. Red dots of light flashed down the streets and through parking lots, making them glimmer in the dark. Sometimes, one of the machine guns' line of fire would stray into a building or rock and tracers would flare up brilliantly, spinning off into the night. It looked like a light show and sounded like an endless roll of Black Cats exploding in the distance.

"Echo COC, Echo COC, this is Post Four, come in Echo COC, over," I said into the radio.

"Post Four, this is Echo COC, send your traffic, over."

"Echo COC, there are shots fired in Shadyville, over," I said, my words coming out clipped between teeth holding a cigarette.

"How many shots fired, over."

"At this point, probably eight hundred, maybe twelve hundred. It's coming from two different machine guns, over."

"Monitor the situation and keep us updated, Post Four, COC out."

"What the fuck do they mean 'monitor the situation'?" Rose said. "We're three klicks away on top of a six-story building, freezing our asses off."

"Who do you think they're killing over there?"

Rose walked away from the window and sat down at the back of the post. My question hung in the air with our breath.

"It has to be the Iraqi Police," Rose said. "Well, at least some of the shooting. They could be slaying civilians over there. Maybe they're fighting off some attack, but I doubt it. Who the fuck knows, man."

I tried the optic on my rifle, but darkness made the magnification worthless. I waited for a tracer to suddenly disappear midair, signifying a hit. I saw it happen a couple times, then watched a stream of tracers chase something down and hold to a spot on the ground for a second before moving on. Suddenly it intensified. The machine guns started to put out short frenzied bursts *Blatatatatatatatatat, Blatatatatata*, followed by a few long ones. *Blatatatatatatatatatatatatatatatatatatatatatatatatatatat.*

"I think this is the finale!" I said. "I should get on the hook with the COC and tell them to blast classical over the comm, Wagner or some shit. That would be fucking unreal!"

Rose didn't give me a response. He was racked out at the back of the post. This happened almost every night. One of us, or both of us, would fall asleep. Usually I was out first, but Rose had spent the day as part of a working party moving boxes of chow around for the company cook.

I pulled out a book and checked to see how the firefight was going. It had died down to a few pops from small arms, the machine guns displaced to wherever they had come from. Leaning against the sandbag wall, I started to read.

After a few hours, I noticed the feral dogs that plagued the country had grouped en masse by the small Iraqi Police (IP) station, a stone's throw south of the FOB.

As if guided by some beacon, they formed a large pack of thirty to fifty animals. For a while, they were content with going through the garbage the IP had left out for the flies. Something changed though and the group turned into a disjointed knot of shadows swirling angrily in on itself. Every few seconds, a sleek shadow would glide closely behind or abreast of another shadow and a yelp would crease the night.

❀　❀　❀

I DREAMT OF nothingness, so saturated it had weight. Echoes of the waking world seeped in and I heard the feral pack in my dream. Their cries cut me deeply, sounding alien, conjuring scenes of hogs being slaughtered. They carried an urgency that made my teeth grind. They lived in wretchedness, crying out for something to listen. My chinstrap dug into my neck. I awoke to the last seconds of shrieking, yelping cacophony.

"What the fuck is going on?" I said.

My voice sounded strange in its familiarity after the sounds of the pack. Rose squinted his eyes against one of the FOB light's orange glare as he leaned against the wall across from me.

"You fell asleep," Rose said. "The dogs woke me up. I watched for a while. A big dog and some of its friends were terrorizing the pack, and then a smaller dog stood up to it. While they faced off, another dog ran out and snapped one of its back legs. I wanted to shoot it."

I remembered hearing Rose's voice yelling at the dogs. Suddenly, I didn't want to talk about it anymore. Rose was freaked out.

"I'm sick of watching that shit show out there," Rose said, spitting chew on the floor. "I'm not going to sleep or anything, I'm just taking a break from watching the feral dog version of *West Side Story*."

He smiled at me weakly, his eyes finally meeting mine instead of looking through them to the blackness beyond us.

I didn't smile back.

EVERYONE SPEAKS BARREL

ULRICH SAT ON HIS HAUNCHES IN SOMEONE'S yard, emptying his bowels. His squat figure looked like a ball of muscle, convulsing in on itself with a tuft of coarse black hair on top; his brown eyes, roving the surroundings, were strained bloodshot. The yard was thirty meters from Post One at the southeast corner of FOB Riviera, so we felt safe. The squad had been patrolling hard for weeks and this long-term exertion had bred complacency through exhaustion. The squad formed a semicircle around him. In our minds, the threat of attack was so small that most of MachineGuns was just milling about, laughing or smoking. None of us seemed concerned that, bunched up, we could be wiped out by a single Vehicle-Borne Improvised Explosive Device (VBIED).

Minutes earlier, the patrol had walked out of the FOB parking lot and down the access road, two parallel columns with Prockop in between. Spirits were high after a breakfast of powdered eggs and slimy bacon. The heat barely pulled beads of sweat from our faces.

A flat blue sky hung overhead, taking a lighter tinge the closer it came to the horizon. The day seemed to hold the promise of adventure. The squad racked rounds into the chambers of our weapons with a gusto more appropriate on safari than in a combat zone.

We hadn't been outside of the Riv more than thirty seconds when Ulrich looked over at Prockop, a mournful expression on his face.

"I've gotta shit, Sergeant," Ulrich said.

Prockop's stride didn't falter.

"We just left the FOB," Prockop said.

His voice carried a lack of inflection customary to Sergeants who had long since burned out. Prockop's first deployment to Iraq had broken his spirit. He didn't bounce back from a Dear John letter, amidst the chaos and violence typical of the early occupation. What held fast was his contract which he was now serving out during another deployment. Prockop was taller than most Marines, although his physicality was diminished by a moderate build and the way his voice didn't carry authority.

"Right now," Ulrich said. "I need to go right now."

The first few men in the patrol took a right on the main road in front of the FOB, heading south toward Saqlawiyah. Prockop craned his neck to see the point man.

"Take a left into that yard!" Prockop yelled.

The front of the patrol swerved sharply into a yard with a well-built house. Whoever lived there wasn't rich, but certainly wasn't poor. The location of the property afforded relative protection because of its close proximity to the FOB, but it wasn't so close as to arouse suspicion that the home's residents were colluding with American forces. I smiled as I trudged into the yard, wondering if the owner had ever suffered for his enviable spot before. If he hadn't, he was about to now in a very strange way.

"Hurry up," Prockop said, before joining a few other Marines on the edge of the property in some shade.

I hadn't taken a defensive position covering a field of fire, not even pretending to be what the military called tactical. Instead, I smoked and watched Rose slowly make his way up to Ulrich.

"That's what you get for drinking eleven milks with your Pop-Tarts in the chow hall this morning," Rose said, before throwing back his head in laughter.

The guffaws bounced off a six-foot concrete wall that ran the east side of the property. A light coat of cement had been applied to the top of the fence and sharp pieces of broken glass, metal, and other dangerous odds and ends stuck skyward. The solution to crossing the hazard was a thick blanket thrown across the top, but we always seemed short on thick blankets while patrolling the wastes. The road in front of the house ran right from the MSR to the north, passed in front of the Riv, and continued down into Saq. The MSR went east to Fallujah and west to Ramadi—it was heavy with traffic.

Ulrich squatted smack dab in the middle of a dusty lawn with sparse patches of the Iraqi version of crab grass. He didn't acknowledge Rose, instead ignoring him to stare at the cars going by with a sour look on his face.

"Urglleahhh," Ulrich said.

The noise was somewhere between a grunt and a groan of anguish. Shit sprayed behind him, making an irregular *splash* and *glop* sound as it hit the dirt. The diarrhea was little more than brown tinted water which pooled around Ulrich's boots.

"Oh, my fucking God," Rose said. "Look at that soft serve shit piling up behind our fat little Chamorro baby."

I shuffled over to Ulrich and looked down at him. Ulrich's call sign Chamorro was the name of his ancestors, Guam's indigenous people; its use often signaled lighthearted teasing.

"Ulrich," I said.

He didn't look up. He just sat there on his haunches, shitting and watching the cars go by. I turned to look at the road, to see if I was missing something interesting, and found traffic had backed up out of Saq. In several cars, children watched wide-eyed, noses squished against the windows, fog jetting out like whiskers.

"Ulrich!" I yelled.

"Fuck. What do you want?" Ulrich said.

More sounds like whimpering followed. He hugged his arms around his stomach, pinching them between his torso and his legs as he squatted. Beads of sweat were rolling down his cheeks and furrowed brow.

"I'm helping you, Marine," I said.

I tried not to laugh as I kicked sand in Ulrich's face. One, two, three, and then four good kicks of sand before I stood back to survey the effect. Ulrich still squatted there, clutching his stomach, but now he was a much paler shade of dust than his usual skin color of light chocolate. He resembled a powdered doughnut. A few Marines in the squad pulled out cameras and snapped photos.

"How did 'I'm helping you' even become a thing?" Rose asked.

The phrase *I'm helping you, Marine* had come from our workup back stateside, in the eastern California wasteland of a base called Twentynine Palms. One evening, we'd been digging in—shallow graves, to aid our sleeping systems in staving off the bitter desert nights. I'd started kicking sand into the grave of the Marine sleeping next to me. *I'm helping you, Marine,* I'd explained. It caught on and spiraled out of control with Marines in MachineGuns screaming *I'm helping you!* while pushing each other off trucks and Marines harassed in porta-johns being told they were just the victims of good Samaritans. It was a running gag that made us laugh when we were miserable and like most grunts in the Corps we were miserable most of the time. I left the question ignored. Another part of the gag was pretending to be ignorant of its existence.

"Goddamn it," Ulrich said. "You come near me and I'll stab you."

Ulrich fished a six-inch folding blade from one of the pockets on his flak and flicked it open with his right hand, while his left hand kept his pants hovering above the pool fading into the earth.

"You're gonna stab me?" I said, trying not to laugh.

I fumbled around in the side pouch on my flak, the one that was supposed to have a medical kit but was actually filled with food, baby wipes, and a tourniquet. I was the kind of Marine who brought most of the things I might need on patrol with me. Marines shit themselves in the desert all the time. I kept baby wipes with me because the moist towelettes did a good job cleaning shit off a person's ass; a plant or stick would leave brown matter behind to rub ass cheeks raw.

"Here are some baby wipes for the little Chamorro baby," I said.

The wipes hit the ground by Ulrich. He looked up at me sheepishly for a moment before putting his knife away and carefully picking up the baby wipes.

"Thanks, Big Head," Ulrich muttered.

I turned away from him as he pulled a wipe out of the pack and started to reach back to clean his ass. Hawkins walked over from standing underneath the shade tree with a crooked smirk. Most white Marines all looked the same in their gear after the desert sun tanned them, but Hawkins' smirk always set him apart. He was an Iowa country boy, ready to drink, fight, and fuck. He wasn't a blowhard though, only speaking when he had something to say.

"Hawkins, did you see those little kids getting an eyeful of Ulrich?" I asked. "I wonder how their parents are going to field those questions. *Daddy, why do the Americans seize control of our country and shit in our lawns?*"

The street in front of us was a little less congested now, the idling cars with peeping children long gone.

"What? Little kids were watching him shit? Jesus Christ," Hawkins said around a chew-stuffed bottom lip. "Have you talked to the guy who owns this dump? He's standing on his front stoop over there."

Rose and I exchanged glances with each other and then with Hawkins. We all three looked down at Ulrich, who had one hand out in front of him to balance and the other behind him with a baby wipe, busy with his ass.

"Should someone go talk to him? I mean, he does live right by the FOB," Rose said. "And aren't we supposed to issue IOU chits to people whose property we damage?"

"Don't look at me," Hawkins said. "You're both senior by a long shot. I'm sure you'll figure out how to smooth it over with him."

Hawkins punctuated his words by spitting a long strand of dark brown liquid in front of Ulrich. Ignoring the interpreter we had with us didn't make a whole lot of sense. I didn't mean to, I'd just forgotten we'd brought one. MachineGuns had a habit of leaving the wire with no interpreter, or "terp" as we called them—whiny pains in the ass. If I wasn't getting through to an Iraqi, all I had to do was stick my weapon in his face. Fear and intimidation worked a strange kind of magic.

"I'll go talk to him," I said.

The man stood, smoking a cigarette, on his stoop. He dressed in garb that wasn't soiled or threadbare; the brand of cigarettes he smoked was better than my own. He had money. The sun left a light webbing of wrinkles on his face. His fingernails looked clean and smooth. He kept glancing from me to Ulrich, now standing in front of his small pile of diarrhea and adjusting his gear. Ulrich had decided to throw the half-dozen baby wipes he'd used behind him. There they lay, haphazardly scattered a few feet from a brown stain that hadn't been there ten minutes before. I glanced from the mess to the man in front of me.

"Hello, sir," I said. "I know that it probably looks a little unprofessional that my brother in arms just shit in your yard ...."

I paused for a moment to eye the man's cigarette.

"Could I get one of those from you?" I asked.

I pointed to the cigarette in his mouth.

"Oh, yes, mista. No problem, no problem, mista," the man said.

He pulled out a pack of Miamis and handed them to me. I carefully extracted a single cigarette out of the pack and handed it back to the man. He offered me a light, but I waved him off, opting instead to find mine somewhere in my pockets. I took a moment to light my smoke and then continued.

"I'm sure you understand that people sometimes shit themselves." I paused to take a drag.

"Yes, mista, no problem, mista," the man said, nodding frantically.

"I mean, my buddy Ulrich didn't leave the wire thinking he was going to shit water in the middle of your property. It's just how it goes sometimes."

"No problem, mista, no problem."

The Iraqi man kept saying "no problem, mista" over and over while he half bowed, ducking his head. The smile on my face faded to a frown. I knew, or thought I knew, I should revel in the thrill of power, but I felt dazed instead.

"I'm sorry," I said.

I didn't want to speak with the groveling man anymore. I turned my back on him, my rifle by my leg as it swung loosely from my lowered arm to look at the Marines behind me. They were forming up beside the road in two-staggered columns, checking and rechecking their gear and weapons, getting ready to patrol into Saq.

"Fall in with your fireteam," Prockop shouted in clipped Sergeant speech.

I fell in behind Ulrich. As we stepped onto the street, Ulrich walked with a strange bowlegged gait. If he was embarrassed, it didn't show. The muddy pile of shit in the Iraqi's yard was almost completely absorbed into the sand now. In a few minutes, even those chunks would be hard to pick out of the rock and trash in the yard. Across the street from us, directly to the south of the FOB, there were several smaller dorm-like buildings with children out on the balconies. The distance was far enough away that I couldn't make out what they were doing, but a few of them had their arms bent up to their faces with flashes periodically coming from their eyes.

"Fuckin' A, those little kids have binoculars," I said. "How the fuck can they afford those?"

The squad had yet to spread out. Rose was close enough to me to talk without yelling.

"Fuck, you're right," Rose said. "The little brown men are always watching us."

"I bet those kids watch the FOB parking lot way more than we want to know," Hawkins said from behind me.

We walked in uncomfortable silence for a few minutes. The children with the binoculars scampered inside, returning to their perches without them. I wondered if they watched us all the time. The FOB was exposed; most Marines realized that. The posts stationed around the perimeter would keep a few intruders out and give us enough warning to repel an attack, but they couldn't stop a rocket or larger exploding round. Echo was sure, as the companies before them had been, that the indigenous population of Saq was too low tech to execute that kind of operation. They didn't have the equipment and our patrols were meant to make sure it stayed that way. Some Marines thought Iraqis were unintelligent, not smart enough to pull off an attack that would cause mass casualties. I knew better. Someone had given those kids binoculars with nefarious intent. I knew the little kids who just watched Ulrich shit in their neighbor's yard were killers. They'd never forget what we did here and when they grew strong enough to raise a rifle or make a bomb, they'd take revenge.

"Do you ever get the feeling that we're out here fucking ourselves?" I asked no one in particular.

"Every day," Rose answered. "And when I'm not out here fucking myself, I'm in the FOB getting fucked by the big green weenie of the Corps."

"Gotta love the dick of the Corps," Hawkins chimed in from behind us. "Always ready to fuck its own by taking away leave or assigning extra duties."

The patrol's banter quieted as we approached the northern part of the town. The marketplace was in full swing at midday. People filled the streets, weaving in and out of the sometimes standstill traffic as they made their way to buy goods. Prockop signaled for the point man to swing right at the roundabout, marked by a fifty-foot tall obelisk covered with ornate carvings. I felt like an adventurer, stepping out into the breech when I patrolled—like going back in time. The most modern buildings the Iraqis lived in were at least thirty years old. Most of the older buildings looked like they were from the 1950s, back when the British occupied Iraq. As the patrol made its way a few blocks west, I thought about how some of the older Iraqis had experienced British occupation as well. I was just the new kid on the block, a new look to the old face of foreign military.

"Take a left," Prockop yelled.

The point man turned left down a road on the west side of the market. I couldn't make out exactly who the point man was, the patrol's dispersion pushing him about twenty-five meters ahead of me with his back turned. I thought it was Larkin, but I couldn't be sure. The rest of the patrol followed until we were all heading the same direction with the busy market to our left. I took a long look into the market as I walked.

Amidst squat concrete buildings the color of old teeth, the market hummed. People haggled loudly for goats in mid-slaughter, their blood and entrails gushing out for the flies. Children ran wildly from stand to stand, yelling parents chasing after them. A few Iraqi Policemen stood, scattered about the chaotic scene with AK-47s in hand. The amount of people in all different kinds of attire dazzled the eye: women clad in head-to-toe black dresses, other women in business suits, poor men in traditional Arabic clothes which Marines called the "man dress," rich men in suits, and a few people dressed like gypsies out of an old movie. The wares being sold ranged from drugs to trinkets, with the former being much more interesting to Marines than the latter. Falafel stands could be easily identified by the small throng of people surrounding them. I never ate falafels—my fear of sickness and broken glass outweighed my hunger pains—but some people couldn't get enough of them. Whenever the chow hall ran short, Marines would come down with chronic diarrhea from eating food outside the wire; the falafel stands were often the culprit.

The market also served as the main source of clothing. Racks of clothes were out for the day, ready to be picked through. Something caught my eye and made me stutter-step. In the middle of one rack were all kinds of uniforms. Some of them were old Iraqi Army (IA) uniforms from before the U.S. arrival. Others were more current uniforms, the kind I saw Iraqi Police and Iraqi Army wearing every day. About to point them out to Rose, I heard Ulrich's voice in front of me.

"Are those Marine cammies?" he asked.

I glanced to the rack ahead of the one I was looking at, directly to the left of Ulrich. Sure as shit, there they were, Marine Corps camouflage utilities. Half of them desert pattern, the kind I was wearing, and the other half woodland pattern. My jaw dropped and hung as I looked at the cammie.

"Owen! Owen, come here for a second," I called out.

Owen was our interpreter for the patrol. Echo had just a few to choose from and only one of them was worth a damn beyond his ability to translate. Owen wasn't the terp that was worth a damn. He hated foot patrols and it got annoying to listen to him beg higher-ups to put him on vehicle patrols like he was some kind of terp superstar.

"One second," Owen said. He trotted up from the back of the column, where he had been lingering.

"How does the market get Marine cammies?" I asked.

Owen glanced behind us at the uniforms. "I do not know, that is a good question," he said, in a cadence that wasn't as smooth as a native speaker's. "There are many ways that someone could come into possession of them. A Marine could have sold them at the market or they could have been stolen. I'm also pretty sure you can buy them on the internet."

I didn't respond, and he walked beside me in silence, glad to have someone in MachineGuns that acknowledged his existence beyond saying *Translate!* while pointing at someone. The roar of the marketplace faded behind us as we followed the road toward the southern part of Saq. A group of children was playing around shot-up, abandoned buildings, common to the cities in Iraq. Dogs yelped and barked in an alley as they dug through garbage, searching for food. Off to our left was the Iraqi Police station and just south of it was what passed for a hospital. The day was hot and sweat stung my eyes. I was glad for a slight breeze coming off the Euphrates.

We were nearing the point in our patrol where we'd turn left and head east along the southern rim of Saq, when a child ran out in the middle of the patrol, right in front of Owen and me. The boy, maybe six, stumbled and fell. He was obese, so large it was almost comical. A chalky substance was smeared around his mouth and covered his bare feet. The child got up and sprinted to the other side of the road, disappearing into an abandoned building.

"Was that kid wearing a fucking G-Unit shirt?" Rose asked before bursting into laughter.

Another child started to run out across the road in front of me but stopped when he realized he was in the middle of our patrol. He was around the same age as the first boy, but very different in appearance. This one was slight of build with fine blond hair and blue eyes that looked up at me like pools in the desert. I stopped in my tracks for a second and we stared at each other. The kid reminded me of back home, looking like so many corn-fed kids in Iowa. I took a step forward and the child turned and walked down the side of the road the same way as the patrol.

"Rose," I said. "Does that kid look Iraqi to you?"

"Fuck no," Rose said. "That kid looks—"

"Is that a fucking white kid up there?" Hawkins interrupted from behind us.

Ulrich twisted his head around to see what was going on behind him and froze, his eyes locked on the child. After a moment, he looked forward and quickened his pace, trying to put distance between himself and the only native white person we'd seen yet.

"Owen," I said. "How is there a white kid walking down the street with us?"

"What do you mean?" Owen asked.

"How did he get here?" I replied.

"He is an Iraqi child."

"No fucking way," Rose said from off to our right. "No fucking way."

"You mean to tell me that two Iraqis knocked boots and that kid was born," I said. "Two *brown* people with *black* hair fucked, and then had a *white* child with *blond* hair?"

"It's like the Christmas story," Hawkins said. "Except with fucking. It's a miracle!"

"Actually," Rose said. "I'm pretty sure Jesus came out white, or at least in all the pictures."

Owen waited to answer as we walked by a large, gutted building that was undergoing construction or reconstruction; it was hard to tell which, since we didn't know if the owner or U.S. forces had gutted the building. Men with hammers pounded away at the cinder block walls. I had no idea what they were trying to accomplish. Construction projects were a rare thing, especially in Saq. Once we had passed, Owen spoke.

"If an Iraqi and a Persian have a child, it can be white," Owen said. "Persians are what you would call, eh ... what is word?"

"Aryan?"

"Yes, Aryan. Persians are Aryan, so it is possible."

"That's interesting. You know who else is Aryan? Big Smith, from Assault. You've met him, I'm sure," I said.

"Yes." Owen said. His voice was quiet, eyes straight ahead.

"How old do you think that kid is, Rose?" I asked.

Rose bound forward a few steps with his long legs to catch up to us. He took a long look at the child walking just ahead.

"That kid is young," Rose said. "I'd guess maybe five years old. Too young to be walking out here with packs of dogs and needles in the dirt."

A young woman ran out into the street and scooped up the child. She looked at the three of us walking abreast from left to right: me, Owen, and then Rose. Fear flashed across her face. The woman must have been in her late twenties, but it was hard to tell. She hurried away, the child in her arms.

"Well, I'll be damned, there she is," I said. "And isn't it something that her child is about as old as the occupation?"

"Oh shit!" Rose shouted. "She must have got some Marine dick!"

Rose made a motion of jerking off an invisible floating cock in front of his face while opening his mouth wide and wagging his tongue back and forth. Owen kept his eyes on the horizon, refusing to look at either Rose or me. I cleared my throat in an effort to get him to look at me, but he wouldn't. I thumped my rifle against my chest and stomped my feet as I walked, but to no avail. Rose kept up his performance on the other side of Owen, his hands jerking back and forth in the air in front of him.

"I guess the real question is, if she wanted it," I said.

Rose's hands slowed, then dropped back to his slung rifle. He looked over at me with a blank look as if the possibility of rape never occurred to him. I stared hard at Owen, but he wouldn't move his gaze. The question hung in the air between us. Owen wasn't like the other terps from other countries; he'd been born and raised in Iraq. His sisters and mother lived in some part of the country where things weren't particularly bad, but it could have happened to one of them. Letting it be wasn't an option for me after goading Owen along my line of questioning. I didn't particularly dislike him, but his vulnerability was like blood in the water. I opened my mouth, but Hawkins interrupted me.

"Big Head," Hawkins said. "That's enough."

I turned around, walking backwards so I could see him.

"Come on," he said.

I watched him walking. In his body armor, Hawkins looked everything like a Marine should look. His chiseled jaw jutted out a little, head leaned back, and eyes blazing at me like embers from beneath his helmet. His gait swayed, absorbing the weight of his gear and weapon gracefully. I remembered how green he'd been when he joined the unit. Now he was so mature. He'd make a fine Sergeant someday.

"We'll have it your way," I said. "I guess it's fucking McDonald's out here."

"I'm pretty sure that's Burger King's slogan, Big Head," Hawkins said with a wry grin.

I turned back around and picked up my pace. Up ahead was the left turn the patrol would take east. The point man disappeared around the corner, as did the second man, then the third. These were the moments we were most vulnerable to attack—when the patrol was cut in half by a corner. I tried not to think about the myriad ways insurgents maim and kill us: roadside IEDs followed by small arms fire, sniper fire to wound one Marine near an IED that detonates when three other Marines run to drag him to safety, or an RPG salvo. Instead, I thought about what I would do to kill us.

I'd take a tailgate from an old beat-up Ford truck, take it apart and put mortar rounds in it hooked up to a cellphone detonator. Then I'd put it back together, put the tailgate back on the truck, and watch for a patrol to walk out of the front gate of the FOB. When I was pretty sure of the route, I'd park the truck where the blast would kill a Marine. If the patrol didn't walk by the truck, it would only take a minute to set up again.

A great rush of air came from the balcony of one of the abandoned buildings to my right. Ulrich had been rounding the corner just ahead of me at a slow walk, carefully looking side to side, but when the air filled with popping sounds he ran. I threw myself into the shallow ditch to my left. My body coursed with ice-cold adrenaline.

"Pigeons," Rose said. "It was just pigeons taking off."

I stood and moved back onto the road. I realized I'd heard the sound that spooked me before, back home while hunting quail, the explosion of wings cupping the air and moving it forcefully.

"We must have pushed a dog up from the street," I said.

My hands fumbled for my pack of smokes. I heard Rose laughing behind me as I lit a cigarette. I took a long drag that burned away a third of it. I rounded the corner without slowing to check my sides, the scare giving me tunnel vision. I was using the butt of my first cigarette to light another one when my eyes focused on what was in front of me. I nearly ran into Ulrich.

Three Iraqi men stood in front of a crumbling cinder block building, talking to Prockop. The leader of the trio towered over Prockop's six-foot-one figure. The taller man had an enormous belly and thick mustache reminiscent of Saddam's—before the dictator donned his last necktie for a long dirt nap. I couldn't hear the discussion they were having, but the big man was using broken English well enough to avoid losing Prockop's attention. The other two men hung back a little ways, letting him do the talking.

"Push forward and get some dispersion, goddamn it," Rose said. "I round the corner to find a gaggle-fuck of Marines acting like it's their first day out of the School of Infantry."

The first half of the patrol moved forward, putting about ten meters between each man while being sure the columns were staggered so no two Marines were parallel on the road. This left the back half of the patrol to catch up, creating an effect commonly referred to by troop handlers as "the slinky."

The patrol took a minute to stabilize. Each man adjusted his gear, did a cursory glance of the surrounding street for IEDs, and checked the rooftops. Everyone settled into a standing position that afforded some comfort in their body armor: shoulders slouched, backs stooped slightly at the waist, knees taking turns bending and stretching. Like any Marine in country, we knew the only thing worse than walking around was standing still. The point man, now ahead of the cluster of Iraqi men and Prockop, turned to face the patrol.

"If only there was someone here that spoke Iraqi."

It was Larkin on point and his voice carried with it the edge of sarcasm.

Owen sprinted to Prockop's side from the back of the column. The other two Iraqis joined in the conversation with the aid of Owen's interpretation.

I looked to the patrol's right, past the single line of decrepit buildings frosted with pigeons, their pock-marked exteriors the face of simple beauty swept away by violence. Inside them a swirl of bats could be heard and the occasional shuffling of dogs or children. Behind the buildings, fields covered with a latticework of deep irrigation ditches stretched to the Euphrates, miles away. Beyond the river would be the town of Habbaniyah with the old British base of the same name now occupied by U.S. forces. Just south of Habbaniyah lay Al Taqaddum and in between the two strongholds was the MSR that ran east and west across the plains. I thought of Al Taqaddum, the true power in the area, a stronghold so unassailable it would never fall. The might of the U.S. Air Force flew from a plateau that rose suddenly from the earth with sheer sides, a geographic anomaly created somehow by the lake that butted up to its southern edges. In my mind, I saw the watchtowers that studded the top of the cliffs and the drones forever circling, always watching.

"What do these guys want?"

Ulrich's voice brought me back to the patrol. He grew impatient and stamped his boots on the packed earth.

"Does it matter?" I asked. "Whatever it is, we aren't going to give it to them."

We stood in silence for a few minutes before Prockop walked over to the patrol and word passed from the front end through the middle to the back that the three Iraqis were diabetics who needed insulin. The hospital didn't have any. The lack of medicine in the hospital didn't surprise anyone—it had gotten hit pretty hard in years past. I never found out who decided to shoot up the hospital, but I was pretty sure it wasn't the Iraqis. Such sights were common—not even the school across the street from the hospital had escaped war's wrecking ball.

The front of the patrol started moving forward along the dirt road.

"Shouldn't we write them a chit or something, so they can go to the FOB and ask for medicine?" Ulrich asked when he passed by the men. They stood there talking to each other in low murmurs.

"There aren't any fucking chits. Everyone stop talking about the fucking chits," I said.

"First Sergeant seems to think there are chits," Ulrich said over his shoulder as he walked. "How we should give them to Iraqis if we damage their properties, and sometimes if they need something. How can we win the hearts and minds if we don't fix the things we break?"

"I thought there were chits, too," Rose said. He didn't sound sure, though.

"Oh really, dumbasses? Where are the chits at? Where can I pick one up? Have you ever seen a chit? Even once, have you ever seen a chit, even one fucking time in your entire Marine Corps career?"

"Well, no," Ulrich said. "But we could write them out."

I waited a beat to hear Rose's answer.

"Fuck ... goddamn it," he said.

"Oh yeah, we'll just write, 'I, Lance Corporal Fuck-Off-A-Lot hereby owe you, Mr. Haji Man, such and such thing,'" I said.

I coughed and spit a glob of something black on the ground ahead of me. Smoking so much wasn't doing me any favors.

"Ulrich," I said. "First Sergeant made me pick a cigarette butt out of a porta-shitter yesterday. Last time I asked him a question, he told me to shut the fuck up. When I asked Prockop about the chits, he asked me the same questions I'm asking you right now. Do you think anyone cares what I think some Iraqi gents should get? Especially medicine—am I a fucking doctor? No, I'm a Machine Gunner. I'm the opposite of a doctor."

Ulrich didn't say anything.

"Ulrich," Rose said. "Big Head's right. There are no chits."

The urban decay slowly turned into houses with lawns, children with patched clothes, and buildings that weren't in disrepair. It wasn't a complete transformation from poverty, but it was much better than south of the market. Cows grazed some of the lawns, goats could be heard bleating, and every so often a group of children would run close by, screeching and laughing. I wanted it to feel like home, but it didn't. Even though this part of town was populated with farms that reminded me of Iowa, it was still alien. The smell of broken earth from the fields and water from the irrigation channels mingled with grass and cow manure, but like dreams that give themselves away, something was wrong. This place wasn't for me. My people's hands hadn't worked the land, tilled the soil, raised the houses, or made the roads. I realized in that moment that I missed home dearly and would do anything to see it again.

The front end of the patrol slowed to a stop; so did the rest of the Marines without losing too much dispersion. I looked ahead and saw that the road took a ninety-degree turn left and went north. The point man, Larkin, was standing in the middle of the road with the turn to his left, a driveway directly ahead, and another driveway to his right. Prockop walked to his side, stood there for a moment, then led the patrol into the drive to his right. Our pace was slow as we navigated the short gravel drive to a large open yard, a small house on one side and a squat building on the other, with farm equipment in between. Prockop led the squad in a circle around the yard and stopped by the house, so the patrol was in a U that had its prongs facing the driveway. I realized it was a move a seasoned Marine would make. If an enemy presented itself in the driveway, the entire squad could open fire.

Prockop started poking around the building. He didn't tell us what he was looking for and I didn't ask. The building didn't seem interesting to me with its rusted sheet metal roof and chickens freely moving around inside. Iraq's agricultural practices were a combination of rundown equipment, third world ingenuity, and crops that easily grew. Many Iraqi farmers had sheds where they could work on their equipment or where they kept their pumps sheltered from the elements while they moved water into irrigation ditches.

Most Marines were sitting down for a break as I walked around the U we made, looking at the farm equipment. I made my way slowly towards the house, taking in as much as I could. A marsh behind the property marked where the Euphrates came closest to Saq which served them well. Their lawn had actual grass, not just sparse spiny shoots. Animals could be let out to graze, taking the burden of constantly having to feed them off the owners. The fertile ground made the land owners rich, while the rest of Saq had nothing but dust, stone, and broken homes. But even with their relative wealth, the people most affluent in southeast Saq at that moment were Marines.

I bumped into a child who'd wandered out of the nearby house.

"As-salamu alaykum, little brother," I said. I extended my gloved hand to the child while greeting him in his own tongue. The child was clean, well-fed, clothed. His brown eyes looked up at me with fear and he leveled a finger of accusation at me.

"Musalaheen! Musalaheen!" The child cried twice before turning to run back inside. He peered at me from behind the doorjamb.

I stood stunned for a moment, arm extended in front of me. I looked at the glove on my hand, blackened from sewage and dirt, torn apart by razor wire and rocks. I realized, if I were him, I wouldn't shake my hand either.

"Musalaheen," Rose said from behind me.

"What does that mean?" I asked. "Do you know? You took those Arabic classes fairly seriously before we came over. I guess I shouldn't have fucked them off."

"It means gunslinger," Rose explained. "Although we got told it meant bandit in the States, it doesn't. The kids always point at us when we ask them who the gunslingers are. Ask them where the mujahideen are, that means freedom fighter, or something like it."

A mother appeared behind the child, pulled the child away and slammed the door.

"I guess that's how it goes sometimes," I said. "The liberators get called bandits while the bad guys get called freedom fighters."

"Makes you wonder which we are," Hawkins said.

The squad stood, shifting and restless. Straps bit them where they were cinched tight, to keep backpacks and armor secured on bodies. Patrolling was long work, usually slow and methodical. Blistered feet and raw skin were the name of the game. The life of a grunt held no glamour off the big screen or out of books. In the desert, life was a struggle, the earth set against us. But near rivers, where green flourished, things were more hopeful; the war seemed distant enough that I dreaded going back to it. But back to the FOB we went. We had nowhere else to go.

RIVER CITY

THE CONVOY PASSED THE IRAQI CHECKPOINT IN
front of the base; from the turret, the Iraqi Police looked
cold as they tried to breathe warmth into cupped hands.
All the Marine posts on the perimeter of the base were
manned, but there weren't any of the normal smoke
trails from cigarettes or dim lights Marines used to read
books. The MRAP came to a jerking stop in front of
FOB Riviera and everyone started to dismount. I heard
something about "River City."

"We're in River City. Did you hear what happened?"

"Fuck," Kistler said. He stormed off to the smoke pit.

"Goddamn it," a Marine said. "Who was it?"

I didn't stick around to find out what was going on.
Hopping down from the top of the MRAP, I walked
into the FOB without bothering to clear my weapon.
Being a Lance Corporal made me a prime scapegoat
for Corporals who didn't want to unload gear. I would
have sprinted up the stairs to my room but slowed when

I saw Seals at the front desk. He had a look on his face that was serious, even for him.

"How was it out there, Big Head?" he asked me.

Seals was steely, the quintessential Marine Sergeant in almost every respect. His only deviation from regulation was fraternizing with MachineGuns in his downtime. MachineGuns had a reputation for telling people, sometimes regardless of rank, to go fuck themselves. We liked Seals though, mostly because he wanted to kill everything in sight. That kind of thinking made the war a lot less complicated. I liked Seals because he reminded me of the old Corps I'd been told about in boot camp, a Corps that existed when wars had been righteous.

"Fucking boring. Thought I was going to shoot two guys in a pickup truck, but then Kistler said no." I looked down at the ground. "I'm pretty sure they were pacing the convoy to get an average speed or—"

Seals cut me off.

"You haven't heard?"

I froze like a deer in a poacher's spotlight.

"What happened?" I asked.

"River City! How do you not know? Some guys over in Golf—" Seals was on his feet. The Company's CO walked out of the wing of the building to the left of the SOG desk.

I moved to the stairs with a purpose and then up them—I didn't want to be underfoot of the higher-ups. Behind me, I heard the CO talking to Seals in a serious, hushed tone. I couldn't make out what was being said as I rounded the first bend in the long flight of stairs that wound up the center of the Riv.

The internet café was in the middle of the second floor, between the two wings of the building that flanked the staircase. If there was a world record for the smallest and shittiest internet café, the one at FOB Riviera would have held it. The café had a total of six computers that barely worked, two phones that only worked half the time, and enough dust to fill a small sandbox. Blaker and the Navy Chief paced in front of the café's outer red wall. I stopped. The Chief wouldn't make eye contact.

"What the fuck happened, Blaker?" I asked.

"Three Marines from Golf Company got smoked," Blaker said.

His face was blank, for the first time since I'd known him. His eyes weren't focused on me, but past me, through the building.

"Wait. What?" I said. I ran my hand over my cropped hair. "Did Viking get hit?"

Viking was the FOB that Golf Company held, a few miles west of the Riv on the MSR. I thought they might have been hit hard with rockets and small arms fire or had maybe even taken contact from a large insurgent force. The battle must have been pitched to leave three Marines on the deck—or had they fallen in the first few exchanges?

"It wasn't like you think," Blaker said.

Whatever the reality of the situation was, it didn't sit so well with the normally energetic frat-boy persona of Blaker.

"Golf was out doing its monthly training to zero their weapons. The Mortar Section was going to fire, but their CO wanted them to practice on targets further away than a few hundred meters. He had three vehicles roll out to set up targets further out," Blaker's voice held no inflection, like some monk chanting. "The first was an MRAP. It rolled over the IED without setting it off. The second was a Humvee. It triggered the pressure plate."

I got the feeling if I had walked away, up the stairwell, Blaker would've stood and talked to whatever his eyes were focused on instead of me, while the Chief shuffled around the internet café's door.

"Fuck," was all I said. The Chief's constant pacing was starting to put me on edge.

"Their Humvee flipped over and started on fire. The green gear pinned them in the Humvee so they couldn't move. The doors wouldn't open. Their friends listened to them scream as they burned."

Gravitas didn't hit me like a ton of bricks, like it evidently had Blaker. There had always been a part of me that thought Marines were being sent here to die for no reason and this was just the curtain pulling back to reveal all my suspicions were true. My stomach began to fill with lead.

Blaker pushed on. He wasn't going to stop until I had heard all of it. I realized he wouldn't have let me walk away. The bigger, more muscular Marine would have grabbed me by the throat, with that blank look on his face, and told me while I squirmed.

"The turret gunner of the third vehicle crawled out of the turret, tried to save them," Blaker stuttered a half step toward me. "When they pulled him off the driver side door, his gloves were smoking. That's how hot it was. His fucking gloves were smoking."

Blaker blinked for a few seconds. Slowly, I could see the spark he usually had in his eyes return—not all at once, but just a glimmer.

"What are you doing standing here?" I asked them.

"I want to call my family and tell them I'm all right," the large Chief said as quietly as I'd ever heard him talk. It surprised me that he could speak so softly. This was the same Chief that had boldly stood up to my Company First Sergeant when the First Shirt violated his own rules and wore gym clothes into the Riv's dingy chow hall, the same Chief who didn't take shit from any Marine, a guy made of iron—now humbled.

Blaker didn't get a chance to answer, as our First Sergeant walked out of the H&S wing to the left of the internet café. He was looking down at some papers as he walked, but stopped just in front of our little group as if sensing us all standing there.

"First Sergeant," the Chief closed the space between himself and the First Shirt in two steps with his long legs. "Will the computer center be open at all? I want to call my family."

The Chief's voice held no trace of the thunder it usually carried.

"It's River City," First Shirt said. He glanced up from his paperwork for half a second to look into the Chief's eyes. "It will be for the rest of the night at least. I'm sorry. Nothing I can do."

"Thank you, First Sergeant," the Chief said. He turned and quietly walked back down the stairwell in the direction of medical. First Shirt was close on his heels, staring intently at the papers in his hands.

"River City?" I said questioningly, looking at Blaker.

"River City is when they lock all of the phones and computer centers down," Blaker answered without missing a beat. "The Corps wants to contact next of kin before anyone else does. If they let a thousand or so Marines from our battalion call home, word would get to the families."

"I can't get into the computer center and call home? You fucking kidding me right now?" My voice quivered with anger.

I made an effort to call home every few days or so, even though the wait for a phone ranged from forty-five minutes to a few hours. It was one thing if the phones wouldn't work, which was half of the time, but it was another if I wasn't going to be allowed.

"It's locked," Blaker said. Sure enough, when I glanced at the door I saw a huge padlock hanging from the little latch that connected the flimsy particleboard door to the makeshift wall.

River City was something I wasn't briefed on before coming over to the sands. It became a strange ritual whenever someone got smoked: the internet cafés locked down, satellite phones stowed away by SOGs at bases across the country. We couldn't plan around River City, because there was no way to tell when someone was going to get blown up or bleed out. Sometimes it would be peak hours of use when the cafés shut down.

The rest of the convoy was starting to filter up the stairs from the trucks. The little lead I had managed to get from the Marines who lived in the same room as me was lost. I guessed it didn't matter, because all the lead was really good for was getting a spot in line at the computer center ahead of them. I turned and filed up the stairs with Mundell and Ulrich.

"Did you hear what happened?" I heard Blaker ask a Marine from his own platoon.

It worried me that Blaker was just standing in front of the internet café, talking about the deaths of three Marines over and over again. Even if it was cathartic, it was strange to see him so hollow.

"I suppose Blaker filled you in on the Golf guys getting hit?" Mundell asked without looking over at me as we trudged up two more flights of stairs.

"Something like that. He seems a little out of it right now. Not sure what's up," I replied. We wound our way up the staircase, our boots kicking up clouds of dust with each stomp.

"Someone from Third Platoon told me the road they'd been sent down was one they shouldn't have been on. I guess Battalion keeps track of when roads get swept for IEDs, and the one they got blown up on hadn't been swept for a long time," Mundell's voice dropped low. "So, basically, they got sent down a road that no one had checked for months to set up targets and got killed."

We fell silent as we neared our wing and formed a single file line which shuffled through the entrance to our little corner of the Riv. Rose split off to his room across from ours, carrying the news with him which the Machine Gunners sleeping there had yet to hear. I walked into my hooch, as rooms were sometimes called, behind Mundell, with Ulrich behind me.

I was exhausted. I lay in bed, instead of looking for cammies to wear that weren't soaked in sewage. Through the day's convoy I had been wearing my flight suit. I'd been told actual pilots somewhere wore flight suits, but I doubted it. MachineGuns wore cammies on foot patrols and we were slated for one tomorrow. I'd be wearing the same cammies for over a month straight. Sewage had turned the lower part of my trousers and boots black.

"What's all the hubbub about?" Larkin asked me as he walked into the room in underwear and a T-shirt. He must have been using a porta-john.

"Some of Golf's vics got hit," I said, exhaustion creeping into my voice and sapping its strength. "A few guys didn't make it."

"Is that what Blaker is going on about in front of the computer center?" Larkin stumbled over someone's boots trying to walk back to his rack in the dark. Just before climbing up to his bunk, he turned with a thoughtful expression on his face.

"I just saw Prockop down at the COC; the Captain was talking to him. You don't think we'll get called out to do some bullshit presence patrol?"

Mundell moaned and rolled over in his rack, "Fuck, Marine, why do you have to say things like that?"

I sat up in bed with a resigned look on my face just as the door to our hooch flew open and smacked against the wall, so hard pieces of plaster pattered against the floor.

"Everyone get the fuck out of bed. Gear up and stage in front of the FOB in twenty minutes," Prockop said. His voice sounded from behind a solid rectangle of light that my eyes hadn't adjusted to yet. "Highers in the COC want us to walk some diesel fuel down to the Marines at the Iraqi Police station."

My eyes slowly made out Prockop in full gear, standing underneath one of the lights in the hall. Behind him in the other room MachineGuns inhabited was Rose, standing as if to crawl up into his top rack. I couldn't make out his face in the dark, but his shoulders sagged so heavily I thought he would fall over. COC stood for Command and Control, and we were their instruments no matter how badly we needed to be human.

"One or two of you load up a bunch of JP-8 diesel from the pump outside and stack the jugs in a Humvee. We'll all walk down with the Humvee to the station and then turn around and walk back."

Prockop turned to look at Rose, then back at me, sitting naked in bed.

"That's your patrol brief," Prockop said looking at his watch. "Nineteen minutes—out front."

RAIN IN THE DESERT

IRAQ DIDN'T HAVE RAIN UNTIL THE WINTER MONTHS, and even then, just a few minutes of sprinkling. The past few days' weather had been unusual; it rained and then misted instead of stopping. The canals grew swollen, the reeds turning a deep green as they gorged on water. The canal roads became treacherous—narrow, flanked by sheer sides that plunged into murky water. A small network of these roads nestled up against the eastern side of Saqlawiyah. The Marines we replaced at FOB Riviera told us not to patrol canal roads after the rain, because the Humvees barely fit. Risking Marines' lives to check on muddy fields and irrigation ditches wasn't operationally sound.

As my squad geared up for a night patrol, I hoped that we wouldn't get tasked out like I thought we would. After getting my vehicle ready, I met Rose in the smoke pit.

"You think we'll get sent out there?" Rose asked. His voice sounded like gravel sliding out of a metal wheelbarrow, from chain smoking.

"We're going to get sent out to those godforsaken roads," I said.

"You'd think that Prockop knowing the Captain would somehow work in our favor, instead of fucking us. Funny how that works."

Rose threw the butt of his cigarette to the ground and stepped on it instead of using the butt can, just a few feet away. Prockop was our squad leader; the Captain, our Platoon Commander, had known his brother in Officer Candidate School. This somehow translated into the Captain giving Prockop the dirty work just to test him.

We stomped through the mud out to the idling trucks. Rose would be my driver, Ulrich in the turret, Doc Bance in the back, and I would be the vehicle commander in the front passenger seat. Rose and I were the same rank, but for the patrol I was in charge of the vehicle because he was driving. Being a vehicle commander wasn't glamorous. It entailed lots of getting out of the truck and moving concertina wire at roadblocks and other control points. The only authority the billet granted was telling the turret gunner to engage a target or instructing the driver. Doc Bance was the highest-ranking person, but since Doc couldn't take leadership or offensive roles in the conflict, he didn't give orders; Rose and I looked up to him and would certainly listen to the blond-haired, blue-eyed, husky Corpsman if he offered an opinion.

The squad left the wire with grim sounds of rounds being racked into weapons—a *clack-clunk* that I'd heard so much I could tell if a round went home or if the chamber was still dry. Command wanted Marines to exit their vehicles and "make ready" their weapons in a safe direction. We ignored this guidance, sending rounds home as vehicles left the wire.

"Sooooooo," Rose said. "Prockop never told us where we're going. I guess I'll just follow the second vehicle?"

We meandered through Saq on a route that kept taking us east, toward the canal roads.

"You motherfuckers didn't have a patrol brief, did you?" Bance said.

I thought about replying with a smart-ass dismissal, but Bance had a real gripe. If we didn't do a patrol brief, which we hadn't, that was a sure sign there hadn't been any planning. Rose and I both knew Prockop started faking the funk a few weeks after we got in country. He'd turn in thoughtless patrol routes and reuse the same alternate routes. We stopped doing patrol briefs because they were, by their very nature, repetitive. Repetition is the lifeblood of soldiering. If flares weren't accounted for, they'd be forgotten. The same went for communication, SOPs, and evacuation plans.

"Am I talking to my fucking self?" Bance said. He looked out the window as he spoke, the mist light enough that dust swirled in the air—the two elements combined to make a brown film on the ballistic glass.

"There's nothing we can do," Rose said. "We can't make Prockop do his job."

I lit a cigarette as the patrol turned onto back roads on the eastern edge of Saq and started to head for the canal roads. There were only a few good entrances and exits to the canal network; small, now muddy, rutted roads that came to a T with a marginally larger canal road. Maneuvering cumbersome vehicles onto the canal road sometimes took an eighteen-point turn. Our

Humvees, the sort used during the occupation, were called up-armored because they were reinforced. The up-armor kit was a couple thousand pounds of armor and ballistic glass bolted onto a regular Humvee with no modifications made to the chassis, frame, engine, or transmission. Overload caused Humvees to wear out, but Battalion didn't have any replacements.

The entire thought process of "stop casualties by heaping armor on our troops" was reflected by our body armor: two heavy sappy plates—one in front and one in back—meant to stop small arms fire, two small side sappy plates, a groin protector, and a face protector in the form of a second Kevlar collar. This body armor—meant for turret gunners, not foot patrols—was issued Corps-wide to Marines. The effects on our bodies were much like the effect the extra armor had on the Humvees, except Marines shrunk. Some of the more diligent Corpsmen, like Doc Bance, measured the height of all the Marines in their platoon pre-deployment; about halfway through the deployment, he reported that most people had shrunk half an inch. The gear compacted the discs of our spines. But command wasn't worried about such things; they were busy sending us out on night patrols, in the rain, on roads barely big enough for a Humvee, overlooking canals on each side.

As our small patrol turned onto one of the access roads that formed a T with a canal road, it started to rain. Not just a mist, an outright rain.

"It's gonna be a bad day," Rose said, then laughed from his belly.

We patiently waited on the muddy road while the first vehicle started to maneuver through the T intersection. Bance counted the number of points in their turn until he hit a dozen, then stared sullenly out the window.

"Sorry if this doesn't make much sense, Doc, but a lot of the stuff we do doesn't make much sense. Not to mention the stuff we don't do," I said, cigarette's ember reflected in my glasses.

"Sweep the town for munitions? House to house, street to street? Haven't done that since we got here three months ago," Rose spoke between chuckles, then turned and looked at me with a leering grin on his face. "Let's go patrol canal roads after dark in the rain. Maybe we'll flip a vic into the water and kill someone."

The vehicle in front us was somewhere around nineteen points and still not close to being able to make the turn.

"I'm soaking wet," Ulrich's voice was muffled, with half of his body sticking out of the Humvee into the turret. "If anyone cares. It sucks."

"Yeah right, you Chamorros love water. You all live on an island for God's sake," Rose said. He punched Ulrich's leg. "Sing me the song of your people, Chamorro boy!"

Somewhere between Rose's chuckles, I heard Ulrich mutter about hating his life. The first vehicle finally made it through the T, leaving deep ruts.

Our Humvee groaned during the ascent to the T. Rose tried to make the turn in one graceful movement, but we ran out of canal road about halfway through the turn. We slowly started to slide backward.

"Fucking brilliant!" Rose bellowed.

He slammed the Humvee into four-wheel drive and started to feather the gas.

"Holy fuck," Doc Bance said. "The patrol just started and we're already having issues."

Rose gunned the vehicle up behind the first truck. When he hit the brakes, our Humvee slid in the mud, coming to rest inches from rear-ending the first vehicle.

"Hey, Rose, why don't you watch what the fuck you're doing," Prockop's voice crackled over the radio.

"Why don't you watch what you're doing," I repeated. My voice pitched to mockery, the singsong cadence of a kindergartener. As I spoke, my cigarette's smoldering ember bounced frantically up and down in front of my face.

"One of those fucking days," Rose said.

"All right, vic three, cross onto the canal road. And try to do it better than Rose," Prockop said.

The rain came steadily down. I told myself to be thankful it wasn't a storm like I'd grown up with back home in the Midwest, as I watched the third vehicle go from point five, to six, to seven, all the way to the upper teens. Finally, without too much sliding, it made it behind our truck. Our little convoy of three Humvees formed a sad-looking procession. The trucks pointed to the network of slick canal roads.

"Chamorro, if I tell you to get out of the turret, you get out of the turret, good to go?" I said. It was one of the rare occasions that I'd flex any muscle as a vehicle commander.

"Won't I get in trouble?" Ulrich said, his voice clearer than before. He'd stopped looking out from the turret, reconciling himself to stare down into the Humvee.

"If there's trouble, it's on me," I said. "It's my order."

Prockop's vehicle started forward and we followed. At first, things weren't horrible, we had a few feet on each side of the Humvees before the road disappeared into blackness. The patrol would sometimes take dirt paths off of the canal roads that went down to ground level but were still surrounded by water. These roads were sort of maintenance roads, between canals. Or would have been, but after the invasion crops stopped getting planted in many of the fields. The maintenance roads hadn't been used by anyone except us for a long time which begged the question we'd been asking the entire time: Why were we out here?

"I think we're stuck," Rose said.

Our Humvee's tires weren't aligned correctly and kept pulling to the right. To correct this, Rose steered to the left. This worked as long as we were accelerating, but as soon as we braked the vehicle would slide to the left in the mud. The mud wasn't a consistent texture or thickness, so the pull right wasn't a constant, making Rose's canted driving a sometimes overcompensation that took us to the left suddenly. We'd hit a patch of firm ground on one of the connecting maintenance roads that had shot us hard left and buried our front left tire in a deep mire at the base of a palm tree.

"*Have you tried four-wheel drive yet?*" Decker's voice came over the radio in a buzzed static from the vehicle behind. Even through the white noise, you could hear the contempt in Decker's voice.

Rose put the truck into four-wheel drive. It shrieked in protest as he violently rocked it back and forth, finally dislodging it from the mud hole with a popping sound I hoped wasn't a tie rod. I looked back to check on Doc and found a cockeyed grin on his face.

"What's so funny?" I yelled. The Humvees were loud and the deployment was deafening me.

"I was just thinking that this maintenance road, tucked away at ground level in these little oases of palm trees, kind of reminds me of *The Island of Doctor Moreau*," Bance said.

"Don't get weird on me now, Doc. You're the only other NCO on this fucked-up patrol, besides Decker and Prockop."

The other two Humvees had left the maintenance road, following it up to another canal road, this one especially narrow. They sat idling in the mud about two-hundred feet away, on top of the dike that held the canal. The rain came faster. Rose pulled us up onto the top of the dike and the patrol started again. We turned west on a canal road, heading further into the medieval irrigation system.

"Where the fuck is Prockop taking us," Bance said. "I hope he walks over to our vic so I can punch him in the goddamn face. We're the same rank—he can't tell me what the fuck to do. I know this patrol isn't up to regulations, and he knows it. I bet we don't even have comm with the COC right now."

I glanced at Rose, who glanced at the green gear. I didn't want to try the COC because we might indeed be out here on our own and because Prockop would hear it and lose his mind. Bance had a good point, chances were high the route we were on didn't at all reflect the route he had turned in to the COC. If we went over the side of the canal road, it would take forever to locate us in the inclement weather, and if someone were to get hurt there would be nowhere to land a chopper for evac. Not that I thought anyone would survive a Humvee falling into a canal.

"There is definitely something wrong," Rose said. "The steering got even worse after I jerked the front left tire out of that mud hole. I'm steering this thing hard left because it's pulling hard right and we're going fucking diagonal."

Our Humvee went down the mud road at a diagonal slant. Every time we braked, the vehicle would straighten out and slide to the right, but there wasn't much room for the truck to slide. We were traveling on a network of canal roads barely big enough for a Humvee. The canals on each side of us were a fifteen-foot drop from the road and full of huge reeds and cattails. Some of them were vibrant green, but others yellow and stiff like spears.

If given a choice between running across a street being lit up with small arms fire and dropping into a canal, I would have gone with the street every time. If the truck went in the water, the sharp edges of the Humvees' interior would split us open like overripe tomatoes left out in the sun.

"Dude!" I yelped, completely losing composure when Rose stepped on the brake, the truck sliding so close to the edge that all I saw was reeds leading down to blackness outside my window.

"There's nothing I can fucking do! What do you want me to do?!" Rose said. He hit the gas and the Humvee jerked back to going diagonal down the canal road.

"Yo, don't follow them so close," Bance said. "These fucks can't drive a constant speed."

Prockop's vehicle must have been having its own problems. It kept speeding up and slowing down. Decker's Humvee was doing the same. As Rose kicked on the windshield wipers to clear the muck, it occurred to me that I might want to put my seatbelt on. I looked out the window at the reeds as I snapped in.

"Real smart. Lock yourself in your seat, so when we go over you fucking drown for sure," Bance said. His voice strained as he braced himself against the ceiling and door, so if we went he wouldn't bounce around the interior.

Rose jerked his entire body to the right as the truck lurched to the left and almost off the road. This correction quickly turned into an overcorrection as the vehicle swerved right and again all I saw was reeds and blackness.

"We're going!" I shouted. I unlatched my seat belt and pushed with my legs against the dash of the Humvee, so my back pressed tight against my seat.

"Pull Ulrich out of the turret," Rose said.

His eyes were locked on the road, although visibility was now down to about thirty feet. Focusing on the taillights ahead of us, which kept turning this way and that onto different canal roads, he looked grim as Ahab chasing the whale.

"Ulrich, out of the turret," I said. "Everyone put your weapons on the deck and hold them there with your feet. They'll fuck us up when we go over."

"When we go over? Thanks for the vote of confidence," Rose said.

Ulrich lowered himself into the vehicle to sit cross-legged, rain following him in.

The patrol continued. I asked Rose and Doc if they thought we were going in circles. Rose said he couldn't tell the difference because of the rain and Doc just shouted, "Fucking Prockop, I'll punch him in his fucking face. This is the last time I go out with MachineGuns!" I didn't ask anymore after that. Ulrich kept wanting to get back up in the turret, but I wouldn't let him.

For some reason, Prockop and Decker kept yelling at Rose over comm to keep up which made Rose's driving even worse. After another real good scare, I pried Ulrich's arms from around my helmet and he stopped asking to go back up. The patrol finally came to a place I was sure we hadn't seen before. Prockop tried pushing straight instead of taking a left and ran out of road. Decker had his vehicle take the left. Rose sat tight.

"Vehicle commanders out of the vics!"

The small radios we used for inter-squad communication crackled and popped with interference from the weather, but I could tell Prockop was scared. The COC had just tried to raise him over the green gear, and although it was coming in broken, I was pretty sure Prockop heard it and ignored it. This was a common tactic used by squad leaders; sometimes the COC was obnoxious, but in this case the head shed just wanted to know our grid coordinates and Prockop couldn't answer, because he didn't know them. There was a chance we were off the map on uncharted roads and that was a big no-no. It wasn't that Marines couldn't handle themselves; it had to do with the logistics of sweeping roads for IEDs. Somewhere at the Battalion COC there was a map of all the roads in our AO keeping track of how long it had been since the roads had been swept for IEDs. Sending us blindly down roads that hadn't been swept for a couple of months was how people got killed.

I opened my door and scraped my rifle off the floorboard. The road was three inches of mud. The rain was now accompanied by a thick mist which fogged my glasses and made my weapon slick to the touch. I tried lighting up a smoke as I walked around my vehicle, doing a quick check of the tires, but the cigarette soaked through. I looked ahead at Prockop's truck and saw him waving me and Decker over.

Decker hustled his portly frame, looking everything like the call sign he hated, "Piggly Wiggly." Prockop stood, arms folded, as he watched me walk at a normal pace. I was cold, wet, and I had just felt my boots soak through.

"Where are we?" was the first thing Decker asked, followed by, "And what are we doing out here?"

I cringed. Decker tended to use a tone of voice that sounded so innocent and naïve you knew it was forced and it came off as antagonistic.

Prockop ignored Decker; his eyes locked on mine through my mist-covered glasses.

"What the fuck is Rose's problem?" Prockop's voice shook with anger.

"Does Rose not know how to put his vehicle in four-wheel drive?" Decker said.

"Rose is doing the best he can. These roads aren't exactly safe in bad weather *or* in the dark," I said. My voice was sharp and my fists clenched.

Decker got a smug look on his face and glanced furtively at Prockop. I had outed myself as someone who wouldn't toe the line. We stood silent with nothing but the sound of rain falling into the canals below us, until Prockop's driver cracked his door.

"Prockop, it's the COC again. They want to know where we are. They sound like they're done fucking around. Should I answer or let them wonder?" the driver asked.

"I'll be there in a second, don't say anything," Prockop yelled, then continued in a low voice to me. "Why don't you drive for him since he's incompetent?"

"I don't think I could do a better job, given the conditions and the way our Humvee is listing to the left as we drive."

"Oh, it's the Humvee's fault, isn't it? Why isn't my driver having the same problems?" Decker asked. "We are all driving the same vehicles, you know."

"Why don't you two monkeys get off my driver's ass. I'm the vehicle commander and Rose is doing the best he can. You two fucks yelling at him is only making it worse. We shouldn't even fucking be out here!"

"You just called two NCOs monkeys," Decker said. His voice oozed wounded pride.

"Not until they acted like it," I said. The words hung in the air with the mist. I knew I'd pay for them later.

"Go stand security!" Prockop said. Veins in his neck bulged. "You too, Decker!"

"Go stand security," I repeated, while looking around at the canal road and into the canals on either side. "Where would you like me to stand?"

Prockop screamed something unintelligible, then stormed over to his Humvee to talk on the green gear with the COC. I looked at the far side of the canal. The opposing dike had a bunch of shrubs and stunted trees on top of it. There wasn't much else to look at. Decker did the same, until Prockop yelled for both of us to get back to our trucks. I stared Decker down as I passed him, my rifle's butt in the crook of my arm with the barrel pointed straight up in the air. I didn't glance back at Prockop. I got in the Humvee and slammed the door. Water dripped off my helmet and onto my soaking wet body armor.

"Well, you fucking owe me one," I said.

"Were they talking shit about me?" Rose asked.

"Sure as shit, they were. Apparently, you don't know how to drive," I said.

"What?" Rose said. "It's not my fault this Humvee hasn't been aligned since the war started."

"According to Decker, we're all driving the same Humvees," I said. "Did you guys hear what the COC said to Prockop over the green gear?"

I held my pack of cigarettes upside down and watched water dribble out. "Well, what a cherry on top of the shit sundae this patrol has been," I said.

Bance tossed me a cigarette that landed on the dash. "Captain is pissed. The patrol is out past its window. COC wants us back ASAP, or most ricky-tick as you Marines might put it," he said.

We sat looking at each other with only the sound of rain coming down through the turret and hitting Ulrich, to accompany our breathing. I tried to light the smoke Doc had given me, but my lighter was too wet.

"What exactly is this window you're referring to?" I asked. "And I need to borrow your lighter."

Doc Bance lit his own smoke and then tossed me his lighter.

"Every patrol has a certain amount of time that it can be in operation. You don't get to just take your squad all over God's green earth," Bance said. "Well, in this case, Allah's brown earth. You have to leave the wire at a certain time and you have to be back by a certain time. You also have to stay on a certain route. So far, I think we've managed to leave the wire at about the right time."

Prockop's vehicle had just completed a fourteen-point turn and was now following Decker's Humvee. Rose pulled up and made a clean turn, bringing us right behind the now second vehicle.

"See? Did you see that fucking turn? It was so smooth it was sexy," Rose said.

I glanced over at him and then said to Doc, "Actually, we left late today. I heard someone in the COC cursing us for it."

"Good. Fuck Prockop," Bance said.

I wasn't sure if Prockop had figured out how to get us back to the FOB, but we started heading in the same direction. The mist stopped and the rain slowed, but it would be a few days before the mud dried back into loose dirt and sand. I felt exhausted, both mentally and physically—the tension of the long patrol taking its toll. The canal roads on what proved to be the way back weren't nearly as treacherous, because Decker's vehicle led with a slow pace.

After twenty minutes of creeping along canal roads, we made it back to some of the more trodden paths on the east side of Saq. I breathed a sigh of relief and saw Rose visibly relax when our Humvee wheels gripped firmer ground, no longer flanked by fifteen-foot drops into brackish canal water. I couldn't tell how late it was or remember why I didn't wear my watch out on this patrol. We had been a little rushed to get our gear on, for no other reason than that Prockop had failed to give us an idea of when the patrol would be leaving the wire.

"Well, I'm glad I didn't get crushed in the turret today," Ulrich's voice sounded far away with half of his body sticking out of the turret. "I guess I should probably thank you for that one, Big Head."

"Well, I'm glad you didn't die either, especially because I'm pretty sure we all would have drowned," I said. Some of the smaller shanties, on the very east side of Saq, started to flash by in the Humvee's headlights.

"Do you think you'll be in trouble when we get back to the FOB?" Ulrich's voice was less distant this time; he must have been speaking down into the Humvee.

I sat silently for a moment before answering. A mosque floated by us in the darkness. Light streamed out the front door into the pitch of night. If the lights were on, then it was around four in the morning. The sheiks and imams got up early to prepare for morning prayer. Judging by some of the coughing and hacking that came from mosques' speakers, they didn't spend much time warming up their voices.

"I'm sure that Prockop will wake someone up and drag me in front of them," I said.

The patrol turned onto one of the main streets which cut north through Saq and went by our FOB to the MSR. It would be time to pay the piper soon enough and I knew it. There was no way that Prockop wouldn't try to get me in trouble for calling him a monkey, however earned it was.

"Bance, would you mind if I dropped your name if me and Prockop get into it with the Staff Sergeant? As an NCO, your word will hold more weight than mine," I said.

"For sure, man," Bance said. "I'll tell whoever wants to know how fucked up and ass backward this patrol was, I don't give a fuck."

The patrol parked the trucks in our section of the FOB's parking lot and we all dismounted. Ulrich and the other turret gunners pulled the machine guns out of the turrets and hauled them inside, leaving the ammo for a second trip. The drivers started to check over the trucks to see if there was any damage to the wheels, then checked the fluid levels before cleaning out the trash. Doc headed inside, muttering something about this being his *last patrol with you fucking morons*. I was told later the first thing he did was walk into his Platoon Sergeant's room and declared he wasn't going out with MachineGuns anymore, because *they fucking tried to kill me out there*. It was the last time Bance went out with us.

I walked up to the hooch I shared with five other Marines, took off my gear and dropped it on the floor. I didn't want to talk to Prockop or Decker. Prockop caught me walking down to the smoke pit.

"Let's go talk to the Staff Sergeant," Prockop said.

This was Prockop's modus operandi.

"It's four in the morning, I'm sure he's asleep," I said. "What is there to talk about anyway? How awesome the patrol was?"

"You thought the patrol was too dangerous, right?" Prockop asked.

I didn't say anything. I just turned back up the stairs and started walking to the Weapons Platoon's Staff Sergeant, Staff Sergeant Gnade. Gnade and I hadn't had any problems before, but I could tell that he wasn't pleased to be woken up. I stood uncomfortably in the room that he had all to himself, Prockop behind me. Gnade had a pretty bad staph infection that splotched his left arm and he was on bed rest. The head doc at the Riv, a giant Chief who didn't take shit from anybody, had told him to take it easy. The doc said if things got worse he'd probably need a helicopter flight to a real hospital, maybe even a jet ride to Germany. Gnade was trying to tough it out though, as ill-advised as that might have been; there was a good chance that if he got pulled into a long hospital stay elsewhere, he would lose his position as Platoon Sergeant.

I don't remember a whole lot of the conversation with Gnade. What I do remember is the tone changing greatly, from condemning my behavior to being more reserved, when I suggested that maybe an official report be taken from Doc Bance. The incident was shelved by Gnade; he said I was wrong for being disrespectful, but that as a vehicle commander I had to voice my concerns for those in the truck. Prockop wasn't happy and stormed off to his room.

I spoke with Mundell, who had been driving for Prockop that night. Mundell was a tall Marine who liked to crop his hair instead of getting a shitty fade like the rest of us. He loved Ultimate Fighting (UFC) and bars with mechanical bulls. He also wouldn't mute the porn he'd watch as he laid in his rack, right next to mine, before running down to the rancid porta-johns to masturbate.

"What did Staff Sergeant say?" Mundell asked.

Mundell openly didn't like me, so his genuine inquiry meant real concern.

"He talked in circles," I said. "So, what do we do if Prockop gets someone killed on some fucked-up patrol?"

"I guess we would say our piece in the reports," Mundell said. His brow furrowed as he thought about the prospect of having to tell higher that someone died due to negligence.

"That's fucking bullshit!" I hissed, spittle flying from my lips. "They'll just whitewash the whole thing. Send some fucking letter about how Ulrich or Terrones or Rose, or you for Christ's sake, how one of us died a hero and served to the utmost."

We stood in the doorway to our room and were joined by Hawkins, who stood as tall as Mundell, but was built more like a professional football player than a UFC fighter. With his high and tight haircut, Hawkins looked like a Marine in a recruiting poster. He had been in Decker's truck during the patrol.

"I'm with Big Head," Hawkins whispered.

Someone from Mortars walked by, squinting against the light as they made their way down to the ground floor and outside to take a leak.

"Let me tell you something. Waiting until someone gets fucking killed, that's fucked up." I said. "That's why I made a stink about it. And if some shit-for-brains gets Ulrich killed for no reason, do you think some cheese-dick letter to his family is going to do him justice? Will it bring him back?"

They both shook their heads. It must have looked comical with me, a short Marine who was stocky even by Marine standards, having two much taller Marines lean down to talk in secrecy. Comical until you saw the look in my eyes.

"If someone gets smoked for no reason, this is how it's going to be," I said. My voice took the tone that Cassius used with Brutus. "You motherfuckers just play it cool and stay the fuck out of my way. I'm going to sprint straight for Prockop's truck and put one in his head."

133

Hawkins' grit held true; he didn't flinch from the idea. Mundell's head snapped back as if he'd opened a sack lunch to find something rotten. He knew what game was afoot, a dirty little secret in the Corps, a tradition that carried on without being written down. It happened in Vietnam more often than most military historians feel comfortable acknowledging, but if you talked to the old Devils they would tell you. If an officer or an NCO was hell-bent on getting everyone killed, he got fragged.

"We'll make something up. I don't know what, but we'll figure it out," I said.

I looked at both of them. Hawkins was down, sick of the risks Prockop took. Mundell was shaken but still standing with us; he hadn't cried out for an NCO or run to get the Sergeant on Duty.

"Okay," Mundell said. "Okay."

Hawkins just nodded his head.

The plan of retaliating if someone was killed due to gross negligence wasn't a good one. We walked away without saying more. I wondered what kind of Corps this was, so bereft of leadership that good men conspired murder. I crawled into my rack and dreamed of a black nothingness for a few hours, before I was woken up to go on post.

HUMVEE CONFESSIONALS

THE EUPHRATES SLID BY ON OUR LEFT FLANK AS
the patrol sat waiting for EOD (Explosive Ordinance
Disposal) to arrive and blow up a small cache of weapons the Combat Engineers found buried in the riverbank. Two Humvees and one MRAP, pointed west,
composed the patrol on the outskirts of Saqlawiyah.
The day's heat radiated from the vehicles in shim-
mering waves that twisted in the breeze coming off
the river.

"You prayed something as we left this morning?"
Owen asked.

I sat in the driver's seat in the last vehicle in the patrol
with Owen next to me and Ulrich in the turret.

"I prayed for my enemies, Owen," I said. "That they
would shoot straight and true, and that we would take
contact."

Owen's eyes widened comically.

"Do you want to die?" he asked me.

I lit a cigarette before responding.

"No. I want EOD to get here, so they can blow the cache and we can get out of the heat."

The patrol had been static for three hours. We'd arrived in the early morning when the air still carried the night's chill, before the desert became a kiln. The patrol rolled in, stopped; the Combat Engineers piled out of the MRAP and swept the riverbank with metal detectors. Forty-five minutes later, they found something.

"Why don't your people pray, Owen?" I asked our interpreter.

Ulrich began to stir in the turret. I couldn't be sure, but he seemed to be waking up. I felt sorry for him; coming to consciousness to find yourself in Iraq as a turret gunner was worse than waking up hungover in jail.

"We pray," Owen said. "What do you mean, we don't pray?"

I watched out the window as Prockop, Hawkins, and some of the Engineers took turns digging the cache out of the ground. When they got the cache halfway uncovered, they sat down by what looked like a small box or suitcase. One of the Engineers waved his detector over it, again and again, until Hawkins gave him a look mean enough to melt wax.

"You aren't even listening to me," Owen said, turning to look out his window at a field of alfalfa.

"Listen, fucker. I'm sorry I can't lock eyes with you every second of this little outing but, in case you missed it, there's a war out there," I said, my left arm sweeping outward as if revealing this to him for the first time. "So, explain to me why your people don't pray or get the fuck out of my vehicle and walk back through town to the FOB. See if you make it."

Saqlawiyah rarely got violent in those days, but Owen had interpreted for the company before us. They'd lost men to hidden machine gun nests and IEDs in trash along the road. Parts of town Marines of Echo Company bopped through were places Marines had bled out less than six months prior, shrieking and pleading with God. While the grunts seemed blissfully forgetful of this, Owen knew, because he'd served with those men before they'd been cut down in the street like dogs. Owen knew the illegal weapons used to snuff out young men's lives hadn't been found during sweeps. He knew the Iraqis killed during the firefight were civilians gunned down in anger, how the real killers faded back into the sand. Owen knew if he got out of the Humvee and hoofed it through town, he'd disappear.

"My people pray," he said again, sounding even surer this time.

"I've been here three months and I've never seen *anyone* pray," I said. "I take that back, I've seen a couple of no-shit bad guys we captured pray while they cried all night before we turned them over to the Iraqi Police."

I took a drag of my smoke and exhaled a cloud. It hung in front of us like fog.

"*Crackle—we—opening the—standby—crackle—*" The small walkie-talkie in my vehicle buzzed with static.

The patrol had the jammers going full bore, something upward of 500hz interfering with our walkie-talkies even at the short distance of thirty meters. We usually ran them to keep radio signals meant for roadside bombs from working, but they also worked to halt cellphone and radio traffic for a few football fields in every direction when we wanted to generate a communication blackout for operational security. Whatever the jammers put out fried anything not military grade trying to compete—Marine Corps jammers even overpowered and destroyed Army jammers.

The small group of Marines and combat engineers kept picking at the ground around the box until the senior engineer squatted in front of the cache nonchalantly, like there was no possibility of explosives rigged to detonate when the lid moved. Hawkins and Prockop didn't feign ignorance; they ducked down on the sloping side of the riverbank near the water just before the engineer opened the box in one smooth motion.

I smelled something burning and realized I'd gotten lost in staring at the engineer, waiting to see if he'd disappear in a flash of light, and let the cigarette pinched between my gloved fingers burn down to the butt. The ember perched on the filter just barely singed my gloves. I opened my door briefly and threw it out into the sands in disgust. Whoever made the decision to open the box before EOD got here hadn't thought about possible consequences. If the box had detonated, we'd have lost at least one person.

"Curiosity killed the cat, but death passes over the Combat Engineer," I said up to Ulrich in the turret.

"No shit," Ulrich said down to me. "I guess if they'd caught on fire the Euphrates is right there."

"The water looks *real* clean," I said with a chuckle. "I'm sure it wouldn't cause some life-threatening infection."

I glanced around the Humvee for something to do but didn't find anything. If Owen hadn't been sitting by me, I would have played solitaire, checkers, or Minesweeper on the PalmPilot that controlled the jammer. The PalmPilot was mounted to the inside of the windshield for easy access. Higher-ups pushed the idea that playing games on the small computers was tantamount to criminal negligence, because if it froze or crashed it could interrupt the jammer. As far as I was concerned, the higher-ups could go fuck themselves and get back to me after going on a few patrols that didn't involve riding a heavily armored convoy to a mega base for chow and a haircut.

"I wonder what's in the box," I muttered.

I resigned myself to watching one of the engineers rifle through the container. Ahead of me, Rose got out of a Humvee and started walking over to the cluster of Marines by the river. I knew he was going to find out what exactly we were dealing with.

"Are you angry?" Owen asked me.

"Angry about what? EOD taking so long?" I asked. "We're waiting for them because they didn't want to leave the wire until after they got lunch at the chow hall in Habbaniyah."

"No," Owen said. "Are you angry at the villagers?"

I turned my head to stare at him. "Why the fuck would I be angry at anyone in Saq?"

"Because of this," he motioned to the small cache on the riverbank. "They were going to use this to kill you."

I laughed, hard. It was Owen's turn to stare at me.

"Or blow them-fucking-selves up," I said between chuckles. "We saved lives here today. Probably the life of some little brown farmer who would have killed himself on accident."

"You aren't upset?" Owen asked.

"Not at anyone in Saq," I said. "I mean, I was kidding with the little brown farmer remark. You're probably right. Someone intended to use those things to kill us."

I paused and gave him an extra serious look. "But you know what?" I asked.

Owen shook his head no.

"I wouldn't blame them if they did, and I don't blame you for hating us."

Owen looked like he wanted to get out of the truck. His face held a mixture of bafflement, confusion, fear. Maybe he thought I was trying to bait him into saying something that would get him kicked out of the unit, or worse.

"But you hate Iraqis," Owen said. His voice now followed a slow deliberate rhythm.

"I don't hate Iraqis," I said. "I'd do the same thing if someone came to my country and told me what to do. This is just a job, man. I don't want to be here."

"Then why are you here?" Owen asked.

"Why am I here? Goddamn it, Owen. You thought I wanted to be here?" My voice was rising and soon I was yelling. "I don't want to be here. I fucking hate this place. I hate the sand, I hate the heat, I hate the way everyone who lives here hates me and wants me to die. I'm sick of worrying about getting shot by a sniper or blown up by an IED. I don't want to fucking be here, I want to be back home."

"Why did you come?"

"That's a good fucking question," I said. "Mostly because when I was seventeen, I signed up. At the time, I thought it was the right thing to do, you know? But now, three years later, and after spending some time in this godforsaken shithole ..." my voice trailed off.

"How was it the right thing to do? Who were you at war with before us?" Owen asked. He used the word "us" instead of "Iraq" or "the insurgents," dropping all pretenses of being a neutral bystander.

"I thought I would somehow defend America and freedom. We seem to use freedom as a truncheon though," I replied. "Soldiering was also just a way to make money, plain and simple. It's complicated—I'm doing a bad job of explaining."

"America," Owen started and hesitated. "What is it like?"

This question from the terps always made me uncomfortable. I'd been briefed by Echo not to tell them I'd help with an acquisition of American citizenship in any way. The terps were helping us for money, of course, but also for the slim possibility that after so many hours of risking their lives and the lives of their families by operating with the Allied Occupation, they'd be granted American citizenship.

I never knew what they wanted me to say. *America, it's pretty much the opposite of this place, not a shithole at all. You can buy food for a few dollars at any moment at a fast food place if you like. Your wife and family wouldn't have to worry about adhering to Sharia law, since no one in Iraq seems keen on it except for the guys with guns on the payroll of imams and sheiks. There are functioning hospitals in America, competent police, roads without dead animals, and garbage everywhere. Shit, it's a big deal to find a body floating down a river in the States.* The conversation couldn't go like that; I just didn't have it in me. When Owen asked about America, he had something in his eyes I hadn't seen before: hope.

"Well," I started, "there are buildings and big cities. Some of the cities are really big, I mean *really* big. I've never been to some of them, like New York City or Washington, D.C., which is the capital where all the decisions come from."

"You have never been to the capital?" Owen asked incredulously.

"No," I said. "I'm from Des Moines, Iowa. Where I live, there isn't much else but corn as far as the eye can see, hog lots, and factory towns. Pretty bleak. But not like here. Fuck, not like here."

"But you take orders from this Washington?" Owen asked. "And what is corn?"

"Yeah, man, I gotta follow orders. When you join up, they give you a contract and you sign your name on the dotted line and then they own you," I made a motion of writing in the air in front of me. "Marines go to a special kind of prison if they don't obey—Fort Leavenworth. From what I hear, the jail is underground and doesn't get much sunlight. And corn is a plant that … is hard to explain. I'll show you a picture of it sometime."

Something in my rearview mirror had caught my eye.

A sheepherder moved up the road toward us. The ground between us told me I had time before I needed to get out of the truck and ruin his day. The man had a flock of about fifty or so sheep with him and a few children. When I glanced to my right, I caught Owen watching me with a kind of wonder, like I was the first Marine he saw as any kind of human.

Before either of us could break the silence, Ulrich appeared as if out of nowhere between us. He'd swiveled the turret to face forward and squatted down to speak with me.

"Hey, Big Head, there is a sheepherder coming. Should I shoot a flare at him?" Ulrich asked.

"No!" I said. "We're in the middle of demolition operation right now, Marine. There is a comm blackout going on, for Christ's sake! Do you think it's a good idea to shoot fucking pyrotechnics into the air to draw attention to ourselves while we sit static for God-only-knows how much longer?"

The question was rhetorical.

"You're right," Ulrich said. "Will you go out and stop him?"

"Of course," I answered. "What else are we gonna do? Send Owen who doesn't have a weapon, who isn't intimidating, and who is probably a spy?"

Ulrich's face split in a big grin and his cheeks showed deep dimples. Those kinds of smiles were rare for him and it made me glad to see it. Owen's face went blank as he looked from me to Ulrich, trying to figure out if we actually thought him a spy.

"What are you guys talking about anyway?" Ulrich asked. "I keep hearing things about back home."

"Is America like it is in the movies with so many people out drinking and having a good time?" Owen asked. "Do you think someone like me could live there? I want to move there. Maybe your government will grant me citizenship. What do you think?"

Ulrich didn't say anything. He just froze in the middle of a motion to stand back up to sit on the turret's seat strap. I think that's when Ulrich started to see it, the realization heading toward every Marine in its own time. I could tell by the look in his eyes. Some people called it the thousand-yard stare; it was the same I'd seen on

Blaker when he'd told me how many guys from Golf had flipped over in their Humvee and screamed while they cooked after they got hit; the same absence I'd seen in salty vets coming in from patrol with their heads still out there with the sands; when someone walked away from a phone call that had made parents and loved ones cease to exist; a blank look that didn't mean things were kept out, but that things were getting in. Nietzsche warned us not to look into the abyss, but in some places, there's nothing else. Without saying anything, Ulrich stood up to peer over the desert. I understood. The desert I could deal with and so could Ulrich. The desert could only kill us.

"Yes," I said. "America is like how it is in the movies."

I couldn't bring myself to tell him any different than the picture in his mind's eye of glamorous people in chic bars drinking, laughing, and dancing. America's complexities and deep-rooted issues didn't seem like something Owen could handle after being at a loss for corn.

"I'd like to go there, take my family with me," Owen said. "Someday."

"You realize there are problems with America, right? It's not perfect." I raised my palms toward the ceiling and looked down to survey my body armor with ammunition and weapons strapped to it. "For instance, here I sit."

Taking a second to light a smoke, I glanced over at Owen with a smirk.

"Now I have to go ruin this motherfucker's day," I said as cigarette smoke started to fill the cab. I pulled my pistol out of its holster and snapped my hand down its spine. The *click clack* meant a bullet had gone into the chamber. We could both tell by the sounds weapons made if they were dry or hot, empty or loaded. Before I shut my door, I turned and looked at him, cigarette in my mouth, pistol in my right hand pointing at the ground. I puffed out my chest and struck a pose.

"'Merica," I said in a throaty bullfrog voice.

The sheepherder froze when he saw me exit the Humvee. The flock swirled from out in front of him back in on itself, to hide behind the herder at the sound of my door slamming. About forty meters of dirt road separated me from the knot of sheep, children, and a man with a staff.

"What do you think, Ulrich?" I asked over my shoulder at the turret while I walked away from the truck. "You think he's on his way to Nazareth with the staff and kids? Or wherever these motherfuckers make the haj to?"

Ulrich waved the 240 Bravo medium machine gun's barrel up and down in its cradle in response. I usually got some banter going when things got a little tense; talking shit usually provided some kind of release, or it had in the beginning. Three months in and it dripped with futility, highlighted the surreal and absurd, even though I was saying the same things I always had.

One of the sparse patches of gravel that splotched the dirt road crunched under my boots. The palm trees fluttered in a breeze from the Euphrates, just beginning to warm. On either side of the road the ground dropped ten feet and turned into farmland. The man stood in the middle of the road with his children and flock behind him, Saq's skyline as a backdrop. I looked over at the men on the riverbank; the engineers were sorting ordinance and contraband from the box onto a sheet while Prockop watched with Rose. Rose felt my eyes and looked up at me, his body language something I could read after hundreds of hours working with him. If Rose stood on the river bank, that left his Humvee without anyone in the driver seat and without a vehicle commander; a weakness of assigning senior Marines to driver roles, something I had pointed out to Prockop several times. I didn't think Prockop would be okay with allowing the flock of Iraqis and sheep to breach security and walk through our lines, especially during an operation where the chances of contact were increasing every minute we sat static waiting for EOD.

About twenty meters away from the group of Iraqis and their livestock, I slowed and stopped. For a moment, I looked at the ground, thinking of how I didn't want to deal with this, didn't want to deal with the language barrier, and knowing the man needed to get through here or he'd have to walk miles around to another road. I kept my pistol behind my back and raised my left fist over my head.

"Roo, emshi," I said, thinking the words meant "stop" and "walk away," but they really meant "stop" and "walk." I thought "emshi" meant away was because I'd been using it in the ville with a dismissive gesture, a flicking of my left hand like I was shooing Iraqis away, while keeping my index finger in place on the trigger with my right hand. If the Iraqis couldn't read my body language, we all knew they could speak barrel.

"Roo," I shouted, then, "emshi!"

The shepherd slowed to a stop when I said "roo" and crept forward a little when I said "emshi." I repeated this a few times until they crept close enough I could spit on them. I knew the man was playing dumb on purpose. There was no way to misconstrue what I wanted to happen. I was standing in the road in front of a Humvee adorned with a grim-looking man staring down the sights of a machine gun, shouting at them to "stop walk." Even if I butchered the language, the intent was obvious.

The man didn't want to walk miles out of his way to go around, obviously. I knew the lay of the land and what roads went where, and west of Saq didn't have many roads running east and west. I couldn't let him past me with so many variables—the animals and children made it too big of a risk. He smiled and started to inch forward towards me again, but suddenly stopped dead-still, smile half faded from his face. His children shrieked and hid behind him, the flock of sheep swirled back in on itself again.

I'd swung my pistol out from behind me and leveled it at the man's head. His group seemed so small and fragile, like a strong wind would carry them away. I was anchored in place by my body armor, ammunition, and weapon. The small, bent figures in front of me didn't have a chance. I heard Ulrich rack a round into the machine gun behind me. The rest of the smile melted off the man's face as he realized my pistol would signal a hail of lead that would leave everything he cared about lying on the road in blood puddles.

I took a few steps toward the man. My gun never stopped pointing at the triangle made by his eyes and nose—the sweet spot. If I dropped a round into that triangle, it was lights out for the man, his medulla oblongata would blow out the back of his head and he'd turn off. At this close proximity, I needed to make every shot count. I didn't have the luxury of standoff, the military term for the ground between my target and me. When I got close enough, I spoke evenly to the man with the staff, his children, and his flock.

"I make the rules here, good to go? You don't get to just walk wherever you want. If I let you walk down this road, there's a chance, due to forces beyond my control, that you or one of the munchkins gets hurt." I paused for a moment and the man opened his mouth, but I cut him off. "So, turn the fuck around and walk away right fucking now!"

As I finished, spittle flew from my mouth and I made a jabbing motion with my pistol at his head. The man said, "Yes, mistah, yes," and quickly turned around. He and his entourage began a slow shuffle away from me. I watched him go and caught him throw a watery-eyed glance over his shoulder. When the group was far enough away, I turned and walked back toward the Humvee.

Ulrich gave me a thumbs up, racked the bolt of his machine gun back, grabbing the round as it fell out, and linking it back to the ammunition belt resting in the weapon's feed tray. I returned the thumbs up as I walked back over the gravel and dirt to the truck. Rose stood, leaning against my door with a bored look on his face.

"Look at you out there, providing rear security," Rose said. "Marine, you are helping win the war against terrorism by telling that goat farmer to go fuck himself."

We both laughed and I handed him a cigarette before lighting my own.

"Yea, I'm not sure what the deal is with our Arabic," I said. "Except that no one listens until I point a gun at them."

"Barrel *is* the international language," Rose said.

"So, what's in the box?" I asked him, nodding my head to where the group of Marines now sat with their backs to the riverbank.

"Grenades, ammunition, explosives, maps, some radios, and a cellphone detonator," Rose said.

"Cellphone detonator," I repeated.

Rose took a long drag of his cigarette before responding. "Yup," he said. "Some kind of receiver that blows when you call it. Maybe some kind of modified beeper."

"What's the word on EOD?" I asked. "Are they ever going to make it out here?"

"I heard they're finally on their way," Rose said, pausing to take another drag. "Interestingly enough, right after noon chow."

We turned our backs to the Humvee to stare south at the Euphrates. When I first set eyes on that river, months ago, it made me realize there was something in Iraq we could never grind away; an oldness that bore the marks of time well before the rise and fall of Britain, centuries before the West rose as a cultural superpower. Now, seeing Marines lounging on its banks in the midst of military occupation, I was never surer we would not be here long enough to alter the course of anything in these lands. The United States could come here and perform acts of military prowess and Sisyphean endurance without rival, but we couldn't span the decades needed to make any kind of real change. The sun beating down on us made every detail seem washed out, as if the image had been overexposed on film.

"Ulrich said you'd been talking to Owen about back home," Rose said.

"And?" I answered. "Am I going to get in trouble for interacting with the terp?"

"You know it's not good to talk about the war right now, not the way you think about it. I'm not saying I disagree with you, but we have talked before about how some things are going to have to be sorted out when we get back." Rose moved his hands a little bit as he got going. "But right now isn't the best time, is all I'm saying. Especially not with Owen. He's probably a fucking terrorist anyway."

With his last statement, Rose rapped on the ballistic glass of the driver side window with his knuckles. Owen looked up from staring down at his boots and smiled widely at Rose.

"Look at that fucking cocksucker," Rose said. "What a lazy piece of shit. Fuck him."

"Owen's not so bad, compared to that skinny fucker who whines all the time," I said. We stood silent for a second. I didn't feel like defending Owen any more than the little I already had.

"Be careful what you say. Not supporting this war effort, or military conflict, or whatever you want to call it, is liable to get you into some trouble," Rose said with a lowered voice. "And I'm not saying that I don't agree. I'm just saying that we're here for five more months—wouldn't be hard for command to send you somewhere else. Someplace you really don't want to be."

Rose was right. There were a few Marines who had disappeared from the company, tasked out to stand guard duty at bases far away, off in the middle of nowhere. Sending Marines to shitty places was kind of like sending them to the gulag.

"Well, anyway, better get back to my truck." Rose laughed. "Hope you have fun with Chamorro Indian boy Ulrich and the traitor." With that he flicked his cigarette butt onto the road and started walking back to his vehicle.

I climbed into my truck and checked the floorboards for my rifle. After making sure it hadn't floated off, I turned and thumped Ulrich on the leg.

"EOD is on its way!" I said with mock enthusiasm. "Now it'll only be a few more hours."

"Great," Ulrich's voice came down from the turret. "I'm glad we aren't inconveniencing them or anything. I'd hate for them to miss a chow."

So, we waited. The Marines on the riverbank got tired of sitting around and swept the ground around the river further to the east. The breeze crossing the Euphrates picked up a little, keeping the vehicles from turning into ovens, the air conditioning in the trucks having broken long ago. Rumor had it that some of Second Platoon's Humvees still had AC that would at least kick out air; most of Weapons Platoon's trucks' AC didn't work in the slightest. After half an hour of me blowing smoke rings, Owen stirred in his seat.

"What do you think Echo will do to retaliate?" Owen asked.

"Nothing," I said. "You realize we pay off the local sheik so we don't get blown up, right?"

Owen shifted in his seat for a moment. When he didn't answer, I continued.

"I know you know the company before us got hit by an IED when they left his house after declining to pay him, one time. I'm not sure what the payment is called exactly, but I think we both know the intention."

"Yes," Owen said. "I remember."

"What do you think would have happened if a Marine had died?" I asked.

Owen looked out the window. His eyes glazed over. "Blood for blood," he replied.

"Most likely, yes," I said. "Or as it is written in my people's book of God's word, 'An eye for an eye.' But today no eyes were lost, so I doubt there will be any retaliation. If anything, whoever tipped us off about these coordinates will get paid and ..."

My voice trailed off as I realized my breach in operational security by telling Owen how we'd gotten the coordinates. Although I doubted he was an actual traitor, I didn't know for sure. I did know there were many rumors about Owen asking Marines far too much: *Where did the patrol go? How long did it stay? Did the patrol find anything? What are the plans for future operations?* Marcus, the only interpreter who'd been allowed to carry his own firearm on patrol, hated Owen and told others when Owen would try to pry information out of him.

"Don't worry," Owen said. He opened his mouth to say something else but then stopped.

Owen's door opened and Prockop's frame filled the space. The look on Owen's face made it obvious Prockop had just interrupted a sensitive conversation. Prockop stood staring at him like a father looking at a child with its hand in the cookie jar.

"What the fuck did you tell that goat farmer?" Prockop asked.

"I'm pretty sure those were sheep," I said. "And I didn't tell him anything."

"Then why the fuck is he back?" Prockop said.

I checked my mirror and saw the man with the staff, children, and sheep had all returned to their original spot. In a single glance, I knew why he was back; he wanted to cross the cordon. The shepherd had walked away to wait for an hour, before coming back to see if the patrol had moved. The gaggle of Iraqis and sheep wouldn't dissipate on its own; it would have to be dealt with.

"Why didn't you let him through?" Prockop asked.

"Let them walk through our lines while we wait for EOD?" I asked back.

"He's gotta clear out. EOD will be here soon and they want a three-hundred-meter cordon set up in a three-hundred-sixty-degree circle around the ordinance," Prockop said.

"Is that even possible?"

"No," Prockop said. "We're going to radio in that we've set up a three-hundred-meter cordon and EOD is going to keep its mouth shut or we'll be here all goddamn night."

The radio hissed and popped with static as a transmission from EOD came across, telling us to be ready in twenty minutes to set up a cordon.

"What the fuck is everyone's deal with having a hard-on for a cordon?" I asked as I opened my door. "I'll make sure this guy fucks off for real this time."

"Do it or it's your ass," Prockop shouted after me as I trudged back to the shepherd.

It was hotter, the three o'clock sun's heat having had enough time to seep into all the rocks and dirt making up the surface of the road. The leaves on the palm trees seemed to have wilted and turned a sickly white color in the blast furnace of the desert. The breeze across the

Euphrates quieted to cool whispers on my neck, the brief respites highlighting the desert's heat. Sweat beaded on my forehead as I approached the man. Twenty minutes until EOD got here. They would want to blow the small cache and get the hell out of dodge.

"Boom," I said, throwing my arms up in the air. I pointed at the cache and repeated the noise and gesture.

The man's eyes grew wide and his children whispered to each other and looked at their father's face. He babbled something at me and motioned to go past.

"No," I said, shaking my head back and forth slowly in an exaggerated gesture. I'd brought my rifle with me this time.

"Boom," I said. I moved the butt of my rifle to my shoulder and pointed it at a forty-five-degree angle at the ground in front of me. With my index finger on the trigger, I pointed with my left hand back down the road.

The man's face curdled with anger and resentment. The hand he'd pointed down the road past the patrol fell to his side. He turned and cuffed one of his children in the back of the head as he started to herd the sheep in front of him, the opposite direction. I stood there with a bad taste in my mouth, wondering how many times my people had turned him back on a road in his own country, and how many days remained until he did something about it. Maybe he'd go and tell someone with a mortar tube where we sat. Our day would turn to shit as soon as steel rained from the sky.

"Fuck," I said to myself. I turned from the group slowly walking away from me and trudged back to the truck.

"EOD is here," Ulrich said from the turret. "Jesus, there are a lot of trucks."

EOD wouldn't pull off the larger road onto the smaller one our patrol's trucks occupied. Five full-sized MRAPs bristling with .50-cals and Mk 19 grenade launchers, not a medium or light machine gun in sight. The EOD element stuck out like a sore thumb in bumfuck-nowhereville Iraq for a couple of reasons. First and foremost, operating along the Euphrates, especially around the parts of the river that started to coil, meant an exposure to water that could only be handled by missions using boats. The Marine Corps being amphibious was almost true in certain parts of the desert where slow, still waters carved the land. Heavy trucks couldn't navigate the canal roads and heavy guns meant fewer ways to warn traffic; medium machine gun rounds were much safer to skip off pavement. Mk 19s would blow things up because they shot grenades. EOD rolled heavy, the personnel having pistols and the latest kit hanging off them. They were the closest thing to actual armor this part of the desert would ever encounter, the greatest manifestation of America's will, outfitted to do two things: blow up ordinance and lay down heavy fire.

I stood outside my truck and watched as a Staff Sergeant walked over to the cache, accompanied by an entourage of varying rank. When he saw the contents of the box laid out on a sheet, he muttered something to a few of the Privates, who ran back to their element to return with rectangular blocks of explosives. The Marines formed a large cluster around the few people from EOD handling the material, crowding in close to see them stacking explosives on ordnance, one of the war's strange rituals. The explosion wouldn't be anything terrific and EOD didn't seem excited as they went about their task, just professional.

After a few moments of EOD moving the blocks into certain positions on the ordnance and pictures being snapped for intel, everyone hustled back toward their respective trucks. For a moment, Prockop and the Staff Sergeant from EOD stopped at the road. I couldn't hear what they were saying. As the rest of the Marines from Echo piled into the vehicles, I realized I needed to get in my own truck or risk being screamed at for not being at my post.

"What's going on?" Owen asked.

I didn't answer, but buckled my seat belt and he followed suit, knowing it as a sign of departure.

"We're striking a blow for freedom, Owen," I said. The corners of my mouth started to twist as I tried to keep from smiling. "History was made here today. We deprived the enemy of its means to fight."

"What are they talking about?" Owen asked, motioning with his chin toward Prockop and the Staff Sergeant.

"Well, I'd imagine EOD is telling Prockop that they're leaving under the impression that we'll set up a three-hundred-meter cordon in a three-hundred-sixty-degree circle around the soon-to-be blast crater," I replied.

"We aren't moving?" Owen asked.

"Fuck no, we aren't moving. Where would we go?" I said.

"But wouldn't it be safer if ..." his voice trailed off.

I lit a cigarette. The radio crackled loudly for several seconds before we could make out any traffic.

"*Spin the turrets, so the back-armor plating is toward the blast, but keep the gunners in the turret for security,*"

Prockop's voice broke up for a second and then continued. *"Close the windows."* Then more static that increased into a whine. I shut off the radio.

"These are the moments I won't make fun of you for praying," I said.

Owen looked like something he'd eaten didn't agree with him. I offered him a cigarette and he accepted.

"Ulrich," I said. "Get out of the turret."

"Prockop said for gunners to stay in the turret," Ulrich replied.

"I don't give a fuck, I'm telling you to get out of the turret," I said. "Are you going to go over there and have a conversation with him about it?"

I clicked back on the radio and an engineer's voice came over the comm. *"—about thirty seconds till detonation—crackle—"*

"Just sit down," I said. "We've been stationary for how many hours? What the fuck are you keeping us secure from? Get in the fucking truck!"

I grabbed Ulrich's pants by his back pocket and gave a couple of yanks.

"Roger, goddamn it, roger," he growled and let himself slide down off the seat strap into the truck.

I watched the cache carefully, ignoring Owen's warnings that it would be safest to duck down. The time passed slowly like the second hand on a factory clock nearing shift change.

"Do you think my camera will be all right?" Ulrich asked.

"What?" I said.

"I left my camera on top of the Humvee to record the blast. Do you think I should go and get it?"

"Fuck no." I said. "Sit the fuck down and shut up. That's an order."

I put my attention back on the cache as it blew, sending out shrapnel, a sound like timber cracking, and a visible sonic boom that swept out and away from the ordnance like a wispy bubble traveling at breakneck speed. A few pieces of shrapnel smacked off the ballistic glass in front of my face, leaving behind a couple of deep pockmarks. The ever-expanding eggshell of the shockwave broke on the trucks in a tumult of vapors and disappeared—the trucks rocked side-to-side, absorbing the energy.

I glanced at the pocks in the ballistic glass and then over at Owen.

"Looks like you were right about ducking," I said.

Owen didn't say anything back. He looked like a turtle, pulling his body armor up with his hands while trying to tuck his helmeted head down.

"Do you think my camera made it?" Ulrich asked as he scrambled back up in the turret.

"Fuck if I know," I said.

I tried to take it all in, the way the clumps of grass in the fields stood like stubble in the sun, how the Euphrates slowly moved past us taking no heed of our actions, the palms, Owen shivering from adrenaline, Ulrich's voice shouting how his camera survived the shockwave and shrapnel. I knew this was a moment that would live forever, in the same place where nightmares swim and twist through what I think I know and remember, coming back to me in shards of dreams and replayed on my waking eyes with the crystal clarity of hallucination.

I glanced over at Owen. He'd stopped shivering and hugged himself. I offered him another smoke and he accepted with a sheepish grin. The truck in front of me started rolling and I threw mine into drive to follow. Glancing into the side mirror, I caught the reflection of myself. For a second, I saw the same stare Blaker had given me, when your eyes don't focus on anything and just look out across eternity. I crammed the heels of my hands into my eye sockets and tried rubbing it off as if it was grease smeared across my face.

"Crackle— jammers off—trying to get ahold of the COC—"

I took a last vain look at myself, trying to see if the stare was still there—I thought it had gone.

"Owen, tap the front of the PalmPilot," I said. "When the screen blinks on, hit the box with the word 'off' in the middle."

Owen did as I told him unsteadily, hands still trembling.

"Are you all right?" he asked me.

"I'm all right," I said. "Maybe you should worry about your own shit, Mr. I-have-Parkinson's-after-explosions."

The patrol headed back through Saqlawiyah, buzzed past the marketplace, bounced over potholes, and lackadaisically made its way around the roundabout with the obelisk in the center at the north side of town. Pigeons cooed in the FOB's parking lot as they scattered their white shit over all the vehicles. The patrol was back behind the safety of the HESCO Barriers filled with dirt and wearing triple-stacked rolls of razor wire as a crown of thorns. The posts stood silent vigil on the surrounding area and the giant camera, posted on a small tower on top of the FOB, hummed as it zoomed in on something in the distance. I looked up at Post Four, at the .50-cal pointed out of its ballistic window at the

FOB's gate. Safety, or something like it, made me relax. A truck moved from its initial spot and parked by me as I stood next to my open Humvee door.

"Wanna burn one in the smoke pit?" Larkin asked me as he hopped out of what had been the second vehicle in the patrol.

"I just smoked a pack on patrol," I said. "I think there's a chance chow is sitting out in the chow hall for the flies, so I'd better get in there."

"First Sergeant said the flies would carry disease from the porta-shitters to the food, but the cooks don't care because they don't eat it," Larkin said.

We trudged into the FOB together and found the food eaten and flies crawling over what remained. Larkin headed out to the smoke pit to kick rocks and smoke. I stood there in the chow hall looking around for something to eat like a dog that keeps looking for the invisible ball its master threw. The boxes of Pop-Tarts stood hollow. The pastries with their cloying honey were gone, the small boxes of cereal were gone—there was nothing.

"Where is the food?" Rose asked from the empty chow containers. "Goddamn it!"

The SOG came in to explain how the company hadn't known when our patrol would get back.

"Are you fucking shitting me?" Rose's voice faded out as Hawkins walked up to me.

"Do you think the food in the dumpster outside is edible?" he asked. I looked at him, shocked for a second, then realized I'd eat food out of the dumpster too.

"I don't know," I said. "It's been sitting out for the flies."

I stumbled up to my room, unstrapped my body armor, and let it fall to the floor—the thud of bullet-stopping ceramic plates, followed by the hollow sound of my Kevlar helmet. Exhaustion, my old friend, come to see me again. I flopped onto my rack, closed my eyes, and rubbed the bridge of my nose. The door smacked against the wall as other Marines walked into the room, dropped gear, and hit the rack.

"What day is it today?" I asked no one in particular.

"Isn't it your birthday?" a voice finally answered, belonging to Ulrich. "Finally, old enough to drink."

The silence broke as people stirred in their racks, digesting the information. On a Marine's birthday in-country, it was customary for the Marine to provide a bottle of liquor for everyone to drink. As counterintuitive as it seemed for the person having the birthday to provide the booze, it made sense. Possession of liquor in a combat zone was a big no-no, so acquiring it fell on the birthday boy because his brothers-in-arms would be too busy fighting a war to deal with the task. Today, that birthday boy was me. A month or so earlier, I'd written a friend of mine with some instructions. Three weeks later, I received a bottle of mouthwash, filled with tequila. "Why tequila?" I'd asked him after. He'd told me Iraq was a desert and so was Mexico, so he figured it would be fitting.

The tequila tasted horrible warm. A tinge of grape, left behind by the mouthwash, lingered in the liquor. The squad huddled around in a small circle in my room and passed the plastic bottle. No one talked. We all just stared at the floor with the bird shit blown in from the desert and the scampering of mice tracked in mud across the tiles. For a second, it seemed like we were mourning at a wake, the brooding was so deep. A few people said happy birthday. Decker asked if there was any more booze. Then he told the whole squad was being pushed out the next day for an all-day operation and to get some rest. Hawkins looked around like he wanted to say something but didn't know what. None of us wanted to think about the war, which seemed like it would never end. We didn't want to think about back home and the recession.

Eight hours later, we geared up and walked back out the door to load trucks for the big operation.

WHITE WHALE

THE TRIBUTARY STRETCHED OUT IN FRONT OF us from the Euphrates, pointing toward the northernmost fringes of Saqlawiyah. Weapons Platoon maneuvered a column of vehicles down from the MSR to a small dirt road that ran parallel to the river. A latticework of paths and irrigation ditches, swollen with water, striped the green plane of farm fields. Halfway down the slope from the MSR to the dirt road, everyone but the drivers dismounted to form up for the sweep: two columns, one on each side of the road. The carcass of a long dead cow, mummified by the desert, crunched as a Humvee's front tire crushed its skull, then ribs. My Sergeant stopped to dry heave.

"Oh my God," Prockop said between gags. "That smell. Fuck. It's rancid."

A few other dead cattle lay along the slope. I didn't know for sure, but I could guess that some bored Marines killed them from behind the guns of a passing convoy. I gathered this from how the carrion scattered out from the MSR, like a herdsman had pushed his small herd up from grassy fields only to have them spooked by diesel engines and gunned down by men half his age. The Humvee's rear tire crunched over the dried bag of bones, pushing more detritus from inside. I started to open my mouth to retch, only to have the blow-dryer heat of the desert push it back down my throat.

"Hell of a start to the big sweep," I said to Prockop.

The Humvee we'd been guiding moved down the slope into position behind an MRAP. The rest of the vehicles sat on the MSR, a few of them idling. There was a pause, while radios crackled and people tried to figure out what was going on. There hadn't been a mission briefing, so I had no idea of the bigger picture. I'd thought about asking for a mission brief before we'd stepped off but knew better.

I'd learned a long time ago that our FOB allowed for some of the habits of garrison to remain a part of our daily lives, despite the threats from the environment and surrounding ville. Captain Vorgang liked the pomp mustered for him in garrison and so did Staff Sergeant Gnade. The Captain liked to tell stories about his last deployment to Afghanistan. Gnade talked about his SWAT (Special Weapons and Tactics) training and fallen comrades.

I didn't buy into it. Everyone in the military has their stories about how the guy they'd just been working next to moments, hours, days, or weeks before just suddenly died and, *Shit, man, it could have been me*. Like most Senior Lance Corporals, I wasn't impressed with stories meant to showcase the sea salt dried on people's collars from long journeys.

The Captain's voice came over the radio, broken with static, as he tried to raise Gnade, who must have been passed out in a Humvee. Prockop held his radio out in front of him, peering above the speaker at the LED that displayed the frequency, channel, battery life, and encryption status. I couldn't believe Gnade. I paced back and forth in the dust, sometimes looking through my ACOG (Advanced Combat Optical Gunsight) at the far bank of the river or up the small dirt road to the plume of green trees on the horizon.

"Where do you think the herdsman is?" I shouted up to Ulrich, who was on top of the lead vehicle, a Seven-Ton truck with a turret jutting out its top. I walked over to a long-dead cow and gave it a few stomps on the head, careful to hold my breath. Rust-colored dust burst out of the eye sockets with the smell of death's long decay. Prockop raised his voice to address the group.

"Both columns are going to punch up to the right side of the road," Prockop said and then looked at me. "Take point and lead out security on that side."

Back in Iowa, cows got killed by hunters who mistook them for deer and their corpses stayed tucked away in the timber. Here in the wastes, the stunted animals that passed for cows were shot out of boredom. A lot of things died like that in the sands: dogs, cows, goats, birds, people. In the States, things seemed to accept death, slide into it like a warm bath. Here, things were wrenched from life, to lie twisted and broken on the scorched desert.

I walked parallel to the road, trying to keep thirty meters of standoff. I wanted to think of home—philandering girlfriend, dying grandmother—but couldn't. If I fucked up or missed something, people would go home in body bags. I always told myself this. Somehow, I left out how people could, and would, go back in body bags no matter what I did. Prockop called it "the nature of the beast," but I didn't call it anything. I couldn't dignify or mystify it.

All I knew was heat and a need to take in my surroundings. The little road saw regular use, that much was evident from the ruts, but it wasn't sturdy enough to support any bigger vehicles. I looked back at the Seven-Ton and wondered how a vehicle that heavy would fare. On the other side of the dirt road lay the tributary and, on my side, fields. Ahead, goats were being herded into a chicken-wire enclosure. The sun was just rising over the tree line.

Behind me, Smith was the first Marine to follow my steps in trace. I would have preferred Larkin, but Smith would do in a pinch. Larkin and I usually shared point and second man, alternating depending on the day and how we felt. We'd found that second man ended up supporting point man so much that it was best to think of the two positions as a team: checking bridges for booby traps, moving concertina wire, and opening gates all took a coordinated effort from the first two men in the element. Larkin and I had made a pact early in our deployment that if one of us got hit by a sniper, the other would immediately sprint over and drag the body to cover.

"Smith, tighten it up," I yelled.

The ground by the small road didn't pose too much of a challenge, but Smith had gotten caught up in a ditch and fallen behind. The vehicles crawled along a little bit ahead of him with the Seven-Ton leading the way.

"Does it matter?" Smith called back.

"Fucking right it matters. If I get hit—"

The Seven-Ton lurched toward the stream. The side of the road closest to the water had sloughed off under the weight. I could see a Marine inside the cab shout into a radio. Ulrich bounced around in the turret like a pinball, caught between the armor plating and .50-caliber machine gun. I couldn't hear the thump of his body armor or when his shoulders took the impact. I couldn't hear him screaming.

Everything slowed down. The ground moved past me and I realized I'd started sprinting toward them. To my left twenty meters Smith was doing the same—but more bodies around the tipping truck would only complicate things.

"Stay the fuck back," I shouted.

Smith stopped. I looked back at the vehicle to see Ulrich disappear over the side. The driver's door swung freely on its hinges, the vehicle's cab empty.

"Get ready for mortars," Prockop screamed while running up to the rear of the truck.

The feeling of falling through a trap made my balls crawl up my insides.

"What?" Smith said, then something unintelligible.

I wondered when the world would start exploding. Were mortar rounds already in the air? I scoped the opposite bank, the alfalfa fields, then the road ahead. It was empty. Just a dusty road, peppered with donkey shit and fields.

"We might get hit! Take cover!" Prockop said.

I dove head first into the nearby irrigation ditch. It was deep with grassy sides. I bounced off one of the walls, twisting through the air like a discarded marionette, and hit the bottom of the trench. The grass disguised many small pools, filled with brackish water, and small brambles hugging the soggy earth. I lay facedown for a few moments with nothing but the smell of damp ground and moldy grass in my nostrils.

"Fucking wonderful," I said, stumbling to my feet. My boots, cammie bottoms, and gear had all turned black.

"They must be using shit as fertilizer," I said to no one.

The top of the trench was three feet above my head. I followed a curve twenty meters around a grassy knoll until it dead-ended, before climbing up the side. After struggling with my sling, failing to level my rifle in front of me, I stopped trying to be tactical and stuck my head up like a groundhog. Behind me, the Seven-Ton listed perilously toward the tributary. The trucks by the MSR had all buttoned up—Marines inside and the turrets swiveling slowly to take in the landscape.

I stumbled from my perch. If I turned and worked my way back down the ditch, I might find Smith. More likely the trench would end, forcing me to break cover and search for Smith above ground. After a few tentative steps, I froze. I thought I heard someone calling my name.

"Big Head ... where are you?"

Ulrich appeared at the earthen lip above me. If he would have stopped and carefully slid into the trench I could have helped him. Ulrich didn't stop, though. He tried to half-slide, half-climb into the trench and tumbled down in a heap. Ulrich got up slowly and surveyed his gear, now tinted black from the bracken water. We both looked like we'd been dipped, facedown, in something putrid.

"No, don't help me get up," he said. "I'm fine. Thank you for asking if falling into this shithole hurt."

I couldn't help but laugh. We both found a place to sit and smoke.

"How the fuck did you survive the fall out of the Seven-Ton?" I asked.

Ulrich blew out a large cloud of blue smoke.

"The side of the road gave out and the truck started going, I mean really started going. For a second I was sure we were going to roll." He paused to look at the glowing tip of his cigarette. "Man, it hurt to bounce around in the turret. I thought I was dead for sure. I looked over and there was the Captain. He kept telling me to jump before the truck rolled on us. I bounced off him before I hit the ground. Then Hewlett comes piling out of the cab with no fucking gear on and the Captain loses his mind. Then we got the fuck out of there."

"He was in there with no gear on?" I asked.

"No shit," Ulrich said. "I don't get why the Assaultmen don't wear their gear, especially with those guys from Golf getting smoked and FOB Viking getting hit."

"The Golf Marines burned to death," I said. "There isn't anything to make us fireproof."

Ulrich took a long drag.

"I heard them on the radio with Camp Hob about getting a wrecker out here," Ulrich said.

Wreckers looked like semis with big tow cables and winches attached to the top and sides; they came with their own entourage of Marines, equipped with radio headsets and armed to the teeth. Now, things were about to get crowded. I glanced down at my watch to see its face read: 0830. The day, and the operation, were off to a bad start.

"Why was Prockop screaming about Mortars?" Ulrich asked.

"People are on edge. The drone saw a squad's worth of armed men mobilize when we were out here a few days ago," I said. "If they have any of the smaller mortar systems, it would be really easy to walk rounds on target, especially if they have spotters and cell phones."

"Do you think he was serious about the incoming or putting on a show for the Captain?"

"You're a lot smarter than you play with other people, aren't you, little Chamorro?"

Ulrich laughed, his smile creasing his face.

"Anyway," he said. "Before I got sent to look for you, I was told we're supposed to sit tight until the wrecker comes."

I climbed back up the side of the trench to peek out over the grassy fields. Nothing had changed, except for a slight morning breeze making the grass ripple and wave like an ocean—I wondered where the sharks were.

"Weird how no one over the rank of E-3 is out on the line right now," I said. "That's how it goes, isn't it? The NCOs and officers sit in the vics while we squat our asses in the bush."

Ulrich leaned his head back against the earth and closed his eyes, not commenting on the rift between NCOs and the rest of the enlisted. After shifting his rifle to lie comfortably across his body, he crossed his legs in front of him. He looked like he was back home in a recliner. I hoped he didn't have a concussion. If he did, there wasn't much I could do for him. The Corpsmen were buttoned up in armored vehicles, being too valuable to expose. If steel rained from the sky and exploded in our midst, then the Corpsmen would come out to try to put the pieces back together, but not before. Ulrich tried to say something else, but his words slurred together. The sun cooked the landscape.

I sat down, facing Ulrich. Exhaustion crept in. My head nodded heavily, but I caught myself. "You've got this," I said to myself. "You've got this."

I lit a smoke.

* * *

A BLEARY TELEVISION showed soldiers on patrol. I sat at the bar by myself, back home, using a fake ID to get into a local dive.

"Barkeep!" I hollered. "Can I get another one?"

A gritty blackness swirled around the edges of everything as if reality barely kept from unraveling. The bartender appeared in front of me.

"What'll it be, Devil Dog?" he asked.

"Give me a Guinness and turn the TV off," I said. "I'm sick of the war."

On the blank TV screen, my reflection faced me in full gear: body armor, Kevlar helmet, Camelbak, tourniquet zip-tied to my shoulder, and about three-hundred rounds loaded into magazines strapped to my stomach, making it hard to belly up to the bar.

"Where is everyone?" I asked.

"At the mall," said a voice to my right.

I turned to find my old friend Adam, sitting there in a tie-dye shirt, adorned with a skeleton Rastafarian riding a mushroom through space, big dreadlocks trailing behind its skull. Adam and I had been pot-smoking buddies in high school, but parted ways when he moved off to a college town to party and I joined the military. Adam's rusty hair was thin, already balding in his early twenties. That, combined with his perpetually red face, made him look like a six-foot-tall Sesame Street character.

I realized I was back at The Den in Des Moines, Iowa, my hometown. The place hadn't changed—same stains on the floor, same dusty signs on the walls, same hillbilly video games in the back where you shot deer with a plastic rifle, and same sleazy dive bar feel with its hot dogs and popcorn and condoms in the bathroom trash can. The place smelled foul and was sweltering.

"What the fuck is that smell?" I asked.

"Shit, it smells like," Adam said.

From the back of the bar, I heard a door slam shut. The bartender walked out of the women's bathroom with a mop in one hand.

"Goddamn women keep throwing their tampons in the toilet. Backed the whole thing up," he said.

I squinted at him as he spoke. His face kept disappearing and reappearing, his voice coming from a long way off. I looked at Adam and started to ask him about the barkeep's face, but the popcorn machine went crazy, popping like a roll of firecrackers. Adam didn't seem concerned about the noise and kept peering into his beer. I felt something on my left and turned to find the three guys from Golf sitting at the bar, one of them still burning. Their faces were charred and cracked like chicken left on the grill too long.

"Did it hurt?" I asked.

The one closest to me worked his jaw, but the only thing that came out sounded like a car tire hissing as it lost pressure. I stared at him for a few seconds while a thick black liquid oozed out of his cheek and down his neck. His right eye couldn't open but the left was mostly intact, milky like an old dog's. The other two were worse. I could tell one had been the turret gunner by the sharp bend in his spine that made sitting at the bar awkward and the other Marine looked like a wax figurine, set too close to a radiator.

"These boys are fucked up like soup sandwiches," I said, turning to find Adam in the middle of throwing down American money, scrawled with Arabic, on the table.

"No one cares about that," Adam said. "I'm heading to the mall. You're welcome to come."

He wouldn't look at me as he said it.

I turned to the dead men beside me, wreathed in their own smoldering.

"It was good seeing you guys. Sorry you didn't make it. Fuckin' ... tough break."

My thoughts were hard to finish, though I couldn't remember drinking too much. My legs didn't want to work as I stood and grabbed my rifle, the floor sticky as fresh pitch. I staggered outside. I was met with desolation—Iraq had followed me.

Everything was shot up: the strip of chain stores to our left looked like downtown Fallujah after a long day of Marines thumping away on their fifties; the Denny's in front of us was on fire and the road to our right looked nearly impassable with torn-open, smoking vehicles. We made our way to Adam's car which turned out to be a Humvee. He wanted me to drive.

"Some things never change."

I tried to keep my voice cheerful, but it cracked. Bodies hung from the streetlight in the parking lot, swinging like macabre ornaments.

"Did we lose the war?" I asked. "And where are the keys?"

"The war came home," Adam said. "And there aren't any keys, it's a Humvee."

A goat herder and his flock blocked our Humvee's path for a moment as we rolled out of the parking lot. I turned toward the mall. The road didn't have any shoulders, instead dropping off into a blackness out of which long, stiff reeds grew up toward the sky.

"Watch out!" Adam screamed.

Ten meters ahead, the carcass of a black-and-white-splotched dairy cow, lumpy and deformed, belly stitched up. I slammed on the brakes, then realized we were in Weapons Platoon second vehicle; the alignment listed badly to the right, making the vehicle start to spin whenever the brakes locked up on mud. The Humvee was sideways when we reached the animal-borne IED. The last thing I saw before the vehicle slid over it was three 155-millimeter artillery rounds packed inside, ready to burst out through the sutures. The blast tore the back half of the Humvee off and sent us spinning through the air. Everything was on fire by the time we hit the ground, hanging upside down by our safety belts. Adam's face started to melt, his lips pulling back from his skull.

"It's just a dream," I screamed as mortars started to rain down around us, making their telltale *crump, crump* sound as they sent shrapnel out in supersonic clouds.

The flames engulfed me, licking my face and hands. I flailed wildly but couldn't break free from the comm gear pinning me against the door.

* * *

I WOKE FROM my sleep with the feeling of steel wool in my mouth, lips tight and cracked. Ulrich was still in the land of nod. Every few seconds, he would make a high-pitched sound in his throat and his face muscles would twitch.

"Where are you guys?" The voice belonged to Decker.

"Ulrich," I said. "Hey! Wake up!"

I pulled out a big water bottle from my drop pouch as Ulrich started to stir. Fumbling around in my gear for a second, I found one of the pink lemonade concentrates. The water bottle turned bright pink as I shook the concentrate into dilution in the bottle. I drank half of the quart and smacked my lips loudly, the sugar's gaudy excess almost sour, washing over my parched tongue.

"Drink the rest of this," I said, tossing the bottle to Ulrich which hit his helmet.

"Great, the bottle touched shit water," Ulrich said. "You bring pink lemonade on ops?"

"Just drink it, smartass," I said. "And look alive, Decker is coming to check on us."

Decker walked up to our position while Ulrich guzzled the lemonade like a cow from its mother's teat. At first, he didn't see us, his instinct to avoid the irrigation ditch entirely.

"Down here," I said.

Decker did a startled bunny hop and swung his rifle around on me.

"You two are really hidden down there," Decker said. "I'm out checking on everyone. The wrecker is fifteen minutes out. Let me know if you need anything."

"It would be easier to let you know if we had a radio," I replied.

"You don't have a radio?" Decker said. "I'll tell Prockop."

The trench's humidity rose and a putrid smell festered. Ulrich and I were both anxious to crawl out and get the sweep moving. Just as the deep rumble of the wrecker's diesel engine reached us, Hewlett stumbled through the grass to our position.

"You guys don't have a radio?" Hewlett asked as he took off his Kevlar helmet.

"Do you think it's a good idea to keep taking your PPE off?" I asked.

PPE stood for Personal Protection Equipment, and referred to the body armor, gloves, helmet, and ballistic glasses Marines wore outside of the wire.

"Yes, I do," Hewlett said. "Because I don't want to wear it."

"God, you and Smith are stupid," Ulrich said. "Just wear the fucking gear! Didn't Smith get his wages garnished for not wearing his helmet on post at the Iraqi Police station?"

The rumble of diesel engines got closer. I peeked over the trench to see the wrecker—a vehicle the same length and size as a fire truck with a crane and several winches—along with EOD's three extended-size MRAPs and a half-dozen Humvees on the MSR. Ulrich and Hewlett bitched about everything, from the heat to girls back home, as we watched the wrecker maneuver into position behind the leaning Seven-Ton. The wrecking crew dismounted and attached winches to the back of the listing vehicle. The Seven-Ton shuddered and it seemed like the vehicle might flip into the river. The wrecker's driver gunned it, yanking the Seven-Ton to safety.

As an MRAP moved up to resume the sweep, radio traffic told the line to punch out and patrol along the road while the combat engineers swept the ground with their metal detectors—the idea was that the MRAP's V-shaped armored hull would absorb the blast from any pressure plate IEDs buried in the road. After fifteen minutes of slowly sweeping, the engineers found a small cache of a few mortars, flares, and grenades near an intersection with one of the smaller roads that made up the fretwork of brown stripes on the fields.

"It doesn't feel right. We need to keep pushing," the Captain said.

I led the column of Marines along the dirt road, until one of the squat buildings in the distance was right in front of me. The sun had reached its zenith and slanted to the west, making the trees cast long shadows against the building. I wiped sweat from my face as I leaned against it, waiting for the rest of the Marines to gather around me. Word had been passed that we'd rally by the stucco barn and then a small contingent of Marines would push up with the engineers to sweep the coordinates intelligence had said would have a big payoff. Crawford, the section leader for Assault, pushed up with the engineers and a few other Marines. They were gone quite a while before anyone thought that maybe they'd actually found something. When the Staff NCOs in EOD started the long walk from their vehicles on the MSR, we knew it was no-shit big.

"What'd they find?" Prockop called to the EOD guys as they walked up the trail to us.

"A white whale," a Gunnery Sergeant answered.

"Then who's Ahab?" one of the Assaultmen asked.

The EOD staff walked by, some not wearing body armor, some just in helmets, some with pistols, and others unarmed. They were a motley crew of upper echelon Staff NCOs. I shook my head at the sight of them, tromping down the back roads. The Captain was the only officer involved in the operation, I realized, as I watched him sitting with his back to the building. He seemed content to let the NCOs take the lead as he slowly rose and followed after them. That left the grunts hanging around with their rifles leaned up against the building. Some of us took a few candid pictures of a scene repeated across the world on many battlegrounds: Marines rallied near an objective, waiting for something to happen. I chain-smoked, as did everyone else who smoked. The air was hot and tense. We wanted to be out of there and back in the air conditioning of the FOB. We'd spent the entire day on a mile-long stretch of road and that wasn't strategically sound. Insurgent activity in Saqlawiyah may have not been "hot," but it existed; a big cache made that undeniable.

"What did they find, Hawkins?" I asked. He leaned against the barn, listening to the old Vietnam War era radio with a big whip antenna he'd been assigned to lug around.

"You won't believe me if I tell you," Hawkins said.

"Why don't you try me?" I said.

"About two dozen 80-millimeter mortars, some mortar tubes, a bunch of 55-millimeter recoilless rifle rounds, Soviet shoulder-fired, armor-piercing rockets, a bunch of rifle rounds, smaller mortar rounds, and artillery rounds," Hawkins said.

"You have got to be fucking kidding me," Ulrich said. "Armor-piercing, shoulder-fired rockets? I bet they go right through the armor on our Humvees."

"The captain is on his way back with pictures," Hawkins said.

Sure enough, the Captain brought back a camera full of pictures of things that would turn our day to shit in a hurry. He said the shoulder-fired rockets were low-tech, like a crazed Boy Scout project. I couldn't imagine getting hit with a rocket—that was unheard of. IEDs and snipers were one thing, but armor-piercing rockets were another. A 55-millimeter recoilless rifle could be set up in a few minutes across from the FOB to shoot exploding shells into Marines' rooms, causing massive casualties. Time passed and slowly the EOD staff trickled back, then the grunts, followed by the engineers. I stood out on the dirt road, waiting for the unexploded ordinance to be detonated. I'd never been around a big explosion full of munitions before, but the Captain had.

"Get your ass off the road," the Captain said. "You're going to get yourself killed standing out there like that."

I sheepishly moved behind the barn as Hawkins counted down to zero, holding the radio's receiver to his ear.

"Do you think it'll be lou—" Ulrich was cut off by the blast.

A sound like a great oak snapping filled our bodies and the ground trembled, while a black geyser of dirt shot thirty stories into the sky. Shrapnel whizzed over the barn and through brush, a few pieces managing to arc just right, so that they gently landed on the helmets and shoulders of Marines smoking and looking uneasy. I heard the shrill bleating of goats coming from somewhere across the river; they might have just been spooked or they may have taken shrapnel. I couldn't tell.

"That would have perforated your face if you'd been standing out there like an idiot," Prockop said.

I took point back to the MSR with a small herd of EOD staff following behind; I'd offered up the polite wisdom that maybe they should fall back to the middle of the column, because many of them barely wore body armor and didn't have weapons. They all nodded in agreement.

I passed out as soon as I got in the Humvee. When I woke, we were back at the FOB. Marines kept asking me what we'd found and where, what we'd done. A squad leader from another platoon got excited as he spoke.

"You guys are helping win the war on terror," he said. "You really are!"

I didn't know what to say. I still smelled like shit from the ditch I'd dove into. I was tired. I didn't feel like I'd helped win anything. When I got up to my room, rats scurried from under the racks to disappear through a hole in the wall. I thought about setting some traps, but I didn't want to start a war in my room. I had the rest of Iraq for that.

OPERATION IRAQI FREEDOM

I WAS ON THE TAIL END OF THE BULLSHIT. I HELPED break down one of the last FOBs. The strategy was the same as the one employed at the beginning of the war in Afghanistan—move into the cities and set up bases. Toward the end of the war, megabases were in place. Camp Fallujah was one of these, a few kilometers northeast of the sprawl of Fallujah itself. It was a monstrosity, outfitted with a helicopter pad and squads of Marines patrolling the perimeter in constant vigil. The base was a labyrinth of twisting gravel roads, leading deep into the oasis of friendly territory.

The chow hall was unlike any other chow hall in our battlespace; it was almost like being back stateside. Giant plasma-screen TVs played the latest sporting events. Paper tablecloths, metal silverware—it was enough to make the most hardened veteran drop his guard. The contrast was stark between the personnel who lived on the base and the transient convoy-goers who ravenously ate there. While personnel stationed at the base were clean-cut and wore pressed uniforms, Marines from outside were grizzled and dirty and carried weapons that were beat up and caked with sand. We looked like a bunch of homeless people eating in a fancy restaurant.

The entrance of Camp Fallujah was in a great dip in the desert, between the road and a far-off ridgeline. The kilometer-long depression in the ground was filled with an assortment of every kind of vehicle on God's green earth, each one torn open and burnt to a crisp. They were countless and stretched to the eastern horizon. After watching them fly by for twenty minutes, we rolled past several checkpoints. Bases with scenes like that at their gates made it so much safer for us in the end. No one in their right mind would try to roll up to that base, not even a suicide bomber. They just couldn't make it.

At the tail end of that bullshit was a mass exodus, including my base, FOB Riviera. Everyone who wasn't attached to a battlespace getting broken down was relocated to a larger camp. This was called an egress or a withdrawal. It couldn't be done fast enough. We wouldn't leave anything for the dinks—except we weren't calling opposition forces dinks anymore. The names we used to dehumanize them had changed though the concept remained the same. We made them different, so we could justify acting like they were no better than the cockroaches that we scraped off the soles of our boots. As we stripped the copper wire that ran all through the base, we cursed them.

We were told that everything we didn't strip would be made into some kind of killing device. That terrorists would wear it into meetings inside Fallujah and smoke half of Battalion 1/5, or 3/5, or whoever was holding down that hornets' nest of pissed-off Arabs. If it wasn't used for that, it would be strapped to a woman who would bear hug an Iraqi Police officer and detonate. Suicide bombers' heads pop straight off like dandelions when they detonate. As soon as heads are blasting off around you like party streamers, you have failed. Somewhere along the line you let yourself down and the hajis knew it. Those clever little guys didn't pull any punches. We were told the time to not blow it was the present, so we stripped everything.

But that's not the picture that got sent up to Battalion. They didn't get a picture of how our fine boys were egressing. Battalion got pictures of me on the front berm of the base, parking my vehicle between posts one and two. We hadn't taken any pictures that patrol; the sandstorm was so thick you could cut it with your bayonet. All we had done was drive around for four godforsaken hours in a brownout, not seeing, not doing a damn thing, and forgetting to take photos of the operation. So, we posed inside of the actual FOB and got a picture of me standing in front of the Humvee. You can't tell from the pic that it was taken inside the base, so Battalion was happy. And that made America happy. That made every jerk-off who was getting laid, high, and wasted stateside as happy as a pig in shit.

The Marines who were there at the tail end knew better. Everyone knew better, except the people in command, who weren't there. They seemed not to have thought about how our leaving would be handled. We just vacated. We did so shorthanded and thus put people in positions that were sloppy, unprofessional, and dangerous. We left entire companies in logistical darkness about how they would not be receiving supplies or about how they would manage a command post with three-quarters of their strength gone and no help on the way.

In the mission briefing, our crooked Sergeant assigned my team leader, Rose, and I to the south end of a double blockade, cutting off all traffic on both sides of the road in town, in order to cover the engineers who were tearing down the berm and gathering up the razor wire. The way things broke down left our Sergeant with no responsibilities and plenty of time to sleep at the north end of the roadblock. As we walked out of the base to the trucks, the smell of diesel, dirt, and the nearby latrines wafted rudely through our noses. Rose informed me that we were doing it severely undermanned; we were getting hung out to dry in the middle of town with no boots on the deck to haul our asses out of the fire and back to the half-torn-open FOB, if Allah willed his children to play rough with us.

We hit the center of town like we owned the place. The roadblock was concertina wire which would tangle people and ensnare cars. We had to dismount and stand in the street, just Rose and me. We had an MRAP at our end of the blockade. Larkin was in the turret behind the machine gun and Doc Martinez was guarding the back door of the MRAP. That left no one in the driver's seat—the vehicle essentially dead in the water—as we cleared out an intersection of cars that had for some reason stopped and refused to move. I put my boots on the ground with my 9-mil already out. Rose took the right side of the street; he was going to kick villagers off their front porches and make them go inside for the remainder of the night. There were few people outside playing soccer or milling about and we were glad for that. I took the left side with the southbound cars standing still, stacked two abreast and more than thirteen deep. I had to move these cars south, across the intersection, so we could set up the blockade.

I went up to someone's car and motioned him forward. No one would move, so I waved my pistol and shouted in broken Arabic. A shop owner who had walked outside to see the commotion clued me in that a giant convoy was sitting across the intersection. The hajis could tell we were trying to clear the streets and I think they wanted us to get the giant convoy out of there as well. The sooner they could go back to gutting animals and readying them for the evening meal, the happier they would be.

I walked over to a beat-up blue Toyota and told the driver to pull forward. He looked at me in panic. He knew I was going to make him ram a vehicle in front of him to clear a path. He understood this. I understood this. Everyone on that street understood this. They also knew that I wasn't going to just start smoking innocents. They didn't know one hundred percent, but it could be assumed that I wasn't going to redecorate his dashboard with the beef-cranberry of his brains, just yet. So the car sat there and the people standing in the dusty street stared at me. I felt heat rise up my back and into my head, my pulse distorting my vision as one thing became certain: I was going to move that man.

Jackie the Iraqi was going to be the link in the chain that forced the cars in front of him forward. This middle-aged haji was going to be heroic, to summon forth fortitude, and I was going to help. I was going to storm over to my vehicle. I was going to tell Larkin to cover me. I would throw open my door and toss the pistol on the seat. I was then going to grab my M-16 A4 service rifle and slam a thirty-round high-capacity magazine into it. I drove my heels into the deck on the way over. Larkin told me that it was apocalypse across the intersection, the unit call sign for the Battalion personal safety attachment, the small army that guarded the Battalion Commander. The first round in my magazine slid into the chamber.

Courage welled up in the Iraqi as he saw me walking back to him. I was about to make this man a hero. Someone who was so brave, he would no longer sit idle at the intersection of his town. He would advance and brave the waiting guns of the apocalypse, be an emissary for those who would no longer let America impose on their lives. He tried to plead with me through the open car window, his calloused hands raised in panic. I would like to think he was pleading for the angel of death to pass over, so that he could go on to take part in some greater glory, that Allah had come to him and told him that someday he would be used for some other purpose than standing up to those who thought they could tower over him. But I don't think that's what he was saying to me. I think he was saying that he wasn't ready to pull forward.

I looked at him and I thought, *No*.

This was the day that he was going to step forward as a man. I wasn't going to give him a choice. As my weapon leveled at his head and hung in the breach of his half-opened window, he knew he was going to be a leader this day. He knew this was the day that Allah had chosen for him to act.

I looked at him and whispered, "No. Forward."

He became the man ahead of his peers and he did pull forward. The cars ahead of him started moving and the cars behind him followed. In that way, the southbound traffic was cleared. I walked over to the truck and Rose told me that the people he had been talking to hauled ass inside as soon as I racked my rifle and put on my business face.

We were happy. We were happy because higher-ups would be happy. Battalion was happy with pictures, it was happy with cleared intersections.

I fell asleep in the truck behind the roadblock, curled into a ball in the driver's seat, dreaming of a sweet nothing, not the nightmare I played out in my waking.

That's how the West was won. It was a victory that hinged on us leaving quickly and efficiently. And that's how I helped win that day, by being a traffic cop who flew all the way around the world, to tell a people that they were wrong to do things the way they were doing them. All the sacrifice, the tears, the blood, the lives and limbs that were left there—they were part of that victory also. A way of saying that America could go anywhere and do anything it wanted. It could walk into your country and force it to be democratic and if you didn't have the courage to like it, we would bequeath you that courage from the 5.56-millimeter hole at the end of our rifles.

ACCESSORY TO GENOCIDE

OMAR WAS WHAT POLITE SOCIETY CALLED A collaborator, what spooks called an informant, what Latino Marines called a snitch, and what some white Marines called a race traitor. Omar was a man of many titles, but only one utility, and I'd forgotten about him in the sweat and sleepless nights of FOB Riviera's breakdown.

When I woke for my last morning in the gutted FOB, the lights didn't turn on; the generator's constant grumble was absent for the first time. I went Condition One—grabbed my M-16A4 service rifle, inserted a magazine, and racked a round into the chamber. We hadn't been briefed on what would happen during the deconstruction phase of our base and had just spent the night providing security for the engineers while they tore down the perimeter fences crowned with razor wire.

Ulrich was the next Marine to go Condition One. Normally it was a big no-no to go into the base with your weapon hot or to go weapons hot inside the ring of wire that circled the FOB. Part of this had to do with weapons safety—it was easy in the close quarters of the base to let a rifle slide from its resting place against a wall and hit the floor—but it also had to do with how rounds in the chambers of weapons taken to the porta-john could lead to suicide, something the Corps wanted to nip in the attempt. I'd gone Condition One because the FOB might not be secure anymore. I wasn't taking any chances and neither was Ulrich.

Slowly, the rest of the squad went Condition One. Then we all geared up in our body armor and helmets. I checked around and found my suspicions of huge gaps in security to be accurate. A farmer was grazing his small herd of sheep in what had been the FOB's parking lot not eight hours before; children ran deftly through the few strands of concertina wire that stood between what was left of the FOB and what was left of Iraq. Only a few Marines manned a single post—a Humvee at the front; the back of the FOB was completely unsecure. Meanwhile, the rest of the MachineGuns squad learned from other follow-on forces that the lion's share of Echo Company was gone. Some Marines said they went to Camp Hob—a dingy camp by a ville just three klicks SW over the Euphrates and maybe forty klicks east on the MSR to Fallujah, then through the city at a diagonal from NE to SW—but others said they'd heard Taq, across the MSR from Hob. Still others thought maybe we'd all end up at Camp Fallujah. The more Marines talked, the more no one knew what was going on.

I grew bored of standing around the gutted FOB and talking about how we'd been left behind and how maybe our extract would be any minute or any day.

Then I remembered Omar and the crowd that had gathered at the FOB's tertiary entrance—the post I'd briefly visited existed so a Marine could sit in the turret behind a machine gun and point it at the group of men, women, and children at the gate, weeping and wailing. As I rushed down the stairs, I thought of how Omar had tried to storm onto the FOB one night while I'd been on Post Two and how one more step was all that had stood between him and oblivion. I'd thought of sending him there regardless, but the FOB's resident spook wouldn't have been happy.

I went to the Humvee and climbed up to sit by the Marine behind the gun. We both laughed at Omar as he cried for us to save him. A man who had dined privately with Echo Company's CO and First Sergeant. A man who had helped America as we'd unleashed hell on Iraq. A man who could be bought. Retribution waited.

"Dead man walking!" We jeered.

He didn't stop crying. He knew his time would come. By then, my heart was so hard I could have stoned him with it. That would have been merciful compared to his rendezvous with death.

FEAR CITY

I'D NEVER EGRESSED FROM A POSITION BEFORE IN my career as a Marine. I couldn't help but feel like I was in retreat. Echo Company being tasked out to a different battlespace didn't have anything to do with insurgents pushing us out of Saqlawiyah. But Saqlawiyah had never really been ours.

The work had just begun. The Corps still needed to cordon off the town and sweep block by block. The cache sweeps had come close to armed confrontation and that was just from sweeping farmers' fields and blowing up their hidden troves of weapons: mortars, shoulder-fired surface-to-air rockets, and cellphone detonators. I couldn't imagine what would happen when Marines went house to house, in search of RPGs and similar, more common weapons of war. But instead of doing this, we left.

The drive through Fallujah seemed to go in slow motion. I stared out of the open-air top of the armored transport, searching the tops of passing buildings for snipers. After about twenty minutes, I couldn't help but gawk at the war-torn buildings pockmarked with bullet holes. Where the fighting had been fierce, buildings bore scars left by tank rounds; entire sections of wall blasted away so that the third story of an apartment complex gaped open, debris spilling out as from a wound. No matter how many times I traversed the city streets and kill zones of Fallujah, the awe never went away, like I'd happened upon the battlegrounds of giants.

When America first rolled into Fallujah, the city had been declared a free-fire zone—a dubious thing under international law. Tanks had fired point blank into the doorways of houses or turned their cannons onto machine gun nests wherever they'd been entrenched. Small arms fire had left its staccato braille everywhere; haggard fortifications had been built and rebuilt, blasted and re-blasted, all along the major corridors of traffic; chipped and marred concrete littered the city, marking an environment too hostile for stone. After U.S. forces pulled out, birth defects added to the pestilence left behind. The armor piercing rounds the tanks fired were made of depleted uranium and the radiation poisoned mothers' wombs.

The Euphrates River glided by undisturbed, as old as the earth, by a city whose origins began before history. Its waters fed the fields of alfalfa and palm groves in the surrounding desert, so that Iraq's Al Anbar province were reminiscent of bedtime stories about sultans and fierce battles in the dunes. Babylonian, Assyrian, and other empires had risen and fallen, wars had been won and lost, while lovers were met and forgotten. Our Bible did not overlook the mighty Euphrates in its texts. Even our annals spoke of its rich history—which most

Marines had forgotten long before they first set their eyes on Fallujah. By then it was too late. Whatever had been was gone, destroyed, and replaced with something beyond horror—desecration.

We descended the only on-ramp left unsealed by coalition forces that connected to the MSR just north of the city and ran all the way east to Baghdad. My vision filled with coils of razor wire stacked on top of fences. The desert wind blew trash up into the thorns. The gutters were filled with garbage, always. Empty boxes, broken pallets, shredded tires, bicycles, and burned-out cars added grisly variance to the filth that coated the streets like a film. Every so often, a rotting animal carcass festered in the heat. But rot in the desert wasn't the same as rot back in the Midwest. Back home, maggots formed writhing pools in animals' stomachs; in the desert and its cities, bodies tended to look more like dehumidified meat as if a twisted taxidermist had mummified the corpses.

The convoy reached the bottom of the on-ramp and I was street-level with Fallujah. I stood up from the bench, cranking my head around to see the opposing on-ramp being used for civilian traffic to and from the MSR. It was gridlock, dotted with Iraqi Police—heat radiating off car hoods in waves as exhaust permeated the air. I dropped back onto the bench as the truck lurched forward, engine whining. The city engulfed our convoy as it plunged into one of the most dangerous places on the planet. Fallujah's horizon was peppered with minarets, to give the people there a visual focal point for prayer. The round, sometimes ornate towers seemed much taller in the city than out in the country. The bigger towers often had clusters of loudspeakers projecting the call to prayer across a torn landscape, chanting words I couldn't begin to understand.

Squinting against the sun, I surveyed the surrounding area. Oily smoke belched into the sky from a fire hidden by buildings. In the distance, I heard the popping sound of Iraqi Police directing traffic with their rifles; they didn't hesitate to shoot a round into the pavement in front of a car if its driver didn't do the right thing. Pedestrians on the sidewalk traveled in pairs with only the occasional lone traveler, usually a businessman or woman, carrying a briefcase or portfolio. A child, walking hand in hand with his father, looked up at me and smiled, his lips moving along with the chant from the minarets. Just before I lost view of them, the little one threw his head back and laughed, joined by his father.

I stared at the rusted floor of the armored carrier for a while to give my eyes rest from the sun, knocked some of the mud off my boots on the steel wall in front of me, lit a cigarette. I fidgeted with my rifle, deftly pulling back the charging handle of my M-16 to see if there was a round in the chamber, before letting the bolt drop back home and closing the ejection port cover.

As I listened to the Iraqis worship, everything seemed biblical. The destruction that surrounded me was what happened when an unstoppable force meets an immovable object. The war's ichor wasn't just gore, but everything that made the landscape hellish, from the garbage to the shelled-out husks of buildings, all of it. Even the few murals I saw as the convoy rumbled past were part of the entropy, looking like sad attempts to keep a last finger's grip on humanity.

The convoy stopped at what had been my favorite piece of art—on one of the sections of gray cement walls topped with razor wire which lined most of the roads segregated for the military. An artist had taken great care in spray-painting scenes of the skyline at night with lights winking out of windows, a palm tree filled oasis, and the bridge over the Euphrates at the south side of town. I thought back to a few months prior, near the start of the tour, when I'd volunteered to go on a convoy with Mortars, from Saqlawiyah through Fallujah to Hob and back. On the return trip through Fallujah, explosions rocked the city blocks ahead of us as suicide bombers walked up to a few Iraqi Police at a checkpoint and detonated.

We had arrived just after errant shrapnel finished raining from the sky and the first responders showed up. Kistler shook me awake in the backseat, the flashing blue and red lights of Iraqi Army trucks filling the Humvee. I looked for bodies but hadn't been sure what I'd seen. Coalition forces were picking up the pieces in a much more literal sense than I had been previously exposed to; their operation hadn't fallen apart, it'd been blown up. The scene flashed through my head, filling my vision for a few seconds, then just as quickly was gone, replaced by the hustle and bustle of the city where the mural once had been.

I never found out if the mural's colors had been splattered with blood, if debris turned shrapnel had marred the wall, or if the mural had simply been destroyed in the explosions. The mural had been something beautiful and precious at a heavily fortified checkpoint. I had naively thought it would be there for the long haul, excluded from the carnage like a totem.

"Goddamn it," I muttered to myself, wringing my hands in my lap. "Goddamn it, goddamn it, goddamn it ..." I whispered that a few more times before I realized I was doing it and stopped. I grasped the foregrip and stock of my rifle, flipping the safety off and then back on like a nervous tic.

When I'd first seen the mural, it had made me smile, given me hope that the people here were more resilient than could be imagined, that they would be willing to work with us to achieve a mutual goal of democracy. It had made me believe in the war, but the war had swept it away. And now, seeing the empty space it left behind and how the city carried on like nothing had ever been lost, I felt despair. If all of this was for nothing, if all our striving and sacrifice was in vain, what were we really doing here? I tried to remember the mural, but already it was fading from my mind.

The armored truck swayed back and forth as its wheels dropped into potholes and bumped over broken pavement. A sharp jolt slammed my back against the backrest as the truck popped a curb, then slammed my head forward against the armor plate in front of me when it came off the curb just as suddenly. My ears rang as I adjusted my helmet, glad for the umpteenth time that I'd had it on while being tossed around inside a vehicle.

"Christ on a crutch," Larkin said beside me. "I was asleep until my head slammed against the truck."

Several other Marines in the truck were cursing and rubbing their heads.

"Did you like that, Larkin?" Rose jeered from near the truck's cab. He was on the other side of the divide which split the truck's bed and served as the backrest for the two benches in the center, facing away from us so that his voice seemed like it came from a distance. "Were you dreaming of that hot little mom of yours?"

"Will you shut the fuck up about my mom already?" Larkin said. "Fucking seriously, it was funny the first month of deployment, *maybe*. Now, it's just fucking stupid ..."

Their voices faded out, replaced by a ringing in my ears. I looked over at Larkin and saw his lips moving. For a few seconds, there was nothing but a high-pitched whine and then slowly voices became more audible, like I was breaking the surface of a lake. But the increase in clarity stopped short, leaving the voices of my squad mates muffled, as if I still had water in my ears. This had been happening with greater frequency in recent months. No doubt it had something to do with operating in and around trucks all day long without wearing ear protection. Not to mention we were all Machine Gunners and had sent hundreds of thousands of rounds down range in our careers.

I kept thinking of the HEARING PROTECTION REQUIRED red placards in the vehicles. Sometimes the signs were blue with white lettering, but usually they were fire engine red. A Marine couldn't operate properly without being able to hear commands and other subtler things, like engines ticking or bullets snapping by. I couldn't imagine trying to do my job with earplugs.

For a moment, the dull ring of a giant bell sounding right above me filled my ears, then the pitch rose to a distant whine. These episodes of not being able to hear anything because of the ringing were becoming more and more frequent. After the war, the ringing would continue and include occasional deafness. Instead of shifting a military radio from one side of my head to the other and then staring at it in frustration when I couldn't hear anything, it would be my cellphone. Bosses, girlfriends, parents, and friends would all become exasperated with moments when I was hard of hearing.

Even though the ride had been bumpy on the metal benches of the armored transport, it was still more comfortable than the strap turret gunners used as a seat, so I considered myself lucky. I could relax and daydream if I wanted, look at my boots when my eyes strained and needed rest. A turret gunner had to be hypervigilant all the time, trying to take in every skyline in search of sniper silhouettes while also inspecting every piece of garbage and carcass by the road which may or may not be an IED. I rolled through Fallujah in the turret many times, staring out over my .50-cal, pounding the energy drinks the Corps provided to its troops in theater. Marines didn't get Red Bull or Monsters—instead we got Rip Its in half cans. They tasted like pixie sticks and sometimes they would make me grind my teeth, sweat profusely, put a tremor in my hands, and make my eyeballs throb. But it was worth it, because they made me feel like I could see everywhere at once, that if I took sniper fire I might be able to return fire before I was taken down.

As I watched Fallujah's street urchins mill about the cracked pavement, I wondered if we were throwing Saqlawiyah and its children to the dogs. With the Marines gone, it was only a matter of time before men with guns came. I knew we were giving that town back to the wild, back to Iraq and the forces that controlled it.

FOB Viking, to the west of us three miles, would have its battlespace double along the Euphrates. As I watched the street, a pack of kids—barely old enough to be left alone for five minutes by American standards—jumped away from a dilapidated building as a chunk of concrete exploded, hitting the sidewalk after falling from stories above. One of the children ran away screaming, clutching his hand to his chest.

It was too late for the little ones, I knew that even then. They would never have normal lives; they would be lucky to learn to read or write. The occupation had been long enough that many of them knew nothing but this devastation in the desert. If the teenagers remembered much about life before the war, I never knew. I didn't ever manage to speak with them; the gulf between us was too wide. The younger children would talk with me. I remembered the kids in Azurdiah, the west suburb of Fallujah, drawing in the dirt the Battalion and Regiment designation of the Marines in their city: 1/5. But the teens were too angry and wouldn't come near us without balling their fists. Fallujah didn't have many teenage boys running around its streets as they were all in the fields working or in uniforms dying.

As I pondered this, a truck painted in the colors of the Iraqi Army surged past the convoy on the shoulder of the road, sending the children on the sidewalk darting away. The only teenage boy I had seen so far that day manned the turret of the truck; he looked about fifteen. I locked eyes with him momentarily, then shook my head, slowly, feeling old at twenty-one.

As the convoy pressed past the center of the city, through what can only be described as mass destruction,

I found myself looking through a devastated storefront, into the mangled entrails of an apartment complex behind. A dull gray building had once stood tall and proud at the intersection with an exterior now so badly perforated it looked stucco. It was falling apart, gutted by an application of force so overwhelming it was almost comical, like the amount of force Wile E. Coyote would unleash on the Road Runner, from an impossible gun with a hundred different barrels.

The convoy stayed its course, south through the town until the road turned to our right, swinging the setting sun straight ahead of us. The last real landmarks were two bridges, bursting into existence as the convoy pushed clear of the dense, urban sprawl and started an ascent to the base of the larger bridge which stretched across the Euphrates. The two bridges stood in stark contrast to each other. While the bridge I traveled on seemed pristine as it rose high out of the hellish scene, the other bridge was built for trains to cross with what remained of two tracks running abreast across it. The tracks' tresses and ties were bent and twisted, jutting up like broken teeth. The bridge bristled with them. I never saw a working train during my tour of Iraq. The bridge had become odious when, early in the invasion, the corpses of four Blackwater mercenary contractors were strung up from the skeleton frame's girders.

I thought back to the first time I'd crossed this bridge. It had been months ago when Echo Company had first left the shadow of Al Taqaddum Air Base and trekked through Fallujah to make our way to Saqlawiyah. The fear I'd felt then was now greatly diminished. Then, it had been as sharp as a knife as the news I'd seen when

I was still in high school clicked into place, the television footage of charred corpses hung on a bridge. The desolation of Fallujah laid bare like a mass grave spread out in front of me.

I was glad to be headed back out into the desert for a while. A palm grove to my left butted up against the banks of the river; to my right was an Iraqi Police checkpoint, its guards begging our convoy with waving hands, hoping to get food, water, or ammunition. We rolled by without stopping. I glanced over my shoulder for one last look at the bridge where mercenaries had hung like animal carcasses after slaughter. Their blood had dripped into the Euphrates to join the crimson tinge left by the once proud people of Fallujah. And in the water their blood mingled—the blood of the sacred and the blood of the damned.

SEMPER FI, DO OR DIE

IN THE WEEKS AFTER OUR RELOCATION TO CAMP Habbaniyah from FOB Saqlawiyah, morale went up. Echo Company's enlisted Marines were happy to eat at an actual chow hall, where the dishes got washed every night. They were overjoyed to use the barn-like structure filled with computers, outfitted with painfully slow internet and six phones with lines that had wait times hours long, and relieved to be able to drop their dirty clothes off at a laundromat and pick them up a few hours later, completely cleaned of filth and fecal matter. Echo Company had actual leisure time for the first time in the tour and Hob had places to spend that time. For a few fleeting weeks, our time was our own.

We lounged around the new-to-us barracks. Instead of small rooms crammed with five to eight men, the living conditions were big squad bays filled with bunk beds, two racks high, with air conditioners filling every available window. The squad bay could get hot around noon when the desert sun drove the temperature into the triple digits. At night though, the bay could get a little chilly, so most Marines threw their sleeping bags on their racks. For the first time during the war, we had room to spread our things out around our sleeping areas. None of us had any more belongings than two sea bags worth of gear, our body armor, weapons, and a laptop, but it was kingly to be able to situate underneath a rack or have shelves made of two-by-fours nailed to the walls over the top bunk. But not having a mission didn't seem like a vacation to me, it seemed like being a chambered round.

While a lot of Marines chose to spend their free time with movies in the rack, playing ping-pong, watching television down at the computer center, or pumping iron in the well-outfitted gym, I ran. Reading no longer held my attention like it had when I was in the smaller confines of FOB Riviera. In the sanctuary of time before the posts were set up and the war resumed for us, I couldn't have imagined sticking my nose back in a book. I wanted to move more than anything. Patrolling on foot in Saq had allowed me some freedom, but soldiering is work and most of the time outside of the wire it had felt like I was part of an armed chain gang with the Sergeants wielding the whip. Suddenly in Hob I could really stride out, and not just a few meters before having to turn back in the confines of some gym or around a small track in the dirt between the base's barracks and its walls. For the first time in months, I could work up a lather on a run, drenching myself in sweat that would evaporate off my body almost as quickly as it appeared.

I couldn't stop jogging around the camp, or the half I was allowed on, at least. Camp Habbaniyah was divided in half, the eastern side being the Marine side and the western side being the Iraqi Army's. The north-south divider that split the camp in two was composed of HESCO Barriers stacked two abreast and four high, crowned with triple-stacked razor wire. I liked to jog this spine of the base, back and forth for hours. Being in a constant state of movement was the only way I could put some space between me and the rest of the company. It would take me the better part of an hour to jog from the northernmost part of the base to the camp's gates.

The camp itself had first come into existence back in the fifties when the British Air Force had tried to bring the Al Anbar province to heel with air superiority. Just outside of Hob's gates were the remnants of the old airstrip the British had used to launch and land their planes, years ago. Now, the Corps used it for refueling stations at the end of the strip, so convoys could access it away from gate traffic. A small cluster of bygone British military style architecture connected to the gate by a hundred or so meters of dirt road. These were the most frequented buildings: the "haji shop" or "haj mart" with its black market wares, the computer and phone center, supply, the motor pool, the intelligence shop where spooks kept POWs in their own private jail, the chow hall, a small church with a badly shot-up steeple, a few dried-up wells, and Battalion HQ. In the center of the Marine side of the base, a little way away from the cluster of buildings, was an old theater that had two levels of seating and an outdoor amphitheater. Not too far away from the theater was a derelict abandoned factory and a few buildings once used as schools by Iraqis before the war with the United States.

During the first few weeks back at Hob, I went back to see if things had changed since I first arrived in country. They hadn't. I walked through the abandoned schoolhouses; the books were still scattered over the floor like a film, but now the dust had settled thicker than before and the sand had risen higher in the corners. No one had come to collect the broken Xerox machine or even thought to shut and lock the doors. I searched the dust for footprints, expecting to find others like me who had come to see the state of things, but the fine icing on decay's cake had not been disturbed since the last time I'd run amok through the base with McShane when we'd first arrived. I checked the factory for life and to see if any effort had been made to restore it to some kind of utility, but it was worse. The crust that surrounded the pools of oil on the floor had hardened and the bird shit had thickened on the gangplanks and walkways of the building. I listened for movement from deeper in the building. I heard nothing, nothing but the inky stillness of things, crumbling slowly in on themselves.

I circled the old church and stuck my head in. Finding the preacher absent, I smirked and walked up and down the aisle and between the pews. The ornaments of the "most high God" hung on the walls and adorned the pulpit. I wondered what made God of the white man any higher than God of the brown man, who prayed facing the minarets as my countrymen prayed facing inward. I walked onto the platform in front of the pews where the preacher would have addressed his congregation of warriors and stood behind the pulpit. At first I just stood there, arms hanging at my sides, hands in my pockets. Then I put my hands on the pulpit's edges and tested it with my weight, leaning over the pulpit hawkishly, raking the pews with my eyes, wondering what it would be like to command the spirits of so many with fire in their hearts.

Whack!

A dull sound echoed through the large room with its crumbling stucco walls and dust everywhere. At first I didn't recognize the sound and thought maybe someone was trying to open the large wooden front door. Then I felt the dull ache in my clenched hand, trembling before me on the pulpit's hardwood top. Again and again, I slammed my fist down on its top, my other hand gripping the edge and pulling it toward me as I swung, trying with all my might to break it into a million pieces. Then both of my fists were going, again and again, the dull sounds filling the room with an echo that seemed to loop for eternity.

I couldn't break the pulpit, I finally realized, and if I didn't stop I'd leave blood on the altar.

A dull roar came from outside and dust billowed against the windows, darkening the sky behind pulled curtains. I jumped down from the platform and bounded with a few light strides to see what was moving by, my boots making a faint *clack* against the hard tile floor. I leaned my back against the wall by the window and cautiously pulled the bottom edge of the curtain with my little finger. Outside, on the dirt road that ran the length of the U.S. side of the base, I could see a convoy of up-armored Humvees rolling by, their ballistic windows flashing in the sun. Then, for a moment, the road was still; the dust settled on the sparse grass of the church's lawn and one of the desert's small birds darted from one bush to the other. I heard another dull roar coming to a stop at the gates. This one struck a fear in me I'd never known before and, somehow, I knew they had come.

We had sat in idleness too long and had been found out. Some higher-up had picked up a roster off his desk far away from the front lines, behind watchtowers, swarms of drones, walls and razor wire, HESCO Barriers filled with their cube of earth, the roads blocked with cement Jersey Barriers standing their lonely vigil, and that motherfucker had tapped the paper with a clean-cut fingernail. He hadn't seen men, he'd seen numbers, and his purposes were not in our best interests. He hadn't thought of our weary backs, our creaking knees, hadn't heard us call out in our sleep while nightmares descended into our minds. Or maybe he had and it didn't matter.

I didn't begrudge him this, though; as a weapon, I expected to be drawn.

For a moment the noise stopped and my heart flooded with relief. I wiped the sweat off my palms on the front of my blouse, feeling like the angel of death had passed over. I threw my head back and laughed, a cackle that bounced sharply off the walls and floors with a harshness that did not flatter. I sounded desperate. I'd heard something pull up to the gate—large vehicles in a group make an unmistakable roar. Maybe the new Humvees were for supply or for the motor pool or for the spooks playing mind games with POWs down at the head shed. But I knew that none of this was so. I tried thinking that the strange peace we had found in Hob would last forever, that we would not be called on to leave the wire again.

The sound of diesel engines firing at the gate filled the air with a dull throb. My hopes crashed down like a child's kite on a windy day, snapping through my mind before breaking on reality. The reverberations grew deeper as the convoy left the gate, after signing in with the Corporal of the Guard. Now it thundered down the road, kicking up a rooster tail of dust two stories high—machines of war, but I didn't know what kind yet. The convoy whipped by, many of them MRAPS. They were new, just like the Humvees, and just like the Humvees they were up-armored with huge plates of steel and ballistic glass. These new MRAPs had something on them I'd seen some units in Fallujah sport as well, a meter-by-meter square of black boards hung out ten feet in front of the vehicle by metal poles hinged from the hood and supported by cables; I wondered if inside the black square boxes were Rhinos with heated coils—the kind that would detonate both IEDs rigged to blow on motion and IEDs rigged to blow from a heat signature. They looked state of the art, sheets of thick steel riveted in place all around the turret to shield the gunner from the concussive force of blasts and the whine of shrapnel, turrets that looked like the tops of towers, large machine guns jutting out of their mouths like lolling tongues, ready to spit smoke and fire.

My mind spun like I'd drunk too much. But it wasn't booze; it was possibilities. I'd just seen thunder rolling by me in the direction of my barracks. How many near-indestructible vehicles had I seen? Enough to be used to take down parts of a much larger city than the one the camp had appropriated its name from. Marines in Fallujah didn't need our help. Even after suicide bombings had cleaved some of their leadership, those men had held firm at their posts; the only thing that would remove their presence in that city would be the indigenous militias wiping them out and I'd never heard of any organization among the people that could challenge the Corps' reign of terror in either of the larger cities in our AO by the Euphrates, Fallujah or Ramadi.

But for me, the map ended at the eastern border of Fallujah. I knew little of the deserts and happenings past the smoking skyline, I realized as I sat in a pew for a moment, lit a cigarette, and searched my mind for answers. I knew they would be waiting for me when I returned to the barracks, answers in the form of trucks ready to make war sitting in our parking lot with their engines still hot. The company would be headed east to Baghdad. I didn't know why, though.

Before I left the church, I looked around the holy room, pews covered with a thin film of dust, the pulpit erect, and cursed myself for not having spent more time around the intelligence shops with my ears open. I'd always distanced myself from spooks, disliking the litany of questions they brought into every conversation and their frowns when the wrong thing was said. Like most enlisted, I secretly regarded anyone that didn't bear the burden of actually carrying out violence with contempt, disdaining their notions of what the Marines Corps was really like. They were rear echelon motherfuckers, always in the rear with the gear. But without them, how would it be possible to hear tidings from abroad? It didn't matter now. All I could do was walk back to the barracks and see what was going on.

The door creaked loudly on its hinges as I left, cringing against the hot desert wind. I pulled my collar up around my neck as I turned to start my trek, through the brownout that had kicked up suddenly as the sun had set. Two figures of Marines stumbled through the dust, rifles slung over their backs, cigarettes dangling from their mouths against all regulations. Both looked furtively at my collar to see if I was an NCO, then relaxed when they saw I was a nonrate just like them.

"What are you doing out here?" one of them asked.

"What did you find out from church?" the other asked, before I had a chance to answer the first. "Any good news?"

"The end is nigh," I said. "Or something like that."

Both Marines roared with laughter, then scurried off down the road towards what I guessed were the barracks past my own, sometimes inhabited by transient units. I shook my head as their bent forms disappeared, silhouetted by halos of sand illuminated by streetlights. When I ran into Marines who had grown strong bonds between them, it was as if they could either read each other's thoughts or finish each other's sentences or both. The pair I'd just run into were the kind who came off comical and strange.

In the parking lot, I could barely make out shapes that looked like big rectangular blocks on wheels. The vehicles were there, the MRAPs with the thin black boxes on metal poles jutting up into the haze—when they were at rest the black boxes were raised upright like a flag. A lone figure was moving from vehicle to vehicle.

"Gunny," I said, announcing my presence as I stalked through the thickening brownout.

"Big Head," Gunny Vance said without looking up from his clipboard.

I slowed my walk as I got within arm's distance but didn't stop until I was a few feet past and then turned back, trying to put some distance between myself and the clipboard so Gunny didn't think I was checking up on him. Such details might seem trivial to a civilian, but in the military, where decorum is often held in high esteem, such details were everything.

"What can I help you with?" Gunny asked, not bothering to look my way as he walked to the next vehicle and checked its license against his list.

"Nothing, Gunny, I was just wondering ..." my voice trailed off. Asking the Gunny about future operations, or the possibility of, was a good way to get yelled at.

"Well? I don't have all fucking day," Gunny said, his eyes blood red under a cocked brow, bottom lip bulging with chew.

"What's up with the new vics, Gunny?" I asked.

"Big Head, don't you do too much thinking for your own good?" Gunny said.

"Maybe so," I answered.

Gunny Vance looked back at his clipboard for a second, before lowering it to his side and pivoting his entire body so his head didn't have to twist.

"We're going to do what's meant to be done with them," Gunny said. "And that's God's work."

"Oorah, Gunny," I said, saluting him verbally with the Marine Corps cry of motivation. I didn't want to appear weak, so it was important that I loved the thought of future violence as much as the next hard-charging Devil Dog.

"We'll need you Machine Gunners," Gunny said, turning away from me and walking toward the next vehicle in line. "That much is sure."

I turned to walk toward the barracks and a gust of wind laced with sand hit me hard enough to put me on one knee. My knuckles bit the ground as I got back up. Brown clouds whipped over the street, followed by twisters of sand and smaller dust devils. As some of the abandoned huts and utility sheds were filled by the sandstorm, rats broke from their cover inside cracked walls, only to dart back. I stopped by the shower trailer before heading into the barracks, turning on the water in one of the dozen stalls shared by the company to see if dust had gotten into the trailer's water reserve. The water ran hot from the broken showerhead, even though I'd turned it to cold. At first, there was just a brown tinge to the stream, then the shower sputtered for a second and the water turned from a light hue of dirt road, to coffee with too much creamer, then to the color of mahogany.

The door slapped open behind me and in walked Mundell. The tall Marine had his Corps issue plain brown scarf wrapped tight around his face, so that only his receding, cropped hairline showed above his ballistic glasses, shining like beetle shells.

"Well fucking Christ on a crutch," Mundell said. "I come back from the gym and can't shower because of this fucking bullshit!"

Mundell held his hygiene kit in front of him, a hand on each end, his arms flexing like he was trying to tear it in half.

"Marine," Mundell said, looking up at me. "I am fucking sick of this place already. Let's go back to the Riv."

I could tell from Mundell's voice that he was serious. He was a fellow Machine Gunner, one of those MMA fighter types, and was one of the Marines I antagonized just to play with fire. I respected him, though, because there was very real intelligence behind his hawkish features. The only times I'd ever seen him shaken were after the bad patrol on the canal roads and when his wife had given him a hard time on the phone a few days earlier.

"She's talking like she wants to end it," Mundell had said. He'd stormed around the squad bay, his hands balled up in front of him on coiled arms, muscles bulging like braids of thick rope. "She was saying how she thought she still wanted to party and stay out all night drinking, that maybe she'd gotten engaged too young."

"What did you say?" I asked. After my girlfriend had Dear-Johned me earlier in the deployment, I never gave advice on other people's relationship problems, figuring questions were the only thing I had to offer.

"I told her I'd be calling her tomorrow and if she still felt the same, I'd fix that shit."

"How?" I asked.

"I'll go to talk to First Sergeant and tell him I need a divorce in a hurry," Mundell said. He swung around on me, his arms shaking, rage on his face. His eyes didn't focus on me, instead staring through.

"I'll end that shit right fucking now!" Mundell had said, spittle flying from his lips.

I'd realized I was looking at a reflection of myself as anger consumed him. I changed the subject.

"Have you seen the new vehicles?" I asked.

Mundell pulled his scarf down around his neck and pushed his glasses up on the top of his forehead.

"There are new vehicles parked in our lot and Gunny is checking their plates to a list," I said. "Some of them are outfitted with Rhinos. The turrets have the left and right ballistic glass panels right by the turret mount."

This kind of turret was something we'd only seen being used by units that were "high speed, low drag," the kind that needed the extra peripheral vision from the turret so the gunner could better engage ground forces charging the truck.

"Are they still out there?" he asked.

"Would I lie to you, Mondoe?" I asked, referring to him by his seldom-used call sign.

Mundell stopped me as I walked by.

"Don't forget to shut the water off," he said.

"Oh, yeah," I said, turning around and twisting the shower knob.

Mundell walked by me on the narrow strip of cement that led from the shower trailer back to the steps of the shitter trailer.

"I'm glad you fucking noticed that, man," I said. "That would have been fucked up."

"You think the company might get mad if you ran the water tank dry?" Mundell said.

I let out a short laugh as I lit up a cigarette. We paused at the parking lot. Mundell peered at the double line of trucks.

"You'd better go have a look-see," I said.

"Yu-up," Mundell said, drawing out the word. "I guess."

I understood Mundell's compulsion to look at the vehicles for himself. He knew that he'd find the trucks as I described them; but they had never been our trucks before. As I walked into the barracks I heard a few

Marines talking about the new trucks, referring to them as "ours." I smiled as I made my way to my rack, thinking about how fast scuttlebutt and gouge manifested and spread through the Marine Corps enlisted ranks. Information was its own kind of currency, especially during hard times or when people got rattled.

I got to my rack and sat down, wincing as my back popped when I bent over to unlace my boots. The air buzzed with noise as Marines milled about the squad bay and the steady bump of rap came from someone's speakers.

"Big Head," Riggan said, as he appeared by my rack with a smile on his face.

"What's up?" I said.

"Did you say one of the hajis sold you booze?"

"It wasn't a haji, it was one of the Indian workers down at the comm center," I said. "Wait around until his shift is over at twenty-three hundred and then ask him."

"What is it he sells?" Riggan asked.

"It's called Five Kings and it comes in a can," I said with a chuckle. "I think you could use it to strip paint or run a car, but it gets you drunk."

"Thanks, man," he said, before disappearing out of the squad bay.

I racked out with earplugs in, blanket over my head.

THE DREAM WAS broken and spread thin over an entire night. As it went on, I got a feeling someone was watching me, hairs standing up on the back of my neck.

I was on top of the hill just north of my parents' property aside the Little Raccoon River, which served as a
property line for the farm at the bottom of the valley, on
the outskirts of Des Moines. I was surrounded by a construction project—razed trees and raised silhouettes of
McMansions in all their unimaginative glory. Before I'd
been shipped off to boot camp, the sky above the valley had
been filled with the heavenly lace of aurora borealis. Now,
the sky was helter-skelter with towering thunderheads.

The front edges of the clouds rolled up like a lip, their
tops seeping out ahead. The storm had crossed over
the lake and become charged, lightning rolling about
in the thunderheads, flashing and belching. As the sky
darkened to black and cold wind whipped the plastic covering the skeletons of houses around me, bolts
filled the night with white light. The plain looked like
a kaleidoscope and thunderclaps blended together like
pebbles in a rain stick.

The dream moved through me in waves, troubling
my sleep. In the end, it became washed out and I don't
know what was destroyed and what was spared by the
white light.

❋　❋　❋

WHEN I WOKE, the squad bay was empty and I had no
idea where anyone was; I'd overslept and been left to
fend for myself. Not that being left undisturbed was
necessarily a slight, it just meant that my actions today
were trivial to the group so I could exist as I saw fit and
was trusted that what I would find fit would be so.

I stood up from my rack, my back creaking in protest. Finding the time to be a little past ten hundred hours, I hit the gym, showered, ate noon chow, and headed back to the squad bay without seeing another person from Echo. I took this as a sign that maybe people I shared my life with had figured out a way to spend their time besides being jarheads. I didn't even think of the vehicles in the parking lot as I moved past them, more marching than walking, driving my heels into the deck like I was trying to crack the world. The day glowed a little bit around the edges, even though I was stuck in the middle of a war zone with an uncertain future; it was as if my nightmares had helped cleanse the worry and tension in my mind. If so, they had done me a disservice. The kind of day I was having wasn't afforded to men of war amidst their dark work.

Not until I sat on my rack with nothing to do did I somehow realize that these were the last bits of sanctuary slipping by. That's why the time was especially sweet. I stood up and paced around the squad bay. I heard the jackboots of my platoon, marching through the dirt outside in discord—there were no formations and organized movements anymore, everyone just gravitated together like a pack.

"What's going on?" I asked Mundell as he walked into the squad bay.

"They're going to send us on a goddamn suicide mission," Mundell said.

Over the course of the next hour or so, I gathered what I missed from the platoon. There had been some general announcement made to the company. The looming situation centered around one of Baghdad's boroughs, just north of the Green Zone. The borough was Sadr City, named after Ayatollah Mohammad Mohammad Sadeq al-Sadr, and run by another with the Ayatollah's surname. There had long been violence and tension in Sadr City and recently the insurgents who inhabited the borough were shooting rockets into the Green Zone just to its south. This had severely pissed off the President of Iraq and he had promised the current Sadr that if rockets didn't stop raining from the sky one of the most powerful military forces in the world, the United States Marine Corps, would lay waste to Sadr City as it had laid waste to so much of Iraq already. The rocket attacks were increasing, though, and the situation was coming to a head. And here Echo was, one in the chamber, waiting to be sent against the enemy.

None of us had ever heard of this place before in our lives, not even a hint of it. But a mission was in the works and we were being slated to "punch it up the gut." We wouldn't know more until after Echo's NCOs returned from their meeting, but the little we knew did not bode well for Weapons Platoon. Sadr City was heavily entrenched, not in the ways of wars of attrition in the past, but in the new ways of heavily armored and arsenaled radicalized Muslims. Weapons had been told to stand by to engage sniper and machine gun nests with extreme prejudice. If they were willing to let the Assaultmen open up with their rockets in a densely-populated area, then all bets were off. Sadr City would be declared a free-fire zone. Most likely the citizens of Sadr would be given a certain amount of time to evacuate, broadcast by pamphlet drops, before it was officially designated an area where it was not only all right, but encouraged, to act out my old School of Infantry company's unofficial motto: Kill Absolutely Everything You See. It would be just like the Battle of Fallujah. We would be asked to wipe them out and we would have no choice but to exterminate or die trying.

The squad bay quieted down for a little bit before evening chow kicked off, a time that coincided with the NCO meeting. Small groups of Marines formed at the front of the squad bay, solemn in their pensive moods. I saw Big Smith writing a letter home, then noticed others doing the same. I didn't know how to feel about the news of our impending doom. I thought about pounding the pulpit in the church the day before, how futile it had been.

I started thinking about what would be next. The company wouldn't just have us board new vehicles and punch east to Baghdad. We'd train first, probably for a few weeks, maybe a few months. Intense training which would go on through all hours of the day and night, just like the training that had spun us up to come over. We would lose men to injury and sickness when their bodies broke under the stress. As I thought about the work to come and the grandiose impending battle, I was surprised at how I felt. I wanted to sing. I wanted to pound my fists against my chest and exalt the heavens. What we had all been waiting for might happen, could happen—would happen? I didn't know the future yet, but it seemed so certain and I didn't care that I'd die for the sake of the Iraqi President's politicking. I felt high, like I was on hard drugs; the feeling in my chest was like a teapot as euphoria shot up and through, like steam ringing out of the spout. I could have fought the world, but Sadr City would do.

"Want to go eat?" I asked Schleur, a Corporal who didn't care if the nonrates didn't address him by rank.

"Naw, man," Schleur said. "Kistler is at the NCO meeting and I want to talk to him as soon as he gets back."

"Why didn't you go?" I asked.

"Because it turned into the 'NCOs that run squads and a bunch of jerk-offs' meeting," Schleur said. "And since I don't run a squad and I'm not a fucking jerk-off, I wasn't invited."

"Oh," I said.

Sometimes I forgot that Marines other than grunts existed in Echo, but there were others. Specifically, the higher-ups who were technically in the company but lived down at the Battalion HQ, at the south end of the camp near the gate. They would be at the meeting, standing around looking more terrified than usual of being outside of their offices. Grunts weren't used to people in the upper echelon leadership looking scared; it made us remember the Corps was full of people just like everyone else and the delusion that we were made of the hardest stuff in existence was bullshit.

I stood with Schleur and waited, not talking much. I tried cracking a few jokes and even poked fun at him to get a rise, but he just stood there with his arms folded and called me an ass. Finally, Sergeant Kistler's smaller form and porn mustache appeared through the barrack's door.

"So, what did they say?" Schleur asked.

"We're fucked," Kistler said.

He didn't look at either of us as he walked back to his squad's bay. Schleur moved quick and caught up to him.

"What do you mean?" Schleur said. "What's going on?"

"It's a suicide mission." Kistler said.

I followed in trace as Kistler and Schleur walked back to the NCO part of Mortar's squad bay. They stopped at Kistler's rack, where he dropped a water bottle and notebook.

"We've got new vehicles, though. Better ones," I said. "And I'm sure we'll get new machine gun—"

Kistler's raised voice cut me off. "You'll die behind those guns!"

Schleur looked shocked at his outburst.

"This is a squad conversation," Kistler said. "Your squad leader will brief you personally."

I looked at him in silence for a second and he spoke again.

"Leave my squad bay."

I didn't say anything back; I turned and left. When Kistler got like that, there wasn't any use arguing. I ran into Prockop right as I left Kistler's squad bay.

"What the fuck is going on?" I asked him.

"We're fucked, man," was all he said.

Now it was my turn to play catch up with my squad leader as he stormed back to his rack.

"What do you mean we're fucked?" I asked, and then again. "What do you mean we're fucked?"

MachineGuns' bay was empty. I sat on my rack and watched my Sergeant pace back and forth, picking things up and looking at them as if wondering if they were his, and then putting them back down. After a few minutes of this, he headed to the back of the squad bay, toward the NCO section.

"They're throwing us to the wolves," Prockop said. "We'll be blown up before we even make it there. They've got copper plate IEDs, practically fucking daisy-chained along the road to the fucking place. Right through the gate we'll be taking sniper fire. And there is just way too fucking many of them for a company. They need to send a few battalions."

That was all I could get out of him. On the way to chow we caught up with Kistler and Schleur and I heard Kistler say that he didn't want to talk about it anymore. I kept to myself during the evening meal. There was a kind of hysteria working up between people which I could almost hear above the high-pitched tinnitus buzzing in my ears. Glances as pointed as bayonets lanced across the tablecloths, hushed conversation in hurried whispers sometimes rising to a panicked crescendo.

Of the riflemen, I remember Sergeant Seals being the best of spirit. His slender figure sat like a railroad spike in his chair, glancing among his squad with a smile on his face, talking and laughing. Some of the other riflemen leadership were not so resilient in the face of possible annihilation and spoke poorly of the proposed operation and the odds of our survival. In Weapons Platoon, the leadership's reaction was a strange mix of resignation to our destruction and elation that we would be allowed to carry out our jobs with complete impunity and no repercussions; it would be like the old days and battles gone by when the Marine Corps was death on a pale horse giving no quarter to white flags.

Crawford, the Assault Section leader, smiled sadly. Did he put his men before thoughts of his wife and children, even while having visions of his section's rockets crushing walls and collapsing buildings with overpressure? The Machine Gunners of Echo broke into splintered groups and spread across the chow hall. Although our feelings about the frontal assault varied from man to man, none of us had any delusions. In Sadr City, we'd butcher people in the streets with our machine guns until we went down. Crass jokes, about which of Echo's staff we'd shoot in the back first, cropped up in the smoke pit outside of the chow hall, raising raucous laughter from Marines. I couldn't help but notice how cigarette cherries trembled in the waning light.

On the way back to the barracks, the sun dipped deeply into the horizon behind me; I found myself walking by Riggan and Low.

"What do you guys think?" I asked.

"Sounds like we're gonna get fucking blowed up," Riggan said.

Low sneered and laughed beside him.

"What do you think, Big Head?" Riggan asked.

"I think it'll be fun to shoot things with the .50-cal," I said.

"Well shit," Low said. "I don't know if I want to go to Sadr City for the president of this fucking country. I don't give a fuck about this place."

"I don't know if I'm ready to die," Riggan said.

I looked at him and saw the fear I felt. Suddenly, I didn't know if I was ready either.

"I wonder what people will say about me when I don't come back home this time," Low said. "He died in a war no one cares about, in a battle no one remembers. That's what they'll say."

We laughed at this as we all lit up another smoke in the pit outside our barrack. Our illuminated faces were desperate and bitter, looking through flame to see if others harbored the same shame at faltering. We smoked in silence, listening to the chatter of other Marines walking to the barracks, hearing the fear in their voices. Being a mere cog in the gears that drove the Marine Corps war machine, I could only go where I was told and try my best to bring myself and my friends back alive. But the more I thought about it, the more I thought that if the battle happened it would be something like destiny, and even if I was afraid that didn't make me a coward; I reasoned that surely those that trudge up Everest do so with fear in their hearts, or why else would they begin the ascent at all?

I finished up my smoke and headed into the barracks for radio watch. I'd heard Kistler say something at chow about an intelligence folder being left out in the company Command and Control room, so that fire team leaders could become familiar with some of the finer details of Sadr City. During my hour-long watch over the radio, I perused the folder and realized it was just as hopeless as some of the Marines had made it out to be. Sadr City, according to the Central Intelligence Agency, was broken up into "blocks"—about forty of them. From the maps I looked at, it didn't appear that the blocks were like Americans think of them. Instead, a block was a square section of the city that had its own school, its own wells, its own minarets and mosques. The estimates for how many people lived in each block of the city ranged from one thousand to three thousand five hundred, and the number of enemy combatants for each block were estimated at around one hundred twenty. According to the report, there were multiple sniper nests armed with .50-caliber sniper rifles staring straight down the main avenue of approach from eight hundred meters inside of the city. IEDs, both copper plate and otherwise, speckled roads on the map, especially the road leading up to the main entrance to Sadr City. I imagined Echo Company's three hundred-ish Marines being rocked by IEDs, armor piercing RPGs, and .50-caliber bullets.

"Hey," Ulrich said, as he walked into the small COC. "Are you supposed to be reading that?"

"They left it out," was my reply.

"Oh," Ulrich said. "Is that the intel report?"

"It surely is," I said. "What are you doing here, anyway?"

"I'm here to relieve you," Ulrich said. "Man, that report must be interesting if you didn't realize an hour went by. What's it say, anyway?" He started walking around the desk as I stood.

"Should I leave the report out for you to read?" I asked.

"No," Ulrich said. "I'm going to watch the weird videos on the battalion network I keep hearing about."

"You mean the videos of Iraqis fucking donkeys and an Iraqi kid fucking a dog?" I asked.

"What?" Ulrich said.

"Mostly the videos are of insurgents getting smoked. But there is some softcore porn that is pretty all right."

"How is this on the battalion network?" Ulrich said incredulously as he took my place at the desk, the computer to his left.

"Well, I'd imagine the other battalions before us had access and no one has bothered to wipe it," I said.

Ulrich grabbed the mouse and started clicking around, seemingly at random on the desktop. I turned and left him to explore the network on his own, knowing he'd watch the horrific sexual degradation along with gore and porn, just like every other Marine. I headed to my rack and was out like a light.

* * *

EARLY THE NEXT morning, training started. We went out to Hob's makeshift range to site in our weapons and were greeted by the soon-to-be-infamous Gunner White, who immediately seized control of training and informed everyone that if we didn't un-fuck ourselves, all of us would die. Over the course of the next four weeks, Echo ran every kind of live-fire drill I had ever experienced and a few new ones. Most Marines took the rigorous training in stride, while others, like Big Smith, decided to shoot a few bursts of automatic fire into Gunner White's truck when he parked it on one of the live fire ranges as an out-of-play obstacle.

Gunner White was interesting, if for no other reason than he was the Regimental Gunner, which meant he was God as far as any of us were concerned. He was a barrel-chested, burly man who'd lived his entire life in the Corps and didn't sugarcoat anything.

"Don't stop shooting until you see brains or spinal fluid," he'd said, during one of the many live-fire, house-clearing exercises. When he saw a few Marines run up to downed targets and mime shooting them in the head, he smiled and asked where we'd learned that SOP.

"It's not really an official SOP," Crawford had explained. "When we went through the Israeli Defense

Forces Counter Terrorism School, their instructors drilled it into us to finish off downed opponents with a round to the head. It's not something we really talk about much, but it comes up now and again during training."

Gunner White smiled wider. "Outstanding."

We trained from sunup to sundown and then into the night with our Night Vision Goggles. We played war games with each other, staging lines of resistance around the abandoned factory and then sending patrols into the lines. Every scenario employed blanks. There were no more Marines pretending to pull the trigger and screaming, "Bang! Bang!" as there had been so many times during stateside training. But as the training went on and intensity increased, casualties occurred. First it was Hawkins with a sprained ankle that had kept him out of training a few days and had the rest of MachineGuns calling him a malingering coward out of spite. Then it was Cheney, becoming deathly ill from fecal matter kicked up with the sand, then drawn into his lungs, making him shit blood. Cheney was rushed to a bird which flew him to a hospital somewhere in Europe to recover.

During the final weeks of training, it became apparent that, from somewhere high above us in the chain of command, the time had come. Although I knew Echo wouldn't be made privy to that decision-making process, I took solace in the idea that our fate was being decided. While Gunner White kept pushing us through drill after drill, range after range, war game after war game, class after class, some of the higher-ups in the Battalion came around. During one exercise, our very own Battalion Commander (BC) appeared, to speak to the enlisted grunts.

"Am I finally going to get to kill someone?" Lowery had asked him. Lowery had been made my team leader for the purpose of training and I stood by him at parade rest, waiting to take part in the rare opportunity we had for a candid chat with leadership while the rest of the company ran through the kill house.

"I hope not," the BC had said. "Jesus, I hope not."

"Uh, excuse me ... sir?" Lowery had replied. "I thought we were going to Sadr City to kill 'em all?"

"Well, that's up in the air right now," the BC had said. "And nothing is certain. It's not up to me, but I wouldn't send you boys into that fire. But if we get the orders, we'll go and it'll be up to you to get this Marine out of there in one piece."

The BC nodded at me as he finished talking.

"Sir," I said. "When will we be able to fire from the defilade?" Defilade was a military term to describe shooting over a piece of terrain at such a trajectory that the bullets fall and strike the enemy, who cannot return fire because of the obstructing terrain.

"Marine," the BC said with a chuckle. "If we go back in time to Iwo Jima, maybe."

The BC shifted his questions and answers to the Marines around us. Lowery and I shot glances back and forth as we walked back to the kill house to run another drill with our fire team.

"What the fuck was that?" Lowery said. "Who the fuck tells a Marine who might go to a free-fire zone that he hopes they don't have to kill anyone?"

"It's kind of like telling a Marine on his way to a whorehouse that he hopes they don't have to fuck anyone," I said.

"Yeah, no shit," Lowery said. "Well, I fucking hope this training ends in the next couple of days, since we really should be practicing how *not* to kill people."

We ran the kill house and, in the last room, when my rifle ran out of ammunition, I threw it to my side so the sling made it wrap around my body and hang behind me, drew my pistol, and put two rounds on a paper target where eyes would have been if it had been a real person. When Gunner White called the kill house cold, or inactive, Lowery walked over to look at my handy work with a grim smile. At no point before this in our training had we been so well honed.

We were ready.

THREE DAYS OF training later, I woke late in the morning and realized I'd been allowed to sleep in. After stumbling around the squad bay while I got dressed, I ran into someone in the lobby of the barracks. Scuttlebutt was that General Petraeus, when presented with a plan outlining Echo's proposed involvement with Sadr City, had rejected it completely. I learned, years later, that the strike force who had been sent instead was composed mostly of armor and that eventually the Iraqi Army moved in and took up positions in the city with some success.

Cheney came back shortly after the training stand down, bringing with him stories of drinking in Sweden and actual American cigarettes. The smokes tasted like honey and it felt good to laugh at his stories. At first, he was wary we'd hate him for missing the hardships, but we were all so physically and emotionally exhausted from the Sadr City scare that no one cared.

"Someone might as well have had a good time," Lowery said, slapping Cheney on the back.

The next day, word came down that the rifle platoons were moving up to Lake Tharthar, far to the north, to do boat operations and vehicle patrols around the lake. Weapons was slated to stay back and become permanent residents of the base, replacing the current Quick Reaction Force (QRF), because MachineGuns knew the heavy and medium machine guns inside and out, whereas the riflemen were still learning. Weapons was ecstatic to be left far behind the company, all to ourselves in a camp with a gym, communications center, chow hall, laundromat, and room to run. Just us, the trucks, the guns, and a decent mission of responding to any emergencies in our AO between Ramadi and Fallujah. Or so we thought. We would find there were things left to fear, in Hob and ourselves.

A BRIDGE TO NOWHERE

IT WAS A FEW WEEKS AFTER GENERAL PETRAEUS canceled Echo Company's suicide mission. I thought about what happened while I sat on post, staring at a dozen decrepit buildings and a parking lot. Echo could have been the main element to roll into Baghdad and punch through the guts of Sadr City. The densely-populated suburb promised small arms fire from thousands of enemy combatants, withering blasts of roadside IEDs, and hidden snipers using .50-caliber rifles. I'd have taken many of them with me in a blaze of glory: .50-cal thumping, eyes wide, screaming like a banshee before I disintegrated into a cloud of blood and pulp. But it didn't happen. Instead, higher had scrapped the doomed mission.

I had half an hour left standing watch outside the small sandbag pillbox. I tried remembering how much time Echo had left in country. The desert was so hot I couldn't remember what month it was, much less the day of the week. The thermometer on post read 120 degrees and rumor had it close to 140 degrees around noon. As the temperature soared, time blurred.

I kept thinking about how I might go home without killing anyone, how I might not be a *real* Marine unless I took a life. I obsessed over it in the free time that being Battalion QRF allowed me when I wasn't stuck on post. All QRF did was sit around and wait to get called out, to either rescue a downed vehicle (this happened often) or roll up to someplace where Iraqis were doing something they shouldn't with the willingness to kill everything we saw (this happened a few times). I thought about it while I walked to the chow hall. I thought about it while I jogged around the dusty base of Habbaniyah. I thought about it while I showered, while I jerked off, while I called home, while I wrote letters. I felt like a fraud when, one by one, I would slide the rounds out of my magazines and then pull the plates off the bottoms, letting the springs relax so they would function properly when I needed to kill someone.

I guessed maybe "need" was a stretch of the imagination, but it was quite possible to take a life within the bounds of the Rules of Engagement. As QRF, we utilized roadblocks, where the main purpose was a show of our presence to the population. Roadblocks interrupted traffic and this confusion increased as Marines tried to keep Escalation of Force protocol straight in their heads—one hundred meters out utilize the Dazzler, a laser, to signal to the cars to halt, at fifty meters fire a warning shot into the deck, after that the vehicle was pretty much fair game, depending on its speed and if warning shots walked up the front to the windshield and then onto the driver's head—all while trying to direct cars off the road to pull fingerprints or check IDs. Some Iraqis got more confused than the Marines and others were too fed up with a scorching commute to comply quickly. Killing someone might not be a need, but depending on the day it could easily be done.

I threw rocks at a camel spider skittering across the road in front of my post as I ruminated, managing to break one of its gangly legs before it disappeared under a vehicle. Unofficial doctrine of the moment was to shy away from engaging vehicles because things weren't hot, and not temperature-wise. Things weren't hot as in there wasn't enemy activity that involved Marines taking small arms fire on a regular basis. Somehow, hot didn't take into account the numerous raids on smaller bases like FOB Viking a few miles to the north or things exploding in Fallujah. If there weren't rounds pinging off walls around you or shrapnel screaming into your Humvee's ballistic glass, you didn't really have much to worry about, or so we thought. I figured it was the complacency of indifference.

Finally, the internal debate had worked itself out enough that I brought it up to my team leader, Rose. He was beside me, flicking water from his Camelbak's hose onto a nearby Humvee, watching the dark spots of water turn lighter and then disappear as they evaporated in seconds. Duties on post included making sure the vehicles weren't broken into and stopping anyone who looked suspicious from coming through the parking lot to our barracks or the neighboring unit's barracks. Our barracks were two buildings, acquired when U.S. forces seized control of the base. We shared Habbaniyah with the Iraqi Army. They had a habit of letting themselves into our trucks and borrowing our gear without return-ing it, so we watched the vehicles. The sun had finished blazing for the day and was now on the steady descent down the western sky. In a few hours, the stars would spell out strange constellations.

"So, I've been thinking, in a few months we will probably go home," I said, then took a long drag of my cigarette. "You know, barring us getting blown up or something."

"Let me have a smoke," Rose said. His arms moved deftly in his body armor as he caught the pack of Miamis—generic Iraqi cigarettes. They cost about a quarter a pack or five bucks for a carton. Even then we paid double the normal price, but the tax didn't bother me. I made more in a month than most Iraqis could dream of.

Rose didn't normally smoke, but whenever a Marine started off a conversation on post with, "So, I've been thinking ..." it signaled a time when having a cigarette to hide behind might be a good idea.

"I signed up to go to war and kill someone, among other things. I think we all did," I said. I kicked rocks idly as I spoke, the tip of my boot barely touching the ground as I leaned way back, in one of the few unbroken chairs dragged out from the post.

"Yeah, I think most of us expected to kill somebody. You don't exactly join because of how great it sounded to sweat in the desert or how you watched a movie about war where they wasted their lives doing nothing."

Rose's eyes were hidden behind dark blue Oakley ballistic glasses, helmet in his lap. He looked straight ahead, puffing on his cigarette with all the gusto of a novice smoker. Pausing for an extra beat between puffs, Rose tilted his head at me and said, "Don't go to jail."

That was all he said. If I wanted to kill someone, Rose just wanted me to be sure that it was justifiable, or at least justifiable enough that it wouldn't get me thrown in the brig.

All our careers, we had been told that at some point we would extinguish the lives of young men much like ourselves. Many of us had gone through basic training with DIs who were veterans of the invasion. They hadn't been gentle about the harsh realities of pulling a trigger on someone who was just going about their business, how even children might become targets. Realistic training exercises had taught us there would be times when the safety of the squad dictated someone die who didn't have malicious intentions. The risk of allowing a car near a checkpoint was always real, because any car could be a VBIED housing multiple 155-millimeter artillery rounds which would kill a handful of Marines. Whether or not this would make me a bad person didn't cross my mind. Good and bad, right and wrong, they were just mirages in the desert. Iraq existed away from them; out here, life was too hard and death too sudden for such novelties.

"I'll try not to end up in the brig," I said as we stood to go to the chow hall.

Two Marines came out to relieve us from post. As they trudged nearer their gait seemed to slow as if they were reluctant to accept the fate of having to sit through another few hours of watching their lives slowly tick away. By the time they made it out, Rose and I were smoking new cigarettes and wore sour looks, dripping sweat. The sinking sun was still scorching. Some of the bats in the palm trees stirred the air, but they wouldn't come out to hunt insects, clustered in the glow of street-lights, until the night was well underway.

"Holy shit, take for-fucking-ever. Seriously," I said, flicking what was left of my cigarette at the nearest Marine's face.

"Watch it, motherfucker," Big Smith said as he casually batted the burning butt out of the air. "You put out my eye and they'll send me home, and then you'll really be in some shit!"

Big Smith was a big corn-fed Marine with blue eyes, a prominent jaw line chiseled from granite, and bulging biceps. He stood a little above six feet which put his face quite a few inches above mine. Behind him was Hewlett, wafer-thin compared to Smith's bulk. Hewlett looked like a college kid with dirty blond hair, who had somehow wandered into a recruiting station and ended up in desert with the rest of us.

"Holy shit, it just took you eight minutes to walk less than forty meters." Rose said. His voice took on the wounded pride of a Marine who has been around for a while and knows when some of the junior Marines aren't pulling their weight. "I don't know how in the fuck that's even possible."

"Fuck off, that's how it's possible. It's not like you guys don't make us wait for you to relieve us," Hewlett said as he sparked up his own smoke. Hewlett and Smith were both part of Assault, another squad that made up Weapons Platoon with MachineGuns and Mortars.

"You Assaultmen are always such martyrs. Speaking of," I said with a grin, slowly spreading across my face.

"Hewlett, wouldn't that God of yours want you to get out here extra early so we could have time to really enjoy the chow hall?"

Rose and I walked away from post and down the road to the chow hall. We ate and joked around with other Marines from our Company. The chow hall could accommodate several hundred people. The servers were Indian men and women, hired from a company that sold long-term labor. Much of the personnel on the base had been contracted from elsewhere. The guards at the chow hall and at the internet café were Ugandan Army, many of whom had seen action during some of the brutal conflicts in their own country and bore the scars to prove it. The workers who helped run the internet café were temporary Indian labor, while the sanitary workers on the base were from the United States—all mercenaries, here to get a piece of war's spoils.

The atmosphere of the chow hall always seemed phony. The fobbits—as those who never left the base were referred to—always in clean, crisp uniforms; officers with spotless pistols, hanging from the newest tactical holsters. Other times there were Marines from beyond the vast Al Anbar province and they might not have had a haircut or a shave in days, if not weeks. Their faces were dirty and their uniforms stained. Marines like me had shitty fades for haircuts, swollen muscles from alternating eating chow and pumping iron, and attitudes that swung from dark humor to something much more volatile.

As I walked under the palms on the way back to the barracks, the bats braved the light, darting out and snapping up insects. The sun threw its last rays over the black horizon, making the trees cast long shadows on the rocky sand. A hot, dry breeze was blowing, but not hard enough to kick up dust. Terrible lung infections could take hold from exposure to winds that carried debris; there were health hazards in the sand, fecal matter from animals, and chemicals from the war. A light breeze allowed for breathing from an uncovered mouth without too much risk.

I started planning as I walked back to the parking lot by the barracks. If I was going to smoke someone at a roadblock, I might get a chance tomorrow. We were supposed to set up between Habbaniyah and Ramadi, the next major city to our west. Following the rules of engagement was imperative and that meant adhering to the different tiers of escalating force. I figured it was lucky I was a turret gunner behind a .50-caliber machine gun. It would make the work a lot easier.

I stopped by my vehicle, in the parking lot in front of the barracks. My knees creaked and my back ached as I hauled myself up the side of the MRAP. MRAPs looked like SWAT trucks on steroids. The vehicle weighed around twelve thousand pounds. Its hull came to a V at the bottom of the vehicle, made of heavy reinforced armor, so if we got hit by multiple 155-millimeter rounds buried in the ground it wouldn't tear us apart. But I'd heard stories that it didn't take much more than five to eight thousand pounds of explosives to flip an MRAP and when that happened pretty much everyone died. Personnel would bounce around inside like jellybeans in a can and the sharp edges of gear, guns, and the inside of the hull would split them to pieces. If the bouncing didn't get them, the flipping upside down and burning to death would; there was no way to crawl out from under the gear. I imagined it felt akin to getting into a tumbling dryer after dousing yourself with gasoline and lighting up.

Sweat poured down my face as I pulled myself up on the side panel and then finally to the top of the truck. The little food I'd just eaten in the chow hall threatened to come up, and my back throbbed. The deployment was wearing me down, making me old, but I had to press on. I hopped into the armored turret behind the .50-cal and checked a few things, to make sure it would fire properly tomorrow. Rooting around the inside of the truck turned up a bottle of lube which I used to douse the bolt of the weapon. I inspected the ammo in the box attached to the large gun, making sure there was no rust, and quickly cleaned off the film of dust that had accumulated since I'd checked it last.

Climbing back out of the turret and on top of the truck, I became afraid someone would see and know what I was planning. I thought about it for a second as I checked the barrel of the weapon to make sure it was screwed in properly to the receiver. I checked my weapon often, much more than the average Marine. Even if someone did see me, they wouldn't think it strange. I lit a cigarette. I felt better behind the smoke as I sat crossed-legged, the truck's hot metal surface making my ass feel like it was on fire.

Rose walked by, laughing with a group of Marines staying in barracks close to ours. He glanced at my truck and saw me sitting on top. Rose didn't say anything or call out, he just looked sad. We locked eyes for a moment and even though we were only a few meters away I knew that if I got up at that moment and ran to embrace him

I would never reach him. As close as we'd become from deployment, this came between us, some kind of gulf. It wasn't that Rose found killing distasteful or wrong. As Marines, we'd been taught that blood made the grass grow. But the decision to pull the trigger on an innocent was like jumping off a high point into a body of water. The first few steps off the ledge to start the descent marked the beginning of a fall that was solitary. Rose couldn't join me in the journey. It wasn't that kind of war, not for us anyway. Maybe taking lives didn't come between brothers in arms during the invasion when everyone was slaying bodies. But this wasn't the invasion—this was the occupation.

I crawled off the truck and wandered over to the designated smoking area. The .50-caliber machine gun was ready, but it was a precaution. Because of the requirements of escalating force, I would start the engagement with my M-16. Usually, I had my Beretta 9-millimeter pistol at the ready while I was in a turret; the smaller pistol was easier to maneuver. I needed to transition quickly between the warning shot and engaging the driver's head with my rifle. Going from pistol to rifle would be hard in the turret behind the large .50-caliber. Using the .50 seemed like overkill and the transition from whatever weapon I used for warning shots to the .50 would take time. I'd heard sometimes Marines would use the .50 for warning shots and skip the rounds off the road into the vehicle. The round would skip off the deck and into the cab, bouncing around and causing multiple causalities. I needed the kill to be a careful application of force, not some turret gunner who lost his mind and sawed a vehicle in half with a machine gun.

I lit a third cigarette as I thought, unsure if I was becoming lost or oriented in all the jargon, protocols, and procedures. I would have to hope for a good field of fire when I set up, which would be a lot of luck. Getting a bad driver could be a showstopper. It could fall in my favor that we would be doing a joint operation. The added chaos would bring opportunities. There wasn't much else to do but wait. I didn't know if I was ready, but I felt ready. After my fifth smoke, my lungs felt like they were filling slowly with tar, so I went inside and lay on my rack.

The barracks themselves were buildings used for businesses prewar. There were three big rooms on the first floor and three big rooms on the second floor, along with a few smaller rooms. The bigger rooms were used to house a squad and called squad bays. MachineGuns had around fifteen people in it. We lived on bunk beds that were only a few feet apart and kept all our belongings either underneath them or overhead on storage shelves we'd nailed to the walls. Three window AC units constantly ran. Their low hum gave the illusion of quiet. But if I sat very still, I realized it wasn't quiet, but brooding. My bunk was the lower one, transformed into a cavern by nailing standard issue blankets on all four sides. I drifted off to sleep and woke to the sound of Marines getting ready to head out on our operation.

We didn't do patrol briefs or any kind of briefs anymore. The SOPs were borderline fictitious in how they thought events would unfold in anything but a maelstrom of hate, if a Marine went down. Eighteen-year-old kids in turrets would be expected to watch their friends get shot, listen to them die over the radio, and then remain calm instead of turning powerful weapons on everyone that wasn't a friendly. We all knew what would happen if a sniper popped a turret gunner's head or if an IED made Swiss cheese of a vehicle—an indiscriminate cull would ensue. People would shout into the radios and shoot at everything in sight.

The vehicle and gun checks flew by. "*Gun up! Truck up! Let's roll!*" Before I knew it, we were rolling through the front gate. "*Echo Four you are cleared and good to go.*" It was a scorching day, just like all the days that summer. The sands would burn your eyes if you stared too long. The breeze was hot and coarse, carrying with it dust and sand. I tried to make myself comfortable in the sling the turret had for a seat. We were moving quickly along an MSR, toward wherever the roadblock was to be set up. It turned out to be a bridge in the middle of nowhere.

We set up on one end of the bridge, facing some of our gun trucks across it so they could use the bridge as a fatal funnel. Some trucks faced down the road the other way; the way traffic wouldn't be allowed to pass through at all. Traffic from that direction would just back up for the next few hours. I stood on the sling, pushing my head out above the top of the turret. Lounging back, using my gear as a buffer between myself and the hard edges of the turret's armor which came up about a foot and a half all the way around except where the gun faced outboard.

"Hurry up, Marines, we don't have all day!" Sergeants screamed into the desert with eyes wide, tendrils of spittle quivering between their teeth.

My MRAP was the main truck blocking traffic from advancing across the bridge. Granted, we weren't actually blocking it, but we were parked just to the side of the road facing down the bridge, meaning our .50-caliber was doing the same. This would be enough to stop most traffic from advancing. The Corps had been controlling the Al Anbar province for a while and it was readily understood that noncompliance could get you killed. Twenty or so meters in front of us was a Humvee from the other unit that had tagged along. I didn't know who was in the turret, but he was behind a 240 Bravo medium machine gun. From what I could tell, watching him pick his nose and joke around, he didn't seem like a killer. On the opposite side of the road, right across from the vehicle that belonged to the other company, was another Humvee. This Humvee belonged to Echo and the turret gunner was Larkin, a member of MachineGuns. Larkin was dependable and had been the point man to my second man quite often during the first half of our deployment when we did foot patrols.

Flicking a smoking butt out into the wasteland, I dropped down into the MRAP. I glanced around the inside quickly, then grabbed my rifle. I turned to close the open back door of the truck to see Terrones looking in at me.

"Hey, I think you are supposed to be in the turret," Terrones said.

He looked exhausted, having ridden in a Humvee with no air conditioning. Terrones was Mexican and we were about the same color because I got so bronzed in the sun, but there was enough dirt on his neck to make a dark ring. The breeze carried enough debris to coat a sweaty person in a few seconds; I was thankful to be stuck in a turret.

"I was just grabbing my rifle," I said.

Terrones hustled off to help signal vehicles across the bridge, so that drivers and passengers could be hauled out to have their irises and fingerprints put into a database. I rose back up in the turret, rifle-first. It was a squeeze, until I situated the rifle to the side of the .50-cal. The action was just getting underway with Marines signaling cars forward and pulling them off to the side of the road at gunpoint, then extracting the occupants. After watching for a few minutes, I realized how badly it had been set up and how confusing it was for the Iraqis.

There was nothing on the other side of the bridge to let Iraqi drivers know what was going on. Essentially, they came up on the bridge moving anywhere from fifty to sixty-five miles an hour, saw my truck with the .50 pointed at them, and slammed on their brakes. After stopping, they would either be signaled forward and get their identifiers harvested or they would be waved through the roadblock. There were two vehicles ahead of mine with Marines in turrets that were signaling people forward across the bridge and it confused everyone, and the Iraqi drivers were having a hard time seeing the two Marines to begin with. The haze of dust cut visibility to about thirty meters. I decided the situation was optimal, blowing dust out of the optic on my M-16 which magnified things four times and allowed for easy aiming through the luminescent chevron floating inside.

I waited and chain-smoked. Like all the other mind-numbing times I'd sat in a turret and waited, except this time there was a purpose. The breeze picked up and the haze thickened. Beneath me and off to my right was where Marines took Iraqis to get their fingerprints and iris scans. From what I could hear it was a tedious process. The machine that took pictures of the iris wasn't in a box and didn't have a shroud, meaning that the blazing desert bore down on the person trying to look into the machine. More than once I heard a Marine tell someone to, "Just hold your eye open," and it made me chuckle when the Iraqis protested about the sand in their eyes.

About forty minutes had gone by when a beat-up red car didn't stop at the other side of the bridge. Instead, it kept going, doing about fifty miles an hour. The bridge spanned about sixty meters and a fourth of the way across the driver must have sensed something was wrong, slowing to twenty or so. My body went cold and mechanical as I grabbed my rifle from beside me and steadied it on top of the .50. I tried pressing the butt stock tight into my shoulder but couldn't get it seated comfortably. My body armor kept getting in the way. The stock felt cold against my cheek as I peered down my optic.

The driver was a middle-aged man in a business suit with a lousy haircut and deep wrinkles creasing his face. The desert had left a heavy mark. His eyes were flashing back and forth, from one Humvee to the next, as he slowly approached our side of the bridge. The Humvee in front of me, from the other company, had its turret gunner waving the man back. At least that's what I thought he was trying to tell the driver, by jumping up and down and flailing his arms. Larkin, across the road, was waving in a vain attempt to get the driver to stop moving and focus solely on him.

I centered the glowing chevron on the man's face. His eyes darted wildly. He signaled to the two Marines with his hands. I put my finger on the trigger and moved my thumb downward in a sweeping motion, as I had countless times before, to take the gun off safety and move the fire selector to single shot, but I didn't feel anything. Canting the weapon to the right, I glanced down and saw that at some point I'd switched the rifle to single shot already. Often things like this would happen; my body would go through an involuntary response and I'd operate on autopilot. The fire selector switch looked alien when I glanced at it, as if it had never been there when the rifle was first designed but was slapped on by someone who wanted to neuter the weapon. My brow furrowed for a second as I struggled to remember if I had ever seen it there before that very moment.

When I looked back into the scope, the man was beginning to dart his car to the left, towards the Humvee in front of me. The turret gunner was yelling, "No, no, no, stop!" over and over. Larkin had his rifle out but didn't look like he was going to use it anytime soon, except maybe to neutralize the Marine across the street from him, screaming incoherently. The driver brought the car to a stop for a second, but the kind of stop all three of us could tell was just a stutter. He kept going. He stopped and started again, and I put pressure on the trigger.

The man looked frightened. He couldn't understand what we wanted him to do. I couldn't tell where he worked, but from the way he dressed it wasn't outside or with his hands. He probably had a family somewhere, kids and a wife. I was cleared to kill him though. I could smoke him, as the saying went, and he would have been like smoke, there one second and gone the next. I would explain how he failed to stop, how he continued across the bridge and defied both forward Humvees when they signaled him to halt. For all I knew, the car had 155-millimeter rounds in the back and he was going to ram a Humvee.

I couldn't take the chance. That's what I would say. I'd talk about how I feared for myself and my fellow Marines, how the fog of war set in when the first Humvee's turret gunner had started to act like a child, causing communication to cease between all three of the vehicles blocking the bridge. I had to end the threat the man in the car represented. The shot would ring out, his head would snap back, a fine pink mist would cloud the back seat and his rear windshield would be covered in the black and red gelatin of brain matter. Somewhere, his wife and kids would be completely fucked. We'd have to pull his car off to the side of the road and take care of the body.

I'd like to say something along the lines of "I couldn't do it" or "I didn't have it in me," but that would be a lie. It would have taken just a few more pounds of pressure on the trigger and the world would have one less Arab. I could have done it and I did have it in me. It's not that simple of course; I'd be dealing with the aftermath of it every day and the fact that it wasn't a righteous kill would haunt me. My dreams would be filled with the man and his family. I'd hear his wife weeping, their children sobbing. Maybe I'd run into him again on the other side, if there is anything over there.

Then I realized, *This guy is just trying to go to work.*

When that hit me, the world stopped for a second. Not the way the world stops when your heart skips a beat, but the way it stops when the concussion of a nearby explosion hits you or when the shriek of rockets fills the air;

when everything is done moving, the little snow globe of reality frozen, the suspended snow looking like sand and there is nothing else but stillness. I recoiled back in the turret, the back plate of my body armor softly thudding against the Humvee's metal. It was a completely original idea, new and pure. I had never thought it before about anything or anyone in my entire life. I felt that man's struggle to provide, thought of the commute and how shitty it must have been, knew his frustration in not being able to make ends meet, saw him at the table with his wife and children, talking about how they would have to tighten their belts to make it through the troubled times.

I carefully put the fire selector back on safety, then double-checked that it was on safe as I watched a couple of Marines haul the man out of his car and slam him on the hood. The guy babbled some stuff I didn't understand and an interpreter hustled over. As I watched the scene, I unloaded my rifle, slowly pulling the magazine out, racking the bolt back, and catching the round that popped out in my hand. Pushing the round back into the magazine, I wondered if I should feel sick, wondered if I should feel anything. I checked my rifle over once more, looked at the man getting sternly talked to, and threw it down into the truck.

"It's your lucky day," I muttered as I stared at the Iraqi man being released to continue his commute. I wondered how much longer he would be tied to this world and if he would depart from it at some other checkpoint or roadblock in the future.

I spent the rest of the operation sitting in the turret, smoking. There really wasn't much for me to do if I wasn't going to do my job. Ignoring the Rules of Engagement, in order to avoid engaging civilians, was a weird paradox. I considered that maybe things were just broken over here. Maybe Iraq really was never-never land, as some people joked. What were we supposed to do? The person in the turret behind the gun would most likely be pay grade E-2 or E-3, Private First Class or Lance Corporal, and fall between the ages of eighteen to twenty-one. The worst part was eventually the car would be a VBIED and I'd watch a Marine get blown out of the turret and slide around on the pavement in his own blood as he tried to get back up.

"Not today?" Rose shouted up at me as he walked by to jump in his Humvee, the roadblock readying for departure.

"It was close," was all I said. It was all I needed to say. He gave a single nod before closing the Humvee door. He stared out of the ballistic glass at me for a second, then down at his hands.

The broken telephone poles, sand dunes, palm trees, Iraqis, and time all rhythmically passed us as we headed back to our barracks at Camp Habbaniyah. I felt numb, the kind of numb you feel when one of your appendages finally starts to wake up. I tried to think back to the point when I'd first gone numb. Maybe it was when I had first rationalized pulling the trigger on someone? How long ago had that been? Years. I thought about the Iraqi man who hadn't stopped, who I'd almost murdered. I tried again to envision the family he may or may not have had, how his wife would react to another story of Americans hauling him out of his car, how his kids would deal with the tension.

I imagined my own father driving to his job at Pioneer, getting stopped by the military, almost shot, and then hauled out of his car; or I tried to at least. I couldn't really imagine it, because it was such a foreign idea. The phantoms I conjured up in my imagination were something that would have filled me with anger and hate if they ever manifested in the real world. We created terrorists by the dozen with our pointless little roadblocks, I was sure of that. Years later, I would try to look back and envision myself in the turret, gazing out over the top of a truck, deciding whether or not a commuter was going home that day. I couldn't. It wasn't possible, because things like that were only possible in Iraq or other war zones where the rules of war collided with reality and left a mangled wreck for kids to navigate while keeping as much of themselves intact as possible.

There wasn't really anyone there to talk to about the way I felt. Maybe Rose, but it wasn't that easy. It would have been like one drowning man turning to another and saying, "Would you please pass me a life preserver?" There wasn't anything any of us could do about it but try to get back home in one piece, even though it was going to take more than that. Our survival was linked more to our humanity than our bodies.

When I hit the rack that night, I didn't have any dreams; those would catch up with me years later. For the time being, my mind was burned out from thinking and my eyes hurt from the sun. I would have plenty of time the next day to ponder how "God, Country, Corps," tattooed on my arm, conflicted with what we were doing.

I didn't think about it the next day, though. I just fell back into the routine of preparing for combat and being constantly ready to leave the wire. I didn't want to kill a man anymore. I didn't want to kill anything anymore. That isn't to say that I wouldn't, or wanted to *not* kill a man; I just didn't want to actively seek out the confrontation. I was content with letting violence come to me. It surrounded me. My entire life revolved around it. I knew it would eventually find me. I could only hope that maybe one day some other kid would pass me up in his rifle's scope. I wondered if it had already happened.

The next day, I felt at peace. I felt alone.

TWO SHALLOW GRAVES

I MET A MAN WHO WAS SOON TO DIE. THE MAN HAD been a farmer or herder before the war broke out in Iraq; that's what I assumed, anyway, as professions were extremely limited in the middle of the desert. I couldn't see his hands to tell if heavy callouses and cracked nails marked him as a manual laborer because they were zip-tied behind his back and I couldn't see his feet because he was on his knees. His head bowed low, he trembled as he sobbed, the noises muffled by the sand bag over his head. What set this man apart from all the other people I met in Iraq who died soon after—Iraqi Police at checkpoints who would disappear into the dark hours of night, Marines I met in passing who would barbecue in their Humvees, Iraqis I barely noticed who'd get run over or disintegrate in a hail of gunfire—is that none of them knew. This man did.

Echo Company had driven many, many miles north of Hob—"a shitload of klicks," as a Sergeant had put it during the half-assed company mission briefing.

Enormous swaths of the desert were to be swept for bomb makers and other lower profile insurgents, who would carry out the violence. During the brief, the Captain had instructed Echo Company to keep an eye out for terrain models, copper plates disguised as ashtrays, wires, and chalky substances, while searching people's houses. When the company's convoy finished the long trek out to the middle-of-nowhere, which took from dawn until midday, the gun trucks formed a large circle and faced outward. All of Weapons Platoon stood post in turrets and driver's seats of vehicles for days, while the rest of the platoons went hunting. Finally, Third Platoon brought someone in.

The man was guilty; his crying gave it away. The Iraqis we brought in who cried were guilty. They knew they'd be turned over to the Iraqi Army or the Iraqi Police and from there, as the Marine Corps saying goes, they would be in a world of shit. The IA's brutality to POWs passed from Marine to Marine, an oral history from those who'd walked into IA or IP prisons outfitted with meat hooks hanging from the ceiling, who'd watched the IA attach jumper cables to scrotal flesh; senior Marines passed these stories to those in their charge. The Marine who told me about the jumper cable coercion also remarked on smelling burnt meat and hair, like a farmer recounting a hog being slaughtered, while the Marine who'd seen the meat hooks just sounded sad. Both Marines were my superiors, veterans of the invasion. Crying wouldn't save the bomb maker, it only let us know he was guilty beyond a doubt—the guilty POWs always cried, the innocent never shed a tear. Not that there was much doubt after his house was swept for contraband.

Third Platoon found a terrain model of an Iraqi Police station, built to scale with ambitious sand castles. Third Platoon also found bomb-making materials: wires, explosives, copper plates, cellphones, beepers, and wind-up timers from old washers and dryers. When Third brought the man in they called him a PUC— Person Under Custody. If we called him a POW, Prisoner of War, in any paperwork, the prisoner would have been granted rights under the Geneva Convention. The man on his knees wouldn't have his status change from PUC for about forty-eight hours, when the United States felt it appropriate, then he would become a POW.

"Who put him on his knees?" I asked Ulrich, who'd been pulled off post to watch the PUC.

"Nobody," Ulrich said, walking forward out of a vehicle's shadow. "He wants to pray."

"He's praying, huh?" I said. "I wonder what about."

The night breeze blew between us with a gentle hiss of moving sand. The man's prayers, interspersed with crying, sounded like nothing more than whispered Arabic to me and I doubted they would save him. How his head bowed made sense now. He was trying to prostrate himself before Allah, but the restraints held him upright. I would like to say that I felt for him, but I didn't. I watched his tears plunging down to become black dots on the desert floor. Great forces had moved us into opposition. I stood on the side of might, and therefore right, while he rested on his knees in the sand with a bag on his head, hands bound. It was like watching a man being swept out to sea by a riptide; there was nothing I could do to save him, even if I was as complicit as the moon.

Looking back now, I wonder how it didn't weigh more heavily on my mind, how I remained so aloof. I knew the man's fate as well as he did, knew it to be morally wrong and a mistake by the standards of agreements and policies written long ago. This knowledge obligated me to do something to stop it, but I didn't. It's easy now for me to forget the hunger, the sun pounding down, sleeping in full gear, the night breeze cracking my skin, how I quenched my thirst with water as hot as a locker-room shower, and the intense solitude of fifteen-hour posts behind a turret, staring out into the desert for ten days straight. Right and wrong had boiled down to survival. At this point in the occupation, insurgent tactics revolved around actions by lone wolves. I wasn't worried about FOBs being overrun, as had happened with one of 2/24 Battalion's FOBs during its first time over. Fox, another company in 2/24, had been overrun, but Echo had been spared the baptism by fire. My main concerns were snipers and copper plate IEDs. This put the man across from me directly at odds with my existence.

As far as I knew, this guy had personally made the bombs that killed the guys in Golf earlier in the tour when they ran over an IED and roasted in their vics after being sent out on a fool's errand by their CO. The man fit the profile of a bomb maker who would funnel IEDs and munitions to the heart of the conflict in the Al Anbar Province. Aside from having the setup and paraphernalia, the man lived far away from the cities where he wouldn't have to worry about the Iraqi Police stopping by his house to discover the large terrain model of their station, nor the blasts from the devices he created. The man had nothing to worry about until Echo formed up its hunting party in a circle facing outwards on the desert plain. Now here he was, on his knees, sobbing prayers to a God who had turned his back on the land between the Tigris and Euphrates. Maybe the man thought about it while he was on his knees, how Saddam's audacity led him to write Allah's name on Iraq's flag as if he had the power to command Allah's blessing; then the Westerners had come with their gun trucks and their young men and their thundering aircraft. War had descended on the land, bringing with it destruction, desolation, pestilence, and finally despair as the Marines rooted out the insurgency like pigs in shit.

The bomb maker was a no-joke bad guy. A mujahideen in the language of the Arabs, a freedom fighter in my own. He'd be put to death as certainly as the harsh desert sun would sweep westward over the sky in the morning. The same sun that had watched his forefathers build and prosper would watch as the IPs loaded him into a truck to take him to a bitter end.

Ulrich and I stood together in long silence; at this point in our tour in Iraq, we'd become like an old couple. As with most old couples, the shadow of death never left us. The war was wearing us down in body and mind, backs aching from supporting body armor for ten days straight. Compacted discs groaned and creaked from the stress. Heels rubbed raw from never leaving their boots. Fleeting glimpses of my reflection in trucks' rearview mirrors showed me I looked like a street urchin. Ten days of sleeping on the desert sand or in the bed of a truck without washing my hands had left dirt smeared across my face, hands, and forearms. Splotches of discolored skin peppered my body. Unbeknownst to me then,

I'd picked up a fungus, which liked the damp seams of my uniform and the sweatiest part of my body armor, along the collar. After the war, I'd go to a store every few months in search of foot cream to slather over my neck and chest; the rash never went away though, only retreated into remission. Ulrich's filthiness was only noticeable by how light-colored the desert's fine dust made him.

I'd been excited on the drive north from Camp Habbaniyah, in the back of a Seven-Ton truck, but now my mind strained. No one had told Weapons we'd be standing post on Echo's perimeter for the duration of the operation, so I'd thought my platoon would help hunt the bomb maker—ten days in and I'd already spent over a hundred and fifty hours on post. During the day, the sun and heat jumbled and confused thoughts in my head. I would sit on post and think back to before I joined, what I thought war would be like. I'd envisioned the desert version of Vietnam which, in hindsight, didn't make any sense because the environments stood in near diametric opposition to each other. Vietnam seemed like the Wild West compared to Iraq's Rules of Engagement and Escalation of Force; it was like bureaucrats wrote the rules this time around with future legalities in mind.

When I enlisted at seventeen, I'd felt like I was fighting for a righteous cause, 9/11 still fresh in my memory. I imagined the towers falling again and again, but unlike before I didn't focus on planes gliding into obelisks of steel and concrete. Instead I focused on the aftermath: the great fall of debris and bodies, the tumult of smoke and great cloud of dust that rose when everything crashed to the ground. This war seemed like a perpetuation of the devastating impact, forever, in all directions, until I wondered if that very aftermath didn't lie before me in the desert. The mission in Iraq, when I'd come over with Echo, had been to snuff out the insurgency through what amounted to an occupation turned witch hunt. And here was a bomb maker, hunted down in desert badlands at the ends of the earth.

The man on his knees in front of me was not a civilian to my mind. I could sympathize with his drive to fight for his people's sovereignty, even as his country was on its back in a pool of blood. I'd felt much the same when I'd first left the States and arrived in Iraq—an event that seemed like some kind of creation myth so remote in my memory. This was the end game, taking down the bomb makers with terrain models on their lawns. The resistance to Allied presence in the Al Anbar Province would now be less capable of doing heavy damage to our vehicles. A plan to attack an Iraqi Police station had been thwarted. I continued to toe the party line that had us calling POWs PUCs and handing them over to Iraqi Army nut-zapping butchers. I acquiesced, because it would have been hugely unpopular—some would have called it treason—to protest.

No one in my squad ever regaled the new joins with the story of the man on his knees who cried all night, whose prayers to Allah were filled with snot and salt. After the war, our memories become selective. People at VA hospitals would ask us if we thought we were blocking out parts of the war. Some of us would answer yes, because on dark nights alone with our drink or smoke or whatever poison we chose to numb the sleepless hours and ward off nightmares, in those moments some of what we pushed down deep would come bubbling up out of our unconscious. The crying bomb maker was one of those memories; the trouble was they often slipped away again like the tide. I would try to hold on by writing them down. I had tried before, but the journal I kept in Iraq wrote right around the memories worth keeping. I penned out how awful a given day was, how my eyes strained on patrol, but not until years later would I glance back through it and wonder why I hadn't written down any of the important stuff. Maybe I couldn't.

The man shifted from one knee to the other, trying to ease the pain of kneeling on rocks. The desert plain we stood on had cracked like a dried-up pond in the hot sun. At some point, months prior, puddles had covered much of the plain. I looked from the man to Ulrich and then back to the man.

"Has anyone shown him the graves?" I asked Ulrich.

Ulrich laughed and lit a cigarette.

"I doubt it," Ulrich said. "Third had him blindfolded the whole time."

Two shallow graves lay just beyond to the southeast. They were the only change of landscape for miles in any direction. I'd first seen them by the ruined walls of a brick house when Echo staged its vehicles single file before orchestrating them into a circle. The twin graves were fair warning and as the trucks circled in a defensive posture the imagery wasn't wasted on me which caused me to think of the old Chinese adage: "When embarking on a quest for revenge, dig two graves." Echo's higher-ups hadn't mentioned revenge and probably didn't look at it as any more than another mission in the desert, but we were a part of 2/24 Battalion and Golf, one of our sister companies, had suffered three KIAs (killed in action) from an IED in the northern part of our AO.

"You think he should be shot and thrown in one of those little graves out there?" Ulrich asked, giving his cigarette's butt end a couple of flicks with his thumb. Ulrich wasn't one for mercy, but when he looked up at me like he was going to continue, he didn't. Instead, he just laughed sadly.

"Nothing like that," I said. "I'm just saying it seems like much ado about nothing to keep him like this, on his knees crying, if all that is going to happen tomorrow is us handing him over to the IA."

Ulrich's cigarette cast his face in a red hue when he took a drag.

"I've heard things could get rough for him," Ulrich said. "Intel has been calling in from Battalion, trying to see if they can see him before we turn him over to the IA."

"Funny how they make zombies look like walking corpses in the movies," I said. "This dude's as close to the living dead as we'll come and he isn't green or trying to bite people."

"Do zombies drink water?" Ulrich asked. "I'm pretty sure zombies don't drink water. This guy keeps whining about how the water is hot. Gunny had me rig up some 550 cord to hang a bottle of water in front of the air conditioner in an MRAP. I'm not sure if it cooled it down very much, but that's what I've been giving to him."

"Is that what the hullaballoo was about earlier?" I asked. "When some of the guys from Third were yelling about POWs getting treated better than Marines?"

"PUC," Ulrich said. "He's a PUC."

My eyes narrowed as I took a drag of my cigarette.

"Who gives a fuck?" I asked. "I could boot this dude in the face and no one would touch me for it."

Ulrich laughed grimly.

"Look at you," I said. "Standing guard in the shadows like a salty devil warrior, ready to defend this man's status as a PUC from those who would accidentally give him rights by calling him a POW."

"Semper," Ulrich said. "Semper Fidelis."

Always Faithful—the Marine Corps motto. I continued without missing a beat.

"Oh yeah, look at you, young warrior from the sea. Between these two Humvees with your head down and your dick hard. You steely-eyed killer. You're going to make sure this guy gets enough to drink, so he can keep crying. Devil Dog, you're going to hang water from the ceiling of the MRAP so this motherfucker here can sip on some cool wat—"

"Big Head," the Company Gunny bellowed, walking up behind Ulrich. "What the fuck are you doing talking to this Marine while he stands post?"

"Gunny, Sergeant Prockop sent me to see how Ulrich was doing on post. He wanted to make sure he didn't need any food or water."

He walked out from behind Ulrich to stand facing the man bound on his knees, who was still crying softly and whispering prayers. New black spots appeared on the sand as the old ones faded to the color of the desert.

"How long has he been crying for?"

"As long as I've been here guarding him, Gunny. So about eight hours," Ulrich said.

"Fucking Christ," Gunny said. "Keep an eye on him. Make sure he doesn't shuffle off somewhere."

"Aye aye, Gunny," Ulrich said as Vance turned and walked away.

I made a gesture feigning masturbation at Ulrich while keeping a serious look on my face.

"Stow that shit," the Gunny yelled without turning around. "We don't need another Abu Grave on our hands."

I stood dumbfounded for a few moments; Vance didn't usually have a flair for puns.

"How the fuck can he see me?" I muttered to Ulrich.

"Marine!" he bellowed, turning to face me this time.

"Aye, Gunny," I said.

"I know you Machine Gunners are thick as thieves, but you're interfering with this Marine's ability to stand post. I suggest you go back to yours."

So I did.

BACK IN MY post, behind a machine gun in the turret of a Seven-Ton, I watched the truck's shadow stretch, longer and longer, before me. I counted myself lucky to be facing outward on the eastern part of the three-hundred-sixty-degree perimeter. I didn't envy evening shifts of looking into the sun while it set. My mornings watching the sun rise left my eyes so fatigued the horizon blurred and twisted. But the first few moments of the sun breaking over crags of desert crust in the distance made me feel connected to the rest of the world. I thought about how people back home were watching it rise as well, even though in reality it was nighttime in America.

That night I thought about the man on his knees and his prayers. I recalled one of the times I had been told to get on my knees and pray. I was six and late one night my mother decided it was time for me to accept the good Lord Jesus Christ as my personal savior. I'd asked questions—*Will God say no? What if I don't? What if I don't mean it?*—to which my mother yelled at me, "Shut up and accept the Lord or you'll go to Hell!" I accepted the Lord because my mom was yelling at me about hell, if that can be called acceptance; when I was older, I realized I had to accept that some people with authority would have me say I accepted the Lord.

Did the man on his knees really believe in Allah? Or was this the first time in a long time he had gotten on his knees to pray? It stood to reason that he was devout, because he actively fought against Christian forces that had come to his land. We could probably find common ground in our fighting spirits, talk about how the war hadn't lived up to the promises of our respective prophets. But I would never really be able to feel his loss. And he would never know the numbness I felt as I watched him cry. I wondered if the man's faith would falter and fade like the day's light.

I surveyed my sector of fire with care, squinting to see as far as I could across the flat, cracked desert. As night fell, Marines on perimeter were supposed to transition over to their NVGs as necessary with the changing ambient light. The NVGs were to be mounted and ready to go, but not activated, because their batteries drained quickly.

I didn't bother putting mine on. If anyone crawled up the front of the Seven-Ton to check, I'd have them on long before they got to the top. Even with the sun just below the horizon the desert sky held enough light to allow me to see eight hundred meters, but that gradually decreased down to fifty as night fell.

A few hours into night watch, I noticed a pack of cigarettes on the dash below me. I squatted quietly, lowering my top half into the cab to find Hewlett, the Marine standing post behind the wheel, sound asleep. I thought about waking him but figured if anything happened my shooting would rouse him. I grabbed the smokes and stood back up, chain-smoking until the pack was empty. Forty-five minutes passed on my watch while I smoked fifteen cigarettes. My lungs felt heavy and my head light. I leaned forward in the turret and rested my helmeted head against the .50-cal's handgrips.

THE NIGHT AIR held the chill of a Midwest autumn. The streetlights of a small-town suburb showed broken sidewalks and dark lawns, in a neighborhood that looked like any other in Iowa. The moon hung full in the sky. People were hunting me. I wasn't sure how I knew, but a horrifying certainty filled my mind, pushing everything else out. I looked down to find myself in a T-shirt and cut-off digital camouflage shorts with an M-16 slung to my body. The street stretched before me for a quarter mile before it blurred in the darkness and ran thirty meters behind me before coming to a T intersection. I turned around and started walking for the intersection, then started running. My breath came in short, ragged gasps. I could hear men running through yards, kicking leaves; one of them stumbled and fell. I spun around, quickly squeezing the trigger over and over in a long arc of fire that swept through the lawns on both sides of the street. The muzzle flash left negative imprints of bright blue and green in my vision. Dark shapes of men fell.

One of the featureless silhouettes stepped onto the sidewalk. I trained my weapon on him and pulled the trigger, but nothing happened. The human form, saturated with blackness, sprinted at me as I frantically racked the bolt back and forth while pulling the trigger, trying to find a round that would fire. As the man leaped at me I took a deep breath to scream and he and my rifle suddenly dropped out of existence like they had never been there at all.

I stood stunned, peering around me in the dim light. The leaves in the yards were upturned where they'd been run through. My breathing returned to normal. From one of the houses, light stretched from the front door as it opened, like a pale carpet reaching out. A strange compulsion drove me toward the door and I knew as I walked across the lawn I was dreaming. The door closed behind me as I dug in my pocket for a pack of smokes. The large entryway of the house was empty, except for ascending stairs and a chandelier above me strewn with thousands of crystals. I heard a soft crying coming from upstairs, a crying that reverberated through the chandelier and made the crystals sound like hail on a tin roof. I got the pack of cigarettes out of my pocket. It was covered in bloody fingerprints. My fingers dripped red onto the carpet. I tried lighting a smoke, but the blood made it hard to work the lighter, eventually soaking the cigarette all the way through. The crying turned to a wail, oscillating the crystals into a hailstorm. Then the wail stopped and everything was still.

"Time to face it," I said.

Somehow, I already knew what I would find upstairs, in the sole room on the second floor of the house. My left hand swung free, splattering blood on white carpet; my right hand felt along the side of the stairwell, leaving behind a streak of blood smeared across the wall. The chandelier's crystals reached a frenzy as I stepped from the stairs to the second floor, dropping onto the carpet like pouring rain.

There was a man on his knees in the room, crying and praying in Arabic. I stood in front of him, my hands still dripping. On the walls around me hung pictures of my family. They fell, breaking on the floor. I held my hand in front of my face, fingers slick with blood. The man started pleading for help in English, told me how his family needed him and that he wanted to see them again.

"I can't help you," I said. "This is a nightmare."

※　※　※

I LOOKED UP to see the first rays of the sun cresting the desert horizon. Yawning, I looked down to see Hewlett slumped over the steering wheel, snoring. I gave him a few swift kicks in the head to help him get started.

"What the fuck, Big Head? You can't wake me up like a normal person?"

"Marine," I said, "Sleeping on post is a very serious offense."

"I woke up in the middle of the night to have a smoke. And guess what? You were having some kind of raving nightmare, after smoking all of mine!"

"A pack of smokes is fifty cents in the ville," I said. "I'll pick some up for you next chance I get, you goddamn crybaby."

"When is the next time we'll be back in a town? Fucking days? Weeks? We've been sitting in this circle for ten days now!"

Hewlett started to say something else, but then his voice trailed off for a moment.

"The Iraqi Army is here to pick up the PUC," he said at last.

I twisted my head to the right to see a dozen Iraqi Army vehicles headed in our direction. About the time they pulled into Echo's circle of vehicles, relief arrived for Hewlett and me. My back creaked as I crawled down from the turret; my joints were aching in a way I'd never felt before. Now I was free to sleep on the sand, try to find an open spot in one of the trucks, eat an MRE, drink hot water, smoke, or relieve my bowels in one of the shitters—two bags filled with a sanitizing chemical. But there was one other thing I could do and it was the most interesting thing to be done. I could watch the bomb maker be handed over to the Iraqi Army as a culmination of the hunt. I started walking towards the center of the circle.

"Sergeant Prockop, I'm going to check on Ulrich," I yelled over my shoulder without bothering to stop and listen for a response.

Halfway to the small group of trucks that made up the COC, I realized my slow trudge was more of a stumble. Fragments of the nightmare I had already faded to almost nothing. *A street*, I remembered, *a street and lawns. There had been a moon, and a man crying on his knees. Had my family been there, with the sound of rain?*

When I saw the man, still on his knees, it was like remembering a forgotten face.

Ulrich stood close by the bomb maker, looking like hell after not having slept for over thirty hours, by my estimate. He'd wiped the desert's white dust off his face at some point but hadn't bothered to touch his neck. Ulrich looked at me as I approached, his face the mask of a Marine on duty. But when I drew close, he relaxed. He tried smiling at me but couldn't manage.

"Time's about here," he said slowly. His eyes held mine, then looked over at the man.

I lit up a smoke and turned to look at the man. Ulrich walked over and pulled the sandbag off his head.

"He won't need that anymore," Ulrich said.

The man looked around, blinking. In appearance, he was much like any other Iraqi male, so it was hard to place his age. The desert made young men seem to be about in their mid-thirties and old men appear much older. The man remained silent on his knees. When he looked at me, I felt the same way I did when barefoot, shirtless Iraqi children with bloated bellies, playing in lots filled with garbage looked at me, the same way I felt when limbless Iraqis with deep scars webbing their faces would look at me, or when I watched Marines hit Iraqis or kill their animals—a nothingness, like the cracked floor of the desert I stood on. I couldn't return his gaze, but Ulrich stared him down the entire time.

A convoy kicked up a rooster tail of dust in the distance to the south. Marines from Third Platoon showed up, to make sure the PUC became a POW with no problems. After several minutes, the IA convoy pulled alongside Echo's perimeter and sent a single vehicle into the circle. The man stopped crying as the IA truck reached him. His jaw set as Marines loaded him in and his eyes searched the sky after they slammed the door. Maybe he took some solace in knowing he'd done what he felt was right. I wondered if I could say the same, if the desert's people took my life tomorrow. I tried to think back to the start of my time in Iraq, months before. I watched the small Iraqi Army convoy fade into the desert's whitewashed horizon. It was just me and Ulrich standing there again.

"I had a strange dream last night," I said.

"What happened?" Ulrich asked.

"I had blood on my hands and he was there," I said with a nod toward where the convoy had disappeared on the horizon.

Ulrich followed my gaze without answering for a moment. The wind hissed between us.

"Sounds like being awake," Ulrich said.

We turned and started walking back to the part of the perimeter where MachineGuns stood post.

"You know, I'm beginning to worry about that," I said.

"Do you think it has something to do with the stress?" Ulrich asked.

"Maybe," I said. "I think it has to do with a lot of things."

When we neared the truck where Prockop slept, Ulrich broke away from me to find out where his post would be. He obviously needed to get some sleep; his words slurred and his syntax jumbled. Whatever was happening in his head wasn't translating to his mouth right anymore.

"Well good luck getting a post that's far enough away you can sleep," I said. "I'm heading over to the small contingent of IA that came."

"I forgot they were with us," Ulrich said.

Four Iraqi Army trucks had been tasked by the IA to come along on the safari for bomb makers so it could be called a "joint operation." In actuality, the IA slept outside of their trucks on cots they had brought; they slept all night and most of the day. I wanted to get their take on the bomb maker, see what they thought and ask if they knew what would happen to him. The four trucks were parked in a row forty meters outside of Echo's perimeter.

"How are you folks?" I asked.

Eight men lay on cots by their vehicles; they were all middle-aged and overweight with bellies that hung over their belts and bushy mustaches. None of the vehicles had turrets and only one of the vehicles was armored. The other three were pickup trucks painted Iraqi Army colors.

"Mista, water?" one of the men said without bothering to sit up in his bed.

The man had more rank on his shoulders than the other men, who hadn't bothered to wake or move at all.

"You don't have any water?" I said in complete disbelief.

"Mista, water, water please!" the man said again.

Another one of the men woke up and started asking me for food.

"I only have enough for me," I said. "I can't help you."

Now more of the men started begging, some of them getting up to show me their empty water bottles and MREs. My mind was boggled. These men, supposed soldiers, were begging the same way Iraqi children begged for chocolate. After a few more minutes of empty water bottles being waved in my face and MRE trash being thrown at my feet, I turned and walked away.

"Mista, water, please!" over and over as I walked away.

"What the fuck were you talking to those hajis for?" Sergeant Prockop asked me when I got back to the perimeter. Someone on post must have told him I'd walked out of Echo's circle.

"They don't have any water or food," I said.

"What?" Prockop said. "You have got to be kidding me."

"I shit you not," I said.

"Go talk to Company Guns and see what he can work out for them," Prockop said before climbing back into his truck to sleep.

I made my way back to the center of the circle to find Gunny Vance, busy looking at maps and personnel rosters. He informed me that each platoon had given up food and water to the IA who had been sleeping by the circle. Now it was MachineGuns' turn.

"I know it shouldn't be this way," he said. "But this is the way it is."

I nodded in agreement, a grim look on my face.

"Prockop always says it's the nature of the beast," I said.

Gunny Vance spit a long tendril of chew from his mouth to the desert floor.

"That's because Prockop knows not to try and make sense of it," Gunny said. He looked up at me from his map. "That's something you could learn a lesson from."

I didn't say anything in response. Maybe he was right and I needed to stop thinking. I looked at the circle of trucks all around me, then back at the Gunny deep in thought over his map, then at the four IA trucks. My walk was more of a stumble back to my post. I had to stand watch during the day; somehow the posts had been shuffled around and I ended up with extra. I let a Marine know to run some of our food out to the IA, then I crawled up in the turret. I lit up a cigarette and stared into the desert, trying not to think about anything.

I was in a turret overlooking the graves. When Echo had first arrived in the desert plain, I'd thought they could be used for whomever we caught out here. Now I knew better. One grave for the bomb maker and one grave for whatever was left of me at the end of all this.

NIGHT RATS

THE DOLDRUMS OF WAR BEAR DOWN ON A MARINE like the desert sun. Echo Company had returned from our operation north of Hob, but the doldrums followed us. Prockop said, "It's the nature of the beast," but he said that about a lot of things, from girls cheating on their husbands, to Iraqi Police being blown up, to how weird everyone was getting—it was all the nature of the beast. Maybe he was right.

When Echo first got to Habbaniyah, we sat for a few days doing nothing. Firewatch was set up by the brass, useless posts to keep everyone from lounging around all day. Stagnation set in, not from a lack of activity—most Marines put on muscle and stamina from the camp's dungeon of a gym and regular food—but from acting out a daily routine without the drama of leaving the wire. Hob wasn't a bad place to be in comparison to an FOB; it had a chow hall filled with servers from India giving us food while wearing outfits strangely reminiscent of bellhops back home. The chow hall loomed large as a barn at a fairground, complete with air conditioning, large plasma screen TVs, a food selection on tight rotation, and a large smoke pit outside the exits.

Being stationed at Hob meant we wouldn't be wearing shit-stained, sweat-crusted, dirt-soiled cammies anymore. A building near the chow hall, adorned with a large hole from when a mortar had blown out one of the top corners, was our salvation from smelling and looking indigent. Someone thought it funny to make a rocket out of sheet metal, paint it red, stick the rocket in the hole, and then hang a sign from it that read Bombs Away Laundry. It contrasted nicely with the giant bunker facilities surrounding Hob—big hanger-like complexes that looked like fallout shelters, once used by Saddam to store weapons and munitions—which had giant, jagged holes blown through their centers by thirteen-hundred-pound laser-guided bombs early in the war.

The other big amenity, a computer center, was in a big white colonial-style barn which also had a movie viewing room on the far east end of the building—I never saw a single movie being run in the movie center. I asked a Staff Sergeant in Headquarters Company when movies would be played; "This isn't an episode of fucking M*A*S*H," was all the reply he gave. Torn-open couches could be moved around to provide more space for games, but no one played games. A little room housed two barber chairs, sometimes manned by Iraqis who made a mint giving Marines bad fades. At the west end of the building, the computers themselves were housed, about thirty of them. They all ran off the same internet line.

Next to them were six phones in large particleboard cubbies spray-painted black. The cubbies had a chair in them and provided only minimal privacy. When a Marine waited in line two hours to check his email, he often spent the first twenty minutes of his allotted thirty minutes on the computer staring at a loading screen and listening to other Marines cry in the phone cubbies. A lot of Marines broke down in the comm center. The problem with having contact with the outside world was that the outside world wanted to forget about us. Significant others made bad decisions at bar closing time and sent electronic notes careening around the world to tell Marines of their indiscretions. Marines would stagger away from Dear John letters, a blank stare on their faces, looking toward the end of the horizon and deep into themselves.

Camp Hob seemed to have a humor all its own, a sardonic smirk accumulated by every Marine who left their mark. The scrawlings in porta-shitters made me chuckle—*www.captainsmith@bitchass.com, www.ltjohn@ pussy.com, you're not going to make it home, ur girlfriend is cheating on you, all of you rear echelon motherfuckers make me sick, short timer*—especially "short timer." That one always got me. A short timer was someone with little time left in country. I was almost a short timer—almost. I was also a "salty dog," now that I'd spent time in country. I knew what to expect of the Iraqi Police and Iraqi Army, what gear needed to go on the trucks for patrol and what could be left behind, to carry extra NVG batteries on patrols along with food and water, that a nail could be substituted in a pinch for a pintle locking pin to secure the turret gun to the truck, that sewage would stain my boots black and blood would stain my cammies brown, how Iraqis would act when confronted by the barrel of a gun, and the animosity many of them felt toward Marines. I also knew the Iraqis would never give up; the insurgents would never stop fighting us.

Knowing some shit presented its own problems though, mostly questions. Maybe it wasn't so much the questions, because a lot of guys had those; maybe everyone asked questions, except the most salty dogs and the KVN mercenaries (Key Volunteer Network). Fitting in with the group required a surrender of sorts, where the warrior in us gave ground, made some concessions about things. My willingness to give ground proved miniscule—I held the line. I stood in my mind under a scrutiny, which laid my soul bare. The venture didn't happen as a plunge into the self through meditation; instead my thoughts sunk inward as a bucket into a well. The realities of the outside world had become too much. When I'd first come over, giving candy to children with their hands out had been a way for me to feel good about myself, but now it was apparent the children would never be fed, would remain beggars forever.

The first time an Iraqi child had tried to steal gear from a fellow Marine and got punched in the face, I blanched, but now I was numb to the violence. Every shot-to-pieces school I saw with textbooks strewn across its floors, every bombed-out hospital where syringes lay scattered across the front lot, all the Iraqis with missing arms and scarred faces—things I withdrew from. I retreated into myself to find an inquisition. I shuffled through chow lines thinking about the war. I jogged countless miles, lifted thousands of pounds, ran numberless drills, sat through myriad classes, but couldn't answer my questions. Other people had them too and they wouldn't go away. I could see it in their eyes, the same way I could see the thousand-yard stare from twenty meters away. I saw it in the chow hall sometimes.

The chow hall opened at midnight when night rations were served. "Night rats," we called them. Feeding during the desert's twilight hours brought out other night rats. The base was frequented by convoys of all different branches of military and national allegiance due to Hob's close proximity to Al Taqaddum, where the overwhelming might of the U.S. Air Force had the biggest, cushiest, most highly guarded base in the region. Hob paled in comparison. Sure, we had a few things going for us, but the Big T had everything. Taq was a hub of commerce and luxury with its basketball courts, Walmart-esque PX, multiple computer centers, and all the brass who weren't at either Camp Fallujah or in Fallujah itself. Marines predominantly occupied Al Taqaddum, nearly all of them POGs (Person Other than Grunt). Grunts lived at the foothills of Taq, five minutes away via an overpass crossing the MSR that ran in between the two bases. Habbaniyah's vacancy sign never went dim, where Taq brimmed with people who cared a lot about rules, uniform regs, and fades. Taq's security wouldn't be happy if they found a small convoy sleeping in the chow hall parking lot. The base COC kept track of visitors—what units, how many packs, what branches of the military. They'd have an expected time of departure; their time on the base accounted for by an itinerary with more on it than, *We'll leave after morning chow.* Hob was more transient friendly.

Night rats would bring the creatures off convoys on long trips, eyes bloodshot, ragged grown-out hair crusted with dirt, flight suits stained with sweat lines like some kind of odd prison jumpsuit with white circles instead of bars. I'd walk in for night rations and there a rat would be, sitting in a sea of white tablecloth and folding chairs. A leer on his face, he'd sit there and push his food around on his plate like it didn't matter, like he had just spent twelve hours in the heat peering at the road for IEDs or staring blankly out over the desert. A lone Marine, tired, openly hostile to the world, or maybe a small group of two or three. This Marine seemed to manifest hostility that went way beyond hate—made hate seem petty. The bare will to smash everything and everyone in sight was all I could make out behind the strangely distant but wanting stare, as if the Marine had crawled all the way to the chow hall on his hands and knees and, in his exhaustion, saw a whorehouse he wanted to use and then burn to the ground.

For many Marines and soldiers, the chow hall was one of the few watering holes that brought them in contact with people outside of their squad. Most Marines only had to pull eight- to nine-month tours of Iraq, but some of the Army and National Guard soldiers counted out eleven months of combat operations in Iraq. The bond between squad mates became so tight that the "us and them" mentality wouldn't dissipate. The Corps, the Army, and the National Guard all bred their grunts to be tough and it showed when they wore down to nothing but little nubs of themselves, points of resistance so hard they'd have pierced God's skin if he'd reached down to pluck them out of the hellacious desert.

Night rats brought me close to some of the people who'd stretched to their breaking point. I came in, shuffled through the food line, and took a seat. A few tables over sat some red-eyed Devil Dog, hunched over his food like an old man, head tilted with one ear pointed straight up toward the ceiling like the guns had finally deafened him. I looked him over once, wondering how long he'd been in body armor that day to be so worn out, when I noticed his stare, ending right in my center. His eyes were unfocused as if he looked at a wall instead of another Marine. I couldn't make out the color of his eyes, black specks in little red spots, sunk back in his head.

I stared back for a while with my hands relaxed at my sides, food forgotten on my plate. At the age of just twenty-one, peace didn't concern me and harmony with my fellow service members seemed a fairytale. If this guy wanted it, I'd fucking give it to him. We continued to stare, and I lost track of time. Maybe fifteen minutes later, other Marines started walking into the chow hall. I'd come just five minutes after it opened and night rats didn't really get busy until an hour in. Maybe it had been longer than fifteen minutes. I got lost in it, like the eyes of a woman or myriad flashes of lightning across a storm front, a force as strong as it was seductive. But fucking didn't cross our minds; the specifics about what we wanted to do with each other so primal it was written in the stars.

I didn't just want to fight him; I didn't just want to feel his jaw fold under the blows of my knotted fists. I wanted to make war against his whole family, to destroy everything he loved with strokes so deft nothing could stand against them. I wanted to drive his people out before me from their homes and watch them wander aimlessly through a wasteland so desolate that men inspired by God wrote great tomes about it which guided the fate of nations for centuries. I wanted a pestilence so thorough and complete that their young would be afflicted with sickness, their unborn children to emerge deformed from the sciences of war, sickness in their animals and crops. I wanted to go to his hometown and break everything with my bare hands, to smear shit through the halls where his forefathers wrote the law and brought order through time untold. I wanted him to feel all his hopes and dreams drain out of him and dry up in the sand.

I felt acid course through my arteries and veins, feeding something primal, akin to aggression, but changed entirely after being cultivated and molded. I wondered if I could get up and vomit the feeling all over the dead-eyed Marine, rub it in his face and cropped hair. I usually only felt this enormous appetite for destruction when I looked at Iraqis or their homes on fire or shot to pieces. When I'd first arrived, the switch inside me had been hard to flip, but now it was stuck. I'd felt it before, walking around the base, but this time stood out. This time someone gave me the same death glare I'd given others, maybe even unaware I'd been doing it. I realized that and wondered if the Marine sitting in front of me with genocide in his eyes knew. From the looks of him, he'd spent too much time in a turret on a long convoy, staring out into the wastes. Maybe he'd finally seen what he'd been searching for out there, flickering like a mirage in the distance, or maybe it was the mangled corpse of a child by the roadside. Maybe war's sheer enormity swelled up over him and came crashing down, sweeping his mind far away from his body in the chair.

He's still out in the wastes somewhere and I'm there with him, I thought.

The Corps always drilled into us how we were the weapon—not the firearms or the vehicles or the bombs, but us. When the spark of life operating the weapons system goes MIA out in the dunes? The Devil Dog just sat looking at me, clearly on autopilot. Just when Rose walked into the chow hall, the Marine slowly pushed his tray away from him and his chair back, stood up, and walked out. When he turned, his eyes didn't lock on mine like a bully's would, trying to exert his will until the last possible second; instead, they remained unfocused, seething straight ahead. Rose sat down in front of me and I realized I'd had my hand on my pistol the entire time.

"What's up with you?" Rose asked. "You look like you've seen a ghost."

"You know how this place can get at night," I said. "All the freaks come out to eat. Well, one sat at the table two behind you and stared at me like he wanted some, you know?"

"Was he one of those fucking loony toons that stumble off convoys all fucked in the head?" Rose asked.

"Kind of," I said, then fell quiet for a second. "You know when you get really burned out and fucking hate the world?"

Rose laughed, spitting some of his food back onto his plate.

"Fuck yeah," he said. "Every fucking day."

"More than that, though," I said. "You know how some people get when they just want to break everything but get stuck idling in neutral."

Rose shoveled food into his face for a few seconds without talking. Someone behind us, near the food line, turned on the giant plasma screen TVs in the center of the room and the voices of several news people discussing the war blared. Clips of fires in Fallujah played across the screen and a few pictures of dead Marines in their dress blues while they had been alive and smiling, before the news cut to sports and the latest celebrity gossip. The television flipped through some other channels to find nothing but static, before turning off.

Ulrich slid up to the table next to Rose. I glanced up at him, not bothering to say hello because we all lived and worked together; instead, I filled him in about the Marine.

"Do you think it has to do with not sleeping?" Ulrich asked. "Maybe it fucks with your head, staying up for days at a time, especially if you are in a turret with the jammers blasting radio waves into your skull."

Rose laughed.

"Fuck, that's a good point," Rose said. "Who knows what any of that shit does to us? I bet the Corps hasn't done any studies because it doesn't want to know."

"Studies?" I said. "The jammers haven't been around more than two years. How the fuck would they do long-term studies on something that new?"

"When he gets back home, do you think they'll put him through some kind of therapy?" Ulrich asked.

"Ulrich, have you ever, in all your years in the Corps, even heard of someone going to a therapist?" Rose asked.

Ulrich's brow furrowed for a second as he thought. Instead of answering, he just looked at his plate and took a bite of food.

"They can't cure this hate," I said, pointing my index finger at my temple. "We were born with it in our heads."

I didn't know it then, but the veteran suicide rate would boom near the end of the conflict in Iraq. Official estimates put the bare-bones number of veterans offing themselves at nearly one an hour. I couldn't have fathomed then, sitting in the chow hall with the only friends I had in the world, that we would be in the demographic at highest risk for killing ourselves after returning home. For many Marines, the beginning of the end started as soon as the landing gear touched down on American soil.

They'd step off the plane, completely naïve of the danger, never knowing the last time they would leave the wire would be when they left the squad and got in the vehicles of friends and family. Years later, the news would murmur reports of a veteran suicide—depression would be blamed and Post Traumatic Stress Disorder (PTSD). Medicines would be prescribed, veteran suicide hotlines manned, and shrinks would say "Glad to see you again" in a way that made you feel it was something they wished they were saying to someone else. When I'd skim the reports, all I'd think about was that guy in the chow hall.

"After fighting the war for so long, we're just starting to see it in ourselves," I said. "And each other."

Rose stopped chewing to stare at me and think for a moment.

"Maybe you're right," he said. "I mean, it has to leave some kind of mark on you."

"The mark of fucking Cain," I said.

"What's the mark of Cain?" Ulrich asked.

"Don't worry about it, little Chamorro baby," Rose said.

Seeing the war from the outside wasn't something we could do yet. We could try to step back from it but wouldn't understand all the implications until much later. Some Marines had an inkling of horrors to come. Ulrich wasn't the first to think about what the lack of sleep might be doing to the electrical circuits in our brains. Lack of sleep combined with stress, food deprivation, sickness, and sand all came together to bear down on our psyches with an amazing weight. Some sleepwalked, their dreams turned to night terrors, while others grew emotionally detached, acting like zombies or soulless marionettes. *Maybe we're all wooden*, I thought, *controlled by strings that stretch all the way back stateside.*

"Have either of you stopped to think about how funny the name of our company is, in given circumstance?" I asked.

"No," Ulrich said carefully, knowing we'd make a fool of him if he lied. "What's so funny about it?"

"Do you mean, have I stopped to think how fitting it is that our company's name is Echo and we are stationed in a camp first built by the British?" Rose asked.

"Smarter than the average bear, Rose," I said.

"How is that funny?" Ulrich asked.

"Echo," I said. "Soldiers in this place are like echoes through time."

"Except, historically, the British air power was stationed here, on the runways out front," Rose said. "Now ours is across the street at Taq."

"You read up on this place before we came here," I said with a chuckle.

"Well, you did first and went on and on about the Sunnis and Shias and how for one Allah is benevolent and in the other he is a vengeful God of punishment—" Rose started.

"Much like the Christian God," I said. "Full of duality."

"—and I couldn't just let you be Mr. Know-It-All. So that's how it's fitting we're in Echo Company, stationed on a British base that operated in the late fifties."

"This place was their Vietnam, right before our Vietnam," I said.

"Speaking of Vietnam," Rose said and then leaned in toward me across the table. "You'd think you'd hear about more atrocities happening."

His voice a low murmur and eyes flitting about the chow hall, he continued after a pause to allow a few Marines we didn't recognize walk by our table on their way out of the chow hall.

"There have been a couple of times an IED has gone off and Marines killed everyone in the area," Ulrich said. "I can't remember the names of the places, though."

"Maybe it's the nature of the war," I said. "There's no jungle canopy here to keep secrets, only the open desert and the sun shining, exposing everything."

"Did the guys in Vietnam ever have to stand tall before the man for their war crimes?" Rose asked.

"Shit, I don't know," I said. "Which means probably not. I mean, how much is a brown life worth over here?"

"How much is a bullet?" Ulrich asked, brown as mahogany, his ancestry going back to Guam.

I chuckled.

"Fuck, let's get out of here," I said. "We are the last ones and the TVs are being wacky."

Rose and Ulrich glanced around to see the TVs hissing gently with static, some of them blinking on and off with a strange rhythm.

"This place is fucking weird," Ulrich said.

"If the guy who sat across from me earlier is outside waiting to eat our brains like a zombie, I swear to God I'm hopping the fucking fence and going to live with the Iraqis," I said. "Fuck it, I can learn to wipe with my hand and herd goats. I bet goat herding has great health insurance and retirement benefits."

The bats whirred through the palms and out to the glowing streetlights to hunt, but there was no rabid Marine with hollowed-out eyes. Just the night and another watch for Rose and me back at the COC. The early morning watches left us with plenty of time to roam around the base and our heads.

While I sat beside an old green-gear radio monitoring the Battalion frequency, I thought about years before, on the other side of the world, during the SOI. Walking out of a chow hall there I'd seen Betts standing by a table of Marines, talking loudly about how he was going on to LAV (Light Assault Vehicle) school and upon completion would be "tracks." Being part of an LAV crew meant never walking again like the rest of us "sticks" as they called us, or "crunchies" after the sound people on foot made when the LAV ran over them. I'd had a bone to pick with him, something that happened back in boot camp when we'd both been in Platoon 3111, or "thirty-one eleven" as we'd chanted together in marching cadence.

Betts had been booted from the platoon for writing a letter home about how he'd taken another recruit's prescribed Vicodin and he'd become "chink-eyed." Our second hat, or second in command, hadn't approved, being Korean. He might have just let Betts go with a thorough thrashing if racism hadn't been present in Betts beyond just words, the kind that he'd tried to keep out of his mouth, but some of the black Marines could tell. How he never sat by them, touched them, laughed with them, or talked to them. Our second hat sensed it as well and the letter was a confession of not only racism, but illicit drug use by the recruit. Stahl didn't press for a dishonorable discharge for drugs, though; instead, he had Betts dropped back four weeks in training when graduation lingered just three days away.

The radio crackled broken traffic from the fringes of Echo's AO as I remembered how gung-ho I'd been, how much I'd believed in the Corps. I felt Betts had wronged me in a way that transcended time and space. He'd breached his duty to me and the rest of the recruits of thirty-one eleven, let us down, abandoned his brothers. The pride inside me couldn't abide and I stopped to spit fire at him in a way only a Private in the Marine Corps can do, biceps bulging, veins in my head standing out, spittle flickering. I told him how wrong he was, what a fuck up he was, that he could go fuck himself. He stood there and watched me, in the same detached way he'd watched Stahl scream at him a few months before. The Marines around us listened in embarrassed silence, knowing that anyone who stood to intercede with the commotion would fight me and the friends I'd made in the MachineGun section I trained with every day for the last two months. I finished my tirade and looked at him for defiance, a spark that would set me on fire. But there was nothing. I marched out of the chow hall.

I got a call from a friend I'd graduated boot camp with. Betts's LAV had flipped over while he was up in the turret and he'd been thrown into a ravine. A training exercise gone bad—killed instantly. Or maybe Trippy tried to say he hoped he died instantly. The flat voice on the other line had made peace with it, regarding the tragedy as fate; a destiny unavoidable for Betts, or it would have been avoided.

My anger dropped through me, my soul wet tissue tearing. I shifted in my chair, on post in the small dingy COC, as I thought about how Trippy had told me to sit down. I'd been thankful for that. He'd heard me yell at Betts but didn't know how I would react to having that anger fold back in on itself. The feeling of numbness, a realization that I'd been wrong and it wasn't worth it became a part of me I stowed away, a wound that kept weeping.

A voice I recognized from Echo buzzed over the comm. Stalter, from Third Platoon, let base command know that a convoy from Echo was pushing up toward the lake, a hundred and thirty miles to the north. Weapons Platoon had been left at the base to cover as Battalion QRF. We'd help anyone in the AO who called out for assistance, for everything from a flat tire to "troops in contact," the code phrase for the COC to send the QRF guns hot right out of the gate. The greatest fear was enemy coordination. A single attack could take a few lives with a larger IED, but a coordinated attack of a roadside bomb, rockets, and small arms fire could devastate a convoy, which grew smaller by the day as the war wound down. No one called it a war anymore, though; I hadn't thought of it that way in months. The might of the USMC waited patiently at Hob, ready to take flight at Taq across the MSR on a great hill. Robin walked into the radio room with a Bible in hand, serene look of divine peace on his face.

"Robin, it's fucking zero five hundred. Why the fuck do you look so happy?" I asked.

Robin stopped in front of the desk before coming around to take my post.

"I guess I'm just excited to read the word of Jesus Christ," he said.

"Oh really," I said. "Do you ever pray and get Allah on the other line instead?"

"No." Robin shook his head with a sad smile on his face.

"Would you tell me if you did?" I asked.

"Well, of course I'd tell—"

"You're a fucking liar," I said. "But anyway, I'm going for a jog. Have fun listening to static. There are some magazines in the desk."

"But command said we couldn't read nonreligious texts on post anymore," Robin said.

I peered around the room, taking in all the dust, rat turds, spider webs, and a floor peppered with sand.

"Who is going to tell on you?" I asked. "As long as you don't fall asleep, you won't miss any traffic."

"You really think people are sleeping on post?" Robin asked.

"Have you ever been so involved in an issue of *The World of Hip Hop* you couldn't hear the radio?" I asked in return.

Robin didn't respond. I left the radio room, changed into running shorts and a green T-shirt, and grabbed my iPod to go for a jog. Hob had a few long roads running along its spine which was a fifteen-foot high wall made of HESCO Barriers topped with three rolls of razor wire stacked on top of each other. The barriers separated the base in half, dividing the Marines from the Iraqi Army. The two armies didn't mingle at all, the Iraqis being told to keep well away from the Marines, the Marines being regaled with stories of Iraqi Army members being sodomized by their own squad so badly they had to get dozens of stitches. Before the Captain had gone up north to the outpost by Lake Tharthar, he'd asked an Iraqi Army Sergeant about the rumors during one of the rare training exercises that brought Marines in proximity to the IA. He came back from a group of IA shaking his head. "I asked them about the stories and they started laughing and pointed to their squad bitch." None of MachineGuns knew what to make of that, adding it to the litany of events that made us wary of working with the Iraqi Police or the Iraqi Army.

I jogged by the northern entrance to the Iraqi side of the base, casting a glance down the road to see if the small post there was manned. A few IA soldiers moved about the shack, smoking and talking, their weapons leaned against the outside. I quickened my pace as I moved by the gate and headed down the dusty road, the spine of the base to my right. When Echo had first come to Hob, I'd been out for a jog and unknowingly headed into the IA side of the base. A Marine Staff Sergeant had stopped me and said, "You look like you can hold your own, but if you head into that side of the base alone, I guarantee you'll come back without your iPod."

I'd changed my course to the one I now followed, down the spine of the base by the detention facility, a place called the "spook shop" or the "head shed," referring to the intelligence Marines that worked there, playing with minds of the detained. I didn't know what happened in the detention facility exactly, but I'd spent some time lingering around it, catching my breath while on jogs—a small courtyard, surrounded by a high fence topped with the usual triple roll razor wire crown, attached to a squat building with a heavy metal door and a sign reading AUTHORIZED INTELLIGENCE PERSONNEL ONLY in gold lettering on a red background.

Before the detention facility, a road went to the theater, a dilapidated relic left behind from the British occupation complete with two huge film projectors still intact above the balcony, the bottom floor with seats facing a stage wreathed in a torn and tattered silver screen. The walls still held some of the chipped paint of a large mural telling of Gilgamesh, stretching all the way around the theater in a U shape. Next to the theater was an outdoor stage with a white wall behind it for a screen and steps leading down to the smaller stage that made for rough coliseum seating. Often at night, the sweet, pungent odor of marijuana wafted away from the theater, or the sound of slurred shouts and bottles breaking. I stayed away from the theater at night; something about its close proximity to the spine, chow hall, and detention facility made me leery of going anywhere near it when I couldn't see, especially with the smell of pot in the air.

On this morning, the base seemed to stir earlier than usual. Jogging down the dirt road, I took a long look at the theater but didn't see any signs of movement. When I passed it and got to the much smaller detention facility

(DetFac), I took a left and started jogging through the cluster of trailers where the intelligence guys, "spooks," lived in front of the DetFac. I got sick of whatever I was listening to and slowed down to change the song. My iPod screen blanked out then came back, on the fritz from all the times I dropped it. As I fiddled with it, the world had turned sideways; someone had knocked me down from behind.

One of the spooks ran away from me, kicking up dust from his boots as he hustled into a trailer and slammed the door after him. I got up slowly, dusted myself off, and looked around just in time to see another spook sprinting into the DetFac. Intelligence people earned the nickname "spook" by snooping around groups of Marines with questions, fading in and out of training exercises, classes, events, and patrols without any explanation offered. We were instructed to act like everything was normal and not mention the presence of intel's eyes and ears. The rank intel people wore changed depending on the day: sometimes an NCO, sometimes a Staff NCO, and other times an officer. Intel Marines were known to gravitate toward action subtly rather than away quickly. If they ran, something was wrong. Most Marines hate to run in boots if they don't have to and these guys hauled ass inside like their lives depended on it. I pulled the headphones out of my ears and listened. A long, slow wail swept over the base for a few seconds and then faded, like a tornado siren back home. Looking down the road, I saw vehicles driving wildly, wheeling haphazardly into parking spots, going much too fast to be safe. Unless something bad was happening.

"Hey!" I shouted. "Hey! What's going on?"

I sprinted to the DetFac door and yanked as hard as I could, but it didn't budge. I stopped and turned as the wail of the siren filled the world again, Armageddon's song in a base full of dust. The wail passed and just as it lifted I heard a dull crackling in the distance. I opened my mouth, letting my jaw hang, and tilted my head back—I'd learned it was the best way to listen to things you could barely hear, using your skull to gather sound. That's when I heard the dull *crump-crump, crump-crump* of mortars. My blood ran cold, my stomach became lead-filled, and I turned to flee. Sprinting with the same panic that had overtaken the spooks, I made it to the parking lot next to the supply shed by Hob's little computer center before I stopped to breathe.

What do I do? I'm with QRF, we'll probably get sent out if people got hit.

I sucked wind, trying to catch my breath and make sense of what was happening. The siren's wail descended on me again. I figured I could probably go hide in the computer center. Marines would be taking cover there under the flimsy sheet metal roof. The only real safety lay back in the DetFac with its heavy roof of cinder blocks meant to protect the high-profile POWs sometimes shackled there, but the reinforced steel door was locked.

Fuck it, I thought and put my headphones back in my ears before I jogged back to the barracks. When I got there, I found out that Taq was being hit with mortar and rocket fire.

"Fuck, I guess all those watchtowers and drones can't stop steel from raining down," I said to Rose while we sat in our squad bay, cleaning our rifles.

"Yeah, man," Rose said. "Shit sounds serious out there. Word is the haj were trying to hit aircraft as they took off from the airfield."

"Did anyone get smoked?" I asked.

"No idea," he said. "But you heard the explosions."

He leaned in closer.

"That's a lot of munitions to pour on that base. With the basketball courts, computer centers, and shopping centers, you'd think somebody would at least lose a leg or some shit. You know what I'm saying?" Rose finished with a long, loud laugh at the end, sad look on his face that slowly faded to nothing.

"No shit," I said. "I guess we'll see."

The next day the computer (comp) center was open; I had walked down just to see if the RIVER CITY sign stood blocking the entrance to the phones. The sign became a kind of penance to us, a totem that higher put out to mourn the dead. No Marine would be allowed to spoil it by online communications; the fine for trying was years of your life in the brig and demotion. I thought back to when Blaker stood outside the comp center at FOB Riviera, telling everyone how the guys from Golf had gotten hit. The distance from the Riv to Hob was only six or so klicks on the other side of the Euphrates, the days there still fresh in my memory.

At the start of the tour, there had seemed to be some purpose; now I'd lost my surety. The learning curve in the Marine Corps peaked during combat operations and reaching the top of the bell curve, allowing me to see over and realize there was nothing else—Echo could have stayed indefinitely, because we'd reached a stalemate in the war. Just like our troops in Vietnam had met resistance that was unbreakable from the indigenous people, we had met the same resistance. The British and the Soviets had learned before us that the desert wasn't a place easily tamed. Iraq was on its second go-round with outside occupation—echoes, just like my own footprints in the rolling dunes.

Whenever higher put the totem up, I would stand in front of it and stare for a few minutes, casting glances at whatever dingy comp center I was at, in whatever outpost our patrols and quick responses brought us to. Marines would say, "It's not going anywhere," but that's not why I stood there. I wasn't impatiently waiting for a sign to disappear so I could get into the computer lab like some people did, so homesick they would wait for hours because eventually the families would know and the sign would be removed so they could shuffle their tired bodies to sit in stiff plastic chairs and check their emails. Some of the Fobbits had the time and would play cards at tables across from the sign. But there was no River City this time. The comp center bustled with bodies—death had passed us over.

I showed up late for chow, just in time to get in line with the Mortarmen's NCOs. Kistler ran the squad, being the only Sergeant. Schleur stood behind him, a Corporal. When I'd first joined the unit, I'd never have been included in the NCO conversations, something else that had changed. Kistler and Schleur were both salty veterans, having done a tour of Iraq together before this one.

"Oh shit, here's Big Head," Schleur said, using my call sign. "He's going to lose his fucking mind when he hears this."

"We can't go telling everyone," Kistler said. "I don't want it to seem like we're spreading scuttlebutt around the base. That's a bad reputation to get."

"You guys already have that reputation," I said.

"Well, that's why we don't want to make it any worse," Kistler said. "Do you understand?"

"Is someone going to tell me what's going on or what?" I asked.

"All right, all right," Schleur said, rasping out a dry reed chuckle. "So, Big Head, check this out. Fucking yesterday, right? So, the POGs that pull perimeter watch on this shithole walk the wire and there's this fucking bomb in the middle of the road."

"Are you shitting me right now?" I said. "There was a fucking bomb on the base?"

"Not just a bomb," Kistler said. "It was an IED in the road. Dug to hit the perimeter patrol."

"Well, yeah," Schleur said. "But it's still a bomb."

"It's not just a fucking bomb. You make it sound like someone threw a fucking firecracker over the wire," Kistler said.

"Anyway," Schleur said. "EOD gets called in and sends out a robot to look at it. The bomb detonates."

"Did anyone die?" I asked.

Schleur paused to scoop some food onto his tray.

"The fucking robot!" He roared with laughter.

"He thinks it's funny," Kistler said. "But I don't think it's funny. I'm not usually one to say someone should get posted over mistakes, because things happen. The bomb was inside the wire, though."

"It's like the wire around this base is a fucking no man's land, I'm tellin' you," Schleur said. "It's not supposed to be like that. There should be Marines in every post."

"There aren't Marines in every post?" I asked.

"They've got the wire set up and posts with cameras on them. Some of them are dummies, though. You can tell if you walk up close to them if they're real or not," Schleur said. "Security walks the wire every morning, to see if it has been cut during the night."

I shuffled along silently in the food line behind them, the setup in front of us reminding me of a high school lunch line. The wire didn't seem so impenetrable here and I wasn't sure why it had ever felt that way. Back at the Riv, at least I knew guys on post had eyes on the wire to make sure insurgents didn't clip the strands and slip through. At Hob, big parts of the wire went unattended for hours at a time, all night and then most of the day. The gamble to use fake security cameras hadn't panned out; the enemy walked the perimeter just like we did, but on the other side, and took note of where they would go undetected. These thoughts did not bring me comfort.

"Feel safe?" Kistler asked as he stepped away from the chow line.

"Not so much," I said.

"Me neither," Kistler said. "But it's the name of the game. We're only here for another six weeks or so. As long as we don't get hit by a mortar or hammered by a copper plate IED outside the wire, we go home."

"Or get hit by a sniper," Schleur said.

"Yeah," Kistler said. "Can't forget about them."

The desert loomed large from outside the wire when I left the chow hall. The boogeymen were no longer content to keep out, venturing through the razored strands to plant bombs on our side. If that was possible, what else could happen? I remembered when I'd first learned I could die of a lung infection from dust in the desert wind, how I'd felt like the whole place was set against me. The air, the sun, the sand, and the people living here all wanted me dead. Every day, all of it circled in a little closer to catch me unaware. Eventually they would.

I had rotated off QRF squad for a few days and thought about hitting up the Indian guys who worked at the comm center. They could get me cans of whiskey, called Three Kings, which burned like turpentine going down. I wondered where they got the whiskey and how they got it onto a base where liquor was strictly prohibited. I could go sit at the comm center for a while and watch the man behind the desk do card tricks. He'd told me he was contracted labor from India and learned magic to pass the ninety-hour weeks he pulled. Eventually his shift would end and we'd walk to his hooch to exchange cash for booze. I went back to the barracks instead, though, to change into gym clothes and head to the dusty weight room next to the comm center. I could see the path I would take in my head. I could see where the spine of HESCO Barriers cut the base in half. The base seemed so small in my head, but was a wide-open space compared to the Riv's little parking lot and backyard of dirt accented by a burn pit.

That night, I jogged past the QRF squad jumping into the vehicles to do crew-served weapons checks. I'd be back in the turret, behind a gun, soon enough. I wanted to feel relieved like in the past, but instead wondered if I'd have to leave the wire to get smoked. Maybe a rocket would fly from the middle of the wastes and arc back to the earth to snuff me out or maybe the hajis would slip through the wire and come for me. As the sun dropped below the horizon that night, the air seemed more chilled. I watched the bats circle out from the palm trees, snapping their wings through cones of light cast by street lamps. What if something streaked out of the darkness of the desert and snapped me up? Living at Camp Hob had lowered my guard. I felt a degree of safety here which just wasn't real.

I jogged around my half of the base slowly before heading into the weight room. At the Motor T lot, a heavy steel door two-inches thick sat in front of the main office which once belonged on the side of an up-armored Seven-Ton. Two dozen quarter-size holes had been blasted through it and someone had spray-painted in yellow letters "Complacency Kills" over the pockmarks. I stopped jogging to examine it, poked my thumb through some of the holes, feeling the sharp edges of the punctures' lips. I nicked my thumb and blood ran down my hand, dribbling into the sand.

YESTERDAY

THE BLADE MOVED ACROSS MY CHEEK IN SMOOTH strokes. I stared intently into the mirror from behind a porcelain sink, one of twelve such sinks in the squad bay bathroom. My gaze held itself in the mirror instead of focusing on the knife in my hand. I had purchased it just hours before, at the San Clemente PX. All the Marines in Receiving bought knives to play with and for protection in the squad bays at night—the six hundred of us stuffed into the single giant platoon grew restless while we waited to fall in on an SOI training battalion starting another cycle.

I'd decided to shave with my knife when I got back to the squad bay. Frustration had been mounting for weeks as I'd waited to cycle into training, but it kept not happening week after week. Receiving Company filled our time with prison games, so I'd spent plenty of hours raking rocks, painting grass green, picking dead grass out of lawns, and cigarette butts out of gutters. Rarely, there would be a call for a worthwhile working party to help stow weapons in the armory, but just as often it would turn out to be a working party to put weights back on their racks in the gym. The frustration turned into latent hostility two weeks into waiting, which was about two weeks ago now.

I slid the knife across my face in another smooth stroke.

When I'd walked by the bathroom, the idea came to me in a flash. I'd shave with my knife. The Corps forgot to mention that I'd be wasting a month of my life waiting around to train? Good! I felt glad just to spite them. I'd show them how much I gave a fuck. They wanted to cram six hundred Marines into five squad bays to watch the turmoil? The time had come to take it up a notch. I wasn't just going to buy the biggest, meanest knife I could find. I was going to use it to clean the stubble off my face, even though I didn't need to shave. I'd already shaved that day, but that wasn't the point.

I sucked my lower lip in and carefully slid the razor edge across my chin.

There might not even be a point. Hell, I didn't know. I'd started shaving because it was ballsy, brash, and a little bit insane. If I erred, applied too much pressure or slipped, it would take many stitches to sew my face shut. I'd suffer Non-Judicial Punishment—get NJPed, as it was called. I didn't care anymore, though. I wanted everyone who walked back into my squad bay from noon chow to see me do it. Every eye needed to take it into account. They needed to know how fed up I was with them.

So, I didn't know why I was surprised to find some-one standing just behind, watching over my shoulder, when I glanced past my reflection. A tall, skinny Latino whom I'd never spoken to before stood watching me. I knew from the company he kept and listening to his stories in the smoke pit that he'd been a gangbanger in L.A. before joining the Marine Corps. He was the kind of person I made a point not to bump into while maneuvering the crowded gangways and corridors.

"Why are you watching me?" I asked him.

"I want to see you cut yourself," he said.

There was no malice in his voice, only wonder.

For a second, I thought of it from his perspective. Tensions ran high in a platoon large enough to be several companies. Just yesterday a Marine from the Southside of Chicago had broken the nose of another Marine for saying the word "nigger." The day before that, Perez, a Marine soul sick with loneliness for his island home, had taken a buck knife and tested its sharpness on the top of his forearm, opening himself deeply. Now today, after going to noon chow, this Marine discovered me shaving my face with one of the meanest knives he'd ever laid eyes on. And not with tentative flicks, but with big, bold strokes across my face, like I had something to prove.

Suddenly, I disliked the Marine standing there, waiting for me to cut myself. Who did he think he was to gawk like that? Anger boiled up in my chest. I was sick of all the machismo and schadenfreude and wanted him gone.

"Get out of here," I said, pointing to the squad bay. "Don't stand there and watch me."

He made a move as if to strike me, but then froze, eyes on the shaving cream covered dagger in my hand.

"What's going on?" Lopez asked.

He'd just walked up from chow as well. I knew Lopez vaguely as a Marine who liked to sleep in his locker while the Company went on runs. Besides that, he was an all right guy and I got the feeling he acted out because he was fed up as well.

"This fool is shaving with a knife," the other Marine said.

Lopez laughed as he looked back and forth from the knife to my face.

"Crazy white boy," he said with a wink. Lopez put his hand on the other Marine's shoulder and led him away into the squad bay. I turned back to the mirror and finished the last stroke across my jawline with a flourish.

* * *

THE SOI WAS the first time I fired a machine gun, the rhythmic jolt of the weapon's bolt back and forth as bullets snapped downrange, my first taste of real power. Sure, I'd fired myriad rifle rounds by the time I touched a machine gun; in kill houses and on ranges I'd leveled my sights on paper silhouettes, but nothing compared to the sheer firepower of a machine gun. Machines that created fire and smoke, whose concussion jolted the dust from the ground, which never grew tired and only sought to sow death forever. As a Marine with the MOS of 0331—03 designating me infantry and 31 specifying machine gunner—I was a reaper, picking up his scythe for the first time. I fell in love.

The Mk 19 sent grenades sailing through the air, barely discernible black spots, which exploded into shrapnel on impact. Suddenly, I had the ability to tear houses apart and disrupt large troop formations. The M2 Browning .50-caliber, almost unchanged since its introduction to war, had a sabot round with tungsten penetrator that pierced six inches of homogenous steel and its standard fire round penetrated three before becoming an "explosive incendiary." The M60, which machine gunners used during Vietnam, had shed weight and become the more reliable M240. Although its rounds didn't explode or penetrate steel, it was easy to use and accurate. I knew all of them inside and out, how they acted when I fired them and how to deploy them in conjunction with other machine guns for maximum effect. Interlocking Fields of Fire, Final Protective Line, Primary Direction of Fire, these were all just words in books I had to repeat on tests. In execution, I came to understand machine gunnery, excel at it.

During a combined night range with riflemen advancing on the ground and machine guns firing overhead, I realized that from the transition from boot camp to SOI Marines had become expendable. My section leader had told me to run a roster to command from Machine Gun hill, where we were digging in the guns to shoot over the riflemen's heads. On the way to the higher-ups at the entrance to the range, I glanced at the roster and saw a box with the words "acceptable loss" and inside the numeral "1." I found myself walking by one of the rifle platoons' squad leaders.

Everyone called him Preach, because he stood over six foot three and had a calm, saintly look about his cropped head. Wizened features betrayed his age. Preach was a thirty-year-old man. I'd heard he needed a letter from his governor to get the age restrictions waived.

"What is it like an allotment or something?" I asked. "How is it okay if someone dies in training?"

"Easy. One of your guns could slip," Preach said, lowering his voice as we approached the tent where the higher-ups stood sipping coffee. "You could dig an arm of the tripod in wrong and send a dozen bullets into the backs of me and my guys."

"More likely an Eleven drops their rifle or negligently discharges into their battle buddy," I said, calling the riflemen by the last digits in their MOS, 0311. "Two months straight of 'I'm up, he sees me, I'm down,' training and you guys still can't get it right."

Preach looked down at me and smiled—gallows humor, pandering to our indignation. Neither of us had to regret the smiles later, because that day everyone made it home.

DOUBLE ENTENDRES

SMITH LAY ON HIS BACK ON THE TOP BUNK OF THE rack he and I shared in MachineGun's squad bay with both of his feet tied to the wooden support beams that ran to the ground. Smith and Ulrich had been wrestling and Smith's boots had come unlaced.

"Tie his boots to the rack! Tie his boots to the rack!"

Laughing hysterically. There were no women among us; just a squad of Machine Gunners who'd been awake for too long on Battalion QRF in Habbaniyah, Iraq. Maybe "pack" was more apt than "squad," because rank no longer mattered. I couldn't imagine returning stateside, as if it were the end of existence. It would be the end of Iraq, the desert, and war. Until then, we'd accepted that Prockop would remain in charge. As for the rest of us, we were more or less equals in each other's minds when it came to matters of rank—especially since besides Prockop, Decker, and Lowery were the only other NCOs. Of course, we were still Marines, so occasionally a senior Marine would lose his mind on a junior for making some kind of juvenile error. But MachineGuns basically held true to the LAV school's motto we'd run past every day back in Twentynine Palms: "The strength of the pack is the wolf; the strength of the wolf is the pack."

Smith was weak. As a group, we had known this for some time. Larkin had also been weak when he first came to the unit, but we'd hardened him with yelling and a few hundred push-ups. Larkin stopped whining and hoping tough times would get better and started pushing through those times when he realized he was stuck with us, when he realized the men he would live with for the next thirteen months required him to rise above adverse conditions and succeed. At some unspoken moment, we decided we'd need to find whatever part of Smith the war hadn't touched—whatever still let him smile his big, lopsided smile—and pound it out as if it were a pea of gold hammered atom-thin over a football field. So, the hazing began.

Yuck Mouth was one of his new names, because his teeth were as yellow as ears of autumn corn. Faggle also seemed to stick to him as a handle—even though it didn't make sense, besides being a play on faggot— or Sméagol or Muck Mouth, nothing that isn't heard on every playground in the world. But our playground was different, because we were in charge of it. I liked it that way. So did everyone else. With Echo Company gone and our Staff NCO in and out of sickbay battling a staph infection, we were Ronin who had to band together every once in a while to leave the wire and assert the dominance of the United States government over the indigenous people of Iraq.

What we didn't like was Smith's stupid smile, reminding us how much of ourselves we'd had to compromise. How exactly we'd come to Smith's boots tied to the rack seemed worth wondering about momentarily, but I knew. Pretending like it was some kind of mystery would have been like acting as if the moon going through its phases to blackness was some kind of magic. How we'd gotten there was simple. We couldn't touch Smith's insides, but everything else was ours.

"Pull his dick out, pull his dick out!" someone screamed at Ulrich.

Ulrich had tied Smith's boots to the posts of the rack, now his arm snaked up the bed and his hand undid Smith's belt.

"Stahp," Smith said. Whenever he got really upset, his slight speech impediment could be heard.

Ulrich didn't stop though and the squad hadn't given him any reason to. Getting to this moment had taken months.

At first, the squad had just yelled at Smith. Yelling might seem like a trivial thing in the Marine Corps, but in a combat zone you spend all your time with your squad. The most Smith could do to escape would be to go to Hob's gym and even then someone he knew would be there. Soon yelling wasn't enough, so a few of us just scrutinized him, patiently waiting for Smith to give away any sign of weakness. Rose noticed that Smith never took off his underwear, unless he was in one of the five dingy stalls in our company shower trailer. Rose pounced on the newfound weakness, stripping naked and dancing over Smith in bed until he woke to Rose's genitals smacking back and forth off his stomach and asshole, inches from Smith's face.

"Oh, you like that, little Faggle," Rose would say. "Do you like that fucking dick? Is it bigger than yours?"

Rose's bursts of laughter always punctuated these episodes, but Smith never found them funny, like he didn't find it funny now that Ulrich was taking his cock out of his pants.

"Play with it!" someone screamed. "Pull it out and play with it!"

Smith's eyes shot wide open and he sat up in his rack, feet struggling to break the laces tethered to the bed. Smith swung a wild right that Ulrich ducked easily. For a second their bodies seemed still as their four hands fumbled around Smith's crotch.

"Yea! Get his little dick hard!"

I turned and followed the voice back to Prockop. I wasn't surprised. It was obvious he meant it. Whatever was going on in our little community permeated all of us.

* * *

BACK WHEN WE first got to Hob, Weapons Platoon shared the building with another platoon that lived upstairs. At the time, Smith's hazing was pretty much kept to the hours before sleep. During the day, we went through drill after drill: house clearing, target shooting, machine gun training, and pistol qualifications. This was before Echo's line platoons pushed north to patrol Lake TharThar. After their success in finding the bomb maker, we wondered what the punishment would have been had we failed, because the reward was permanent duty in hell, far away from the nearest amenity. In those days, time to mold Smith had been short and most people participated out of boredom. Ulrich found a padded baton for self-defense training and we'd all taken turns hitting Smith with it for hours, especially when he was trying to relax in bed. When that stopped being effective, we bought a Taser which shot sparks and electricity between its two exposed metal knobs. Smith would startle awake, gasping and panting as we raked it up and down his ribs.

One day, Prockop muttered something about going upstairs to do some lines with First Platoon. I couldn't really tell whether he was serious or not. Drug use was rampant and the Iraqis who shared the base with us had no qualms about selling dope to Marines.

I gritted my teeth as he walked out of the squad bay. We were on a rolling QRF which hadn't yet settled into the slower rhythms we adopted when we became permanently assigned. Prockop was squad leader for the next twelve hours, until changeover. Prockop had said things like this before. He'd come back hours later to toss and turn in bed, then get up and ask us for smokes between muttering, "I'm fucked up," over and over. Half an hour went by. I was getting up to make sure Prockop didn't get completely fucked out of his head on drugs when Fleming walked over to me.

"Have you seen Prockop?" Fleming asked. "He borrowed my camera before he went upstairs and I think I've decided I don't want him to use it anymore."

Fleming, although technically junior to me in rank, was twenty-seven to my twenty-one. If he'd changed his mind about letting Prockop borrow the camera, he'd probably actually thought about it and not just done it on a whim.

"You know what, I'll go get it for you. Okay?" I answered.

"It's all right," Fleming said. "You don't need to get up or anything, I'll just take care of it."

"No, really," I said. "I think they might be doing naughty things up there, so I'll go grab it."

"Uh, oka-ay?" Fleming said slowly.

I headed upstairs and into Second Platoon's main squad bay which kept the first two squads while the third slept in an auxiliary storage room down the hall. Second Platoon's racks were arranged in a semicircle that obscured the back part of the room from sight. The semicircle was not in military order and racks staggered haphazardly. I moved on through, noticing how many Marines were lounging in bed with earphones, while the ones who weren't wouldn't meet my gaze.

Surely, they aren't just blowing rails out in the open, I thought. The idea was just too ludicrous. A few Marines getting coked out of their brains could be kept a secret, but if everyone here saw it then it was public knowledge.

A group of six to eight Marines came into view, standing at the back of the room around the squad leader and team leader racks. They all had their shirts off and were wearing the Marine Corps authorized Physical Training short shorts that barely covered their butts; I couldn't yet see the men facing me on the other side. I slowed my walk as I approached the back of the room. The Marines in the racks around me looked neither at me, nor where the men stood.

I was known for breaking the balls of Marines in the other platoons. Often, they were guarded in conversation when they saw me watching. What I saw in their eyes now was unsettling. Some of them looked like I was about to walk in on their parents fucking. The tension took hold of my mind and I wished I'd brought my pistol.

I balled up my fists and set my jaw as I walked up to the circle of men. Billy, a squad leader in Second Platoon, stood in the circle looking down through a digital camera. His shirt was also off and his right hand was down at his cock, pumping back and forth. I looked in blank astonishment from man to man, each one with his throbbing dick out. I knew some of the men in the circle; I would have trusted my life with them in a combat situation. Marines I'd known for over three years now stood with vacant eyes, their junk hanging over the elastic of their green PT silky shorts.

"What the fuck are you guys doing?" I asked.

"Fluffing ourselves," Blaker said. "Come on, join the party."

In the circle, Billy snapped a picture of his dick next to another Marine's. I looked at Prockop. He had his erection out.

"What are you doing?" I asked.

"Seeing whose dick is bigger," Prockop said. His expression was relaxed, his face flushed. I couldn't tell if he was high or not and didn't know if it mattered anymore.

Hendricks stood across from me. I'd known him for a few years, but I hadn't seen him naked before. Nor had I seen him red-faced, eyes glazed, stroking his rock-hard erection in a circle of other Marines doing likewise, while his squad leader took pictures.

My alarm wasn't from morals. This wasn't my first time encountering Marines doing drugs and acting out behavior most of them would have reviled in public. Back at FOB Riviera, Marines I'd gone to high school with asked

312

me if I wanted to do lines of Xanax with them. It had come out recently that two old vets on their second tours spent time on post staring into each other's eyes while they masturbated. But there was no manual written on how to handle this, no codes of conduct regarding a circle jerk. While Marines stood around me fondling themselves, I reasoned that at the very least the rules concerning fraternization were being infringed. If these Marines had mixed up drugs somewhere along the way to standing in a circle with Fleming's camera, that would be even more trouble.

Prockop must have seen some flicker in my expression because his hand slowed down, leaving his dick to wobble back and forth in front of him. Blaker stood beside him, stroking like a maniac.

"Oh yeah, baby. Look at my dick," Blaker said. He thrust his hips so his cock bounced up and down, hitting his stomach with loud smacking sounds.

Some of the other Marines' erections weren't faring so well—the tension in the room was making them lag. Hendricks looked confused, like he wondered how he'd come to have his half-flaccid member in his hand. Instead of waking up in bed, he'd woken up to a nightmare where he was playing with himself in front of a bunch of men whose respect he needed, whose mettle he had to count on outside the wire.

My own feelings rolled through me like thunder. I didn't know what to think. I felt the loneliness of the deserted and betrayed. These men had left me behind while they made some kind of escape. They were supposed to be my leaders, some of them Marine Corps Sergeants and Corporals, NCOs who made up the backbone of Marine command structure. But they had left duty behind, abandoned their oaths. Or was it that simple? I didn't know and couldn't tell from their flushed expressions and bloodshot eyes. I turned away from the circle of Marines without saying anything.

Walking back through the racks, I could see a few of the Marines in Second Platoon hide their faces behind books and laptops. Just when I thought none of them would say anything to me, someone pulled their headphones out of their ears.

"There isn't anything we can do about it," he said. "If we say anything, our world turns to shit."

I tried to open my mouth to say something, but nothing came out. My jaw seemed stuck and as much as I tried it wouldn't budge. I walked by him mutely, my mouth still open.

The Marine who spoke was right. The lower-ranked men in Second Platoon had to rely on the good graces of their immediate squad superiors outside of the wire. Marines who caused trouble for their NCOs were safe enough inside the wire, but outside things were different. Our squad leaders reigned supreme in the streets and fields of the countryside.

I ran into Corporal Lowery as he walked out the front door of the building in shower flip-flops, towel in hand. Lowery was the one of the three NCOs in the Machine Gun section of Weapons Platoon and that gave him quite a bit of clout around the company. The Machine Gun section had over twenty people in it total, compared to a rifle squad of twelve men or less.

"Guess what Prockop is doing upstairs," I said.

"Is he getting all fucked up again?" Lowery asked, his voice deadpan. Lowery didn't have a problem with people drinking off duty, but doing drugs on duty was a different thing altogether—the general consensus in our section.

"Well, I don't know about that," I said. "Because when I went up there a bunch of Second Platoon's leadership was standing around with their dicks out, getting them hard and taking pictures."

"Prockop was doing this?" Lowery asked. "He was actively participating, not just watching?"

"He had his dick out," I said.

Lowery's face turned red and he shook his head. Without saying anything else he turned and walked out the front door of the barracks, toward the shower trailer. Back in the squad bay, I told Fleming what his camera was being used for. He shook his head the same way Lowery had and left to find out what was going on for himself. When he came back he tried to pass by my rack without saying anything, but I called him over. Fleming was my junior in rank by about a year and a half; it didn't give me much authority over him, but enough that when I called he answered.

"So, what did you find?" I asked.

"Uhhh, well, I went up there and there they all were in a circle," Fleming's voice was more high-pitched than normal. "But their dicks were all put away. It did look like lots of them still had boners. Prockop got all embarrassed when I got my camera back from him. He started to say something—"

"Have you looked at the pictures?" I interrupted.

"No," Fleming said. "Why?"

"Get it out and let's look," I said.

"I don't want to," he said. "Not now. Some other time."

"That's an order," I said, sitting up in my rack. "Get the camera out. Now."

Fleming reluctantly pulled the camera out of his pants' cargo pocket and turned it on. He kept looking up at me to see me crack a smile, let him know I would relent.

"Now go through the pictures," I said.

Fleming flipped through some of the pictures. In some of the pictures we could clearly see Marines we knew standing side by side with throbbing members, while in others the pictures were close up on the privates. There were no pictures of drug use or of Marines touching each other. I hadn't thought far enough ahead to know how the pictures could be used, but some interesting possibilities presented themselves. Prockop might start seeing things my way and maybe I wouldn't have to stand any more midnight posts. I could get everything I wanted from him and still shoot the images to Battalion in an anonymous email or just print them for a drop off. They could be mailed home to media outlets, a few of which would have loved to run a story about drug-laden homoeroticism in the Marine Corps. Fleming stopped going through the photos.

"What do I do with them?" Fleming asked.

"Erase them," I said. "And keep your mouth shut about this."

"Uh, yea. This wasn't something I planned on bringing up to anyone," Fleming said.

He stared at the black screen on the back of his digital camera.

"Why did you let me go up there?" Fleming asked.

I bared teeth at him.

"Why shouldn't you know?" I said. "It was happening, wasn't it? Our squad leader keeps getting fucked up while serving as QRF Sergeant on duty and you are part of that QRF squad, so you tell me why you shouldn't know."

※　※　※

I WATCHED ULRICH trying to fish Smith's dick out of his pants. The shouting and hollering in the squad bay made it difficult to think, much less understand what was going on. If Ulrich had pulled Smith's dick out and started playing with it, I'd have let it happen. I'd have sat and watched while Smith, my brother-in-arms, was sexually assaulted, because he hadn't lost what we had. He could still smile like he meant it, like there was some-place inside of him the war hadn't corrupted. It made me furious. I wanted to break his stupid smile with its yellow teeth and stuttered words, so he could feel the loss and know how things really were. If degradation was what it took, I would bear witness.

"Stop it!" Smith cried out again, his words slurred.

Smith sat up in the bed suddenly and whipped his hand up above his head. There was a sharp clicking sound. Smith had a knife in his hand and he'd just opened it, the blade flashing in the squad bay's lights.

"Watch out, Ulrich!" Larkin yelled from his rack.

Smith's arm came down quickly, twice in succession, cutting each of his bootlaces free. Ulrich hopped away as Smith jumped down from the bed, holding the knife out in front of him in a fighting stance.

"You motherfucker!" Smith screamed. "I'll kill you!"

Ulrich's face went pale. He moved backwards, his arms raised in front of him as if to ward off an animal's attack.

"You'll what, Smith?" Ulrich said. "I couldn't quite understand you."

Ulrich might have backed up, but he wasn't backing down, not by joking about Smith's stutter. Smith whipped the knife back and forth in front of him a few times as he walked toward Ulrich. From the look in Smith's eyes, I knew he was serious. Tears streamed down his face, his breathing unsteady as he held up his undone pants with his left hand.

"I can see your dick, Smith!" Ulrich cried. "Hey look everyone! It's Smith's little wiener!"

Smith was bawling as he advanced on the backpedaling Ulrich. The squad bay's length allowed them to move about fifteen feet before Ulrich ran out of room.

"Shud uh!" Smith screamed.

Ulrich looked around for something to defend himself with.

"Ulrich, grab an M-16!" I yelled at him. I didn't know whether he would swing it like a club or shoot Smith, but it was the best idea I had at the time.

"Stop!" Prockop yelled. "Smith, stop right now!"

Smith kept advancing on Ulrich, who had fallen back into defense posture and no longer fled. They were going to kill each other. Smith had a knife and his first blow could be a fatal one, but if his knife thrust wasn't true Ulrich would snap his arm like a toothpick and, after that, his neck. Ulrich was five-foot-five and two hundred twenty pounds of bulging muscle to Smith's gawky, lanky body of fat rolls. Smith crouched down, gathering himself to make a final lunge.

"Smith! Drop the knife *now!*" Prockop bellowed.

Smith froze for a second, then threw the knife away, sending it spinning under someone's rack. Smith let loose with another animal scream then swung around to face us. His first few steps back to us were jerky as if he were a marionette. The look on my face must have seethed contempt and he must have seen the same look in everyone else's face as well. His face twisted angrily as he sniffled, snot pouring out of his nose and onto his shirt.

Lowery sat in front of me, on a bottom rack against the wall. When Smith had turned and given us all the death glare, Lowery had pulled out his pistol and clicked the safety off, pulling the hammer back to half cock. Smith saw it and came to a stop. He stood upright and hung his head, turned to the wall and buried his face against it in his arm, sobbing.

Lowery looked back at me and I gave him a nod of support. If Smith pulled any of that crazy shit on us, Lowery would put him down and we'd all have told the MPs how Smith had lost his fucking mind due to the stress of being on QRF. *For no fucking reason, he just snapped*, I would say. The whole squad would square away our stories. Sure, we'd probably have to sell the Assault section on the fact that Smith needed to be put down, but it wouldn't be hard. They hated Smith as well and didn't even have to live with him like we did. Maybe we'd say he was talking to people who weren't there with the same names as the Golf Company Marines who had gotten blown up.

We wouldn't tell the MPs how he'd kept his fucking stupid yellow smile and his dumb laugh. We wouldn't tell them about the months of hazing, how for days at a time we wouldn't let Smith sleep, until he broke down in tears and begged us to stop waking him up every fifteen minutes. The time he chased me down the squad bay with a rifle and tried to spear me with it would slip my mind.

But Lowery didn't put Smith down like a rabid dog. He didn't have to. Smith slowly limped out of the squad bay, staring at the ground. I'd never seen so much shame before. All of us had hurt Smith badly, so maybe things had turned out like we wanted. But there was still a voice of reason in my head that told me otherwise; something which had stayed true to when I'd first come over, to find schools and hospitals shot up, and syringes dumped in abandoned lots where children played; something which had held the course when I tried to rationalize how SOPs for escalation of force put the lives of both Marines and law-abiding Iraqi citizens at serious risk.

Prockop followed Smith to lecture him about his temper. Lowery holstered his pistol and looked around at the rest of the squad. Most Marines wouldn't meet his gaze, but I did and so did Rose. Ulrich couldn't get his eyes off the ground. His shoulders slumped forward and there was a frown on his face.

"Holy fucking shit," Lowery said. "I thought Smith was going to kill Ulrich."

"Yeah, no shit," Rose said. "Maybe we shouldn't fuck with Smith anymore."

Hoarse laughter echoed throughout the squad bay, followed by silence. The sound of boots nervously scuffing the ground filled the room.

"Well, I'm gonna go have a cigarette in the smoke pit," Lowery said. "And if Smith wants to get froggy, by God, he's gonna get it."

Lowery moved toward the door, then hesitated.

"It's bad enough we've got to worry about getting killed when we leave the wire, or maybe by an IED the hajis plant inside the wire, *or* in some mortar or rocket attack on the base," Lowery said. "But killing each other over dumb shit? This is too much."

Lowery turned and left before anyone got the chance to point out how easy it was to say that Ulrich forcibly playing with Smith's penis was "dumb shit," when it wasn't you tied to the rack. No one brought up how what had just happened was sexual assault. No one brought up how we'd made his life hell for months on end. There were some nights, after a day where we'd been especially hard on him, when I'd lain in bed wondering, *Is tonight the night Smith waits until we're asleep, slips out of bed, flips his M-16 to burst mode, and goes from rack to rack?*

None of it was said because it didn't need to be. Every Marine knew the extent of what we were doing to Smith, how we were breaking him down a little bit more each day, and how things kept escalating. Explaining to another squad would be as simple as saying, "It's his stupid smile, like the kid who loses the dodgeball game for his team would smile. Smith's a shitbird who doesn't get it."

Smith out there on patrol, what a joke. A Marine on patrol was supposed to be sharp and intelligent, never missing anything—like a wire sticking out of an empty pop can which could be an IED, or the carcass of a dog that had stitches where insurgents had sewn a bomb into it, or the sun's flash off a sniper's scope. Smith wasn't out there patrolling though; he was just following the man in front of him around with that stupid fucking smile on his face or staring at the ground, refusing to take it all in.

I knew this with the same certainty as I knew that if I walked out of the wire by myself and into the ville, I'd never be seen or heard from again. I knew he wasn't paying attention or he would have asked himself some of the same questions that had dimmed the light in so many of his brothers' eyes. He would have thought about the implications of an occupying force leaving behind war children—all the implications. Smith had rolled down streets in Humvees, past shot-up hospitals and bombed-out schools and, in his mind, that was normal for war and had nothing to do with us. He'd driven the MSR which ran through the heart of Fallujah so many times he knew its turns and bends, but the gutted buildings, twisted rebar, burned-out houses, and bullet-riddled walls didn't consume his thoughts. I wondered if he realized what waited for us, outside the wire; I knew he didn't realize what it had done to us on the inside.

Smith was the Marine every Drill Instructor screamed at in boot camp while the rest of his platoon did push-ups in the dirt. He was what the DIs called "the one," the one guy in the squad who somehow manages to keep believing enough to have a goofy smile on his face. Our little redheaded fuck-up, a real Blue Falcon, or buddy fucker. Yuck Mouth, aloof above the existential chaos of war.

From then on things were different, not just because of what we did to Smith but also due to concerns about Prockop's leadership. The Marines in MachineGuns continued to haze and berate Smith. It didn't stop until after we got back home when Smith finally had enough of Rose's drunken bullying and beat him badly in retaliation. All the senior Marines in MachineGuns congratulated him then. I told Smith it was what we wanted out of him the whole time, for him to show a little fighting spirit—but that was a lie. What really happened was that enough of us wanted to see Smith break that we tried. What kind of effect this torment had on Smith's psyche I'll never know, because I never asked. Smith is a young man in his late twenties now, living his life in a small town in the wastes of southwestern Illinois.

Would he tell me the truth if I asked? Would he forget all the terrible things I did and watched others do to him, become suddenly vulnerable and bare his soul to me about how much it had all affected him? Would he admit that he'd never forget our faces, because he saw all of us in nightmares that repeated on a continuous loop night after night? Maybe he'd have sought out help at a VA Hospital near him and heard enough psychobabble to call them night terrors. I'm afraid I'd tell him about my own nightmares and realize how similar we both are. All I can do is hope the parts of Smith I hurt healed long ago without him even noticing. I want to believe that.

Our concerns about Prockop's leadership were nothing new, but now it wasn't just his work ethic we were questioning. Many of us wondered if Prockop was cracking up, doing drugs, and acting out fantasies with NCOs in other platoons while on duty. Could I trust Prockop to make the right decisions under pressure outside the wire? I had to remind myself that Prockop was just a young man, barely older than me. This rumination brought more inner turmoil than peace, because it could have easily been me making the same fucked-up decisions as Prockop. The extent of my service was only half of Prockop's since this was his second deployment and his first had been rougher, more violent.

"I'll be back to the squad bay in a second," I said as Lowery and I passed each other at the barracks door. "I need to take a leak and have a smoke. Then we gotta talk."

Lowery grunted an acknowledgment over the sound of his flip-flops quietly padding back to his rack. A feeling of déjà vu came over me; I had run into Lowery on the way out of the barracks after the incident with Prockop a few weeks before and had the same thoughts in my head.

We couldn't report what happened to Smith; something like this could break the company up. Echo would never be the same if someone walked down to Battalion HQ. I'd heard rumors of Companies disbanded over widespread breaches in conduct. Every single Marine in Weapons Platoon had at one time believed in the war and everything it stood for: America righting wrongs and saving the day. Prockop once believed, his first time around, before he was a Sergeant. But that was a long time ago at this point. As our superiors let us down, we let ourselves down, again and again.

THE DAY BEFORE YESTERDAY

SOME NIGHTS, AFTER THE PLATOON HAD CLIMBED into bed, Stahl told war stories. His Coraframs clicked as he walked the squad bay, demons on his heels. He told us of children in firefights, how if one scrambled for a gun lying in the street "they got cut in half." We knew some of Stahl's old platoon by name, especially the troublemakers and the ones that didn't make it. Stahl would talk about the battles he'd fought in Iraq, how we slept safe behind the walls of USMCRD while Marines were out there "hooking and jabbing with the enemy."

Stahl pleaded with us to understand his methods, words slurring. When the platoon was told to "hit the beach"—run around the showers in our cammies, then head outside to roll around a sand pit—that was to build discipline. When Stahl made us breathe through the cammies we'd just worn back from the gas chamber, that was to toughen us up. When Stahl kicked the feet out from under Recruit Torres for rolling his eyes, it had been to maintain order. When he tried for months to wash out one of the Collins twins so their blue-collar parents would have to choose which graduation to attend, it was to illustrate how individual failure affected the whole. When a recruit tripped during a hike, he screamed, "Don't help him up!" to foster self-reliance and destroy the expectation of assistance. And when we stood in line and Stahl slowly walked down my side of the squad bay, *click-clack click-clack*, with an answerless riddle followed by a cuff across the face, it was done out of a necessity—I needed to know life wasn't fair.

Looking back on the draconian measures, Stahl was right. The future loomed cumulonimbus, our small conception of war nothing but patriotic figures standing at the POA facing a storm front of decisions that would put lives in jeopardy. Our own lives and those of everyone around us. Stahl understood there was no way for us to really know the fear of sirens forecasting inbound mortars, feel the small sonic boom of passing bullets, hear a friend cry out in battle, and want to shrink away. Stahl knew men broke and hearts proved callow. Some nights, when it all bore down on him, he wept.

Graduation day marched closer with complete disregard for our preparedness. When I graduated, I was ready to fight the world. I'd never felt prouder than standing on the parade deck in formation when Stahl put the Eagle Globe and Anchor in my hand, ceremoniously making me a Marine. Of the one hundred twenty recruits Platoon 3111 started with, ninety graduated. I tried to remember faces but couldn't. When Stahl told 3111 to fall out of its final formation, I wish I'd taken a picture. The moment before our bodies sagged out of the POA and into the real world of being wartime Marines should have been savored. But I didn't care. My knees came unlocked, my muscles relaxed, and the instant passed. Our war had just begun.

SHORT TIMERS

NEAR THE END, WE WERE SHORT TIMERS. OUR attitudes had gone through the arc that veteran Marines predicted. In the beginning, every piece of garbage on the road was a possible IED and every silhouette in a window a sniper. In the middle, the fear gave way to boredom, even when operations were dangerous; war wore us down and stretched us thin, making Marines wish they'd get hit so they'd either die or get sent home. But as Echo Company neared the end of its second deployment, Marines became hypervigilant of any threat and avoided going outside the wire as much as possible. I wasn't sure what the rest of the company was doing since Weapons Platoon had been left at Camp Habbaniyah, near the center of Iraq, as Battalion QRF. The rest of the Company went north to a big lake to do God only knew what. How they were handling it I don't know, but the Marines in Weapons Platoon who didn't have wives and children back home did their best to fill in for those who did when we got slated to go outside the wire. But sometimes it couldn't be helped, like when QRF got called out.

"I'm not going back outside the wire," Gunther said. "I stripped all the gear off my flak jacket, took the SAPI plates out, and packed everything in my sea bag."

Gunther was a Sergeant in Golf Company. Earlier in the deployment he'd lost three guys to an IED, two of them vets of the first deployment. Their Humvee had flipped upside down and caught on fire, killing the turret gunner instantly. The patrol listened to them scream while they cooked, unable to pry open the heavy, armored doors. He looked like he hadn't slept in weeks, dark bags sagging under his eyes. His skin was yellowish, waxy.

"I'm telling my LT, 'No more,' when I get back to the barracks," he said. "What the fuck are we doing outside the wire anyway? I'm not getting blown up this close to going back. Fuck that."

I took a long drag of my cigarette and kicked rocks with the toe of my boot. When I looked up, Gunther had the expression I'd grown so accustomed—the infamous thousand-yard stare.

"I've got a wife and kids," he said, but not to me. Not to anyone. "I've got a wife and kids," he repeated. "And ain't nothing going to bring me back if I cross over. And for what? What did Rodriguez die for?"

The three men he'd lost had died when Golf CO had decided their Mortarmen needed targets set up for practice. A few vehicles had been tasked to take the targets downrange, on a road that hadn't been swept for IEDs in a few years. The MRAP didn't trigger the IED, its enormous weight evenly distributed in a freak act of physics so that it passed over unscathed. The second vehicle was a Humvee which wasn't so lucky. Unlucky to have been tasked to go down a road that was listed as "red" because it hadn't been swept in ages. Unlucky that the MRAP, a vehicle which would have survived the blast, drove over the IED in a one-in-a-million way and the bomb didn't blow. Unlucky to flip upside down and catch on fire, instead of killing them all instantly. Unlucky in death, the last moments of their lives a screaming delirium of pain. Gunther had listened to the two that survived the rollover, watched them thrash, clawing at the windows as their skin charred and sloughed off. I'd heard one of the turret gunners in the third vehicle had come to the rescue and tried to wrench the driver's door open, that Marines had pulled him off the vehicle, his gloves smoking.

Had it been Gunther to pull the young Marine back to safety from the ensuing eruption of diesel in the truck's fuel tank? I'd never asked. I didn't really know him, except from sometimes seeing him around Camp Habbaniyah. I kept quiet as he muttered again and again that he wasn't going back outside the wire, lighting his next cigarette with the dying ember of the last. After he repeated the process five times, he calmed down. The muttering stopped. He ground the last butt under his boot heel and walked away. The deployment had been rough on Golf and especially rough on Gunther's platoon. They'd been hit by suicide bombers early on, before the IED, and some of the guys hadn't recovered psychologically. One Marine in particular, whose name I didn't know, couldn't sleep and didn't socialize with others, instead sitting by himself and staring off at the horizon. I'd made the mistake of asking him why he couldn't sleep, and he'd described the attack, suicide bombers' heads flying like dandelions thumbed from their stem.

I'd first heard the story about the IED from Blaker, just after walking in from a long night patrol, the 240 Golf medium machine gun hanging heavy in my hands. I'd shrugged off his manic account of what he had heard from the higher-ups about what had happened—dying is part of what Marines do. But now, watching Gunther walk away from me with his shoulders sagging, I wondered if he was right. What were we doing going outside the wire still? If I asked someone new to country or some boot Lieutenant (LT), they'd belt out the tired slogans—"Winning the hearts and minds," or "Taking the fight to the enemy," or maybe I'd even hear, "Boots on the deck, good to go?"

I ground my cigarette out with my boot and headed back towards the barracks. I wondered what would happen if Gunther refused orders to gear up and lead his squad out of the gate. Cowardice in the face of the enemy was punishable by death, which everyone knew. And it wasn't like sitting on the base meant you'd be safe. Just recently Hob and Taq had both been targeted with rocket attacks. It wasn't just death from above that could get you inside the wire, because the wire itself wasn't exactly impermeable. So far only one IED had been found inside the perimeter, but it was enough to keep everyone on edge. Marines had started walking the small desert base with multiple magazines of ammunition instead of the standard one. My pistol was always condition one— magazine inserted, round in the chamber, safety on—no matter where I went. The Ugandans who guarded the chow hall or dusty internet center never said anything to me about it. They understood the way few people could, their own country being war-torn.

"They're sending an element to Ramadi," Schleur said. He stood in the smoke pit by the barracks, sucking on a cigarette in earnest.

He paused to take a drag. If I never saw another smoke pit again after deployment, it would be too soon. I was getting sick of fitting in my conversations around drags of cigarettes, but there was no way to quit in country.

"Prockop's taking names for who's going," Schleur continued. "God, I hope he doesn't pick me. This is exactly the kind of dumbfuck thing that would get me killed."

"What's the mission?" I asked.

I'd never heard of our battalion doing any operations that far west. I remembered everything I'd heard about Ramadi before deployment, none of it good.

"We're supposed to be showing the guys replacing us where it is," Schleur said. "Because I guess seeing it on a fucking map isn't enough."

I wanted to go. The deployment would be over in a few weeks and I wanted to be able to say that I'd been to Ramadi. I knew it was stupid and I hesitated to tell Schleur.

"What is it, Big Head?" he asked me.

"I want to go," I said.

"What the fuck," Schleur said. "You have lost your fucking mind, Marine. Why the fuck would you want to go to that shithole and risk getting blown up this close to going home? Seeing Fallujah just isn't enough for you, eh? You're a fucking war tourist."

Schleur cackled and shook his head.

"Well, take my fucking spot then," he said. "I'm pretty sure they're going to make me drive the lead Humvee."

In the squad bay Prockop was on the prowl, looking for Marines to send to Ramadi.

"Fleming," Prockop said. "You're going to Ramadi."

Fleming sat up in his rack, rubbing sleep from his eyes. Many Marines had post in the radio room during the night, watching the battalion network for news from higher and listening in case we got called out to help a downed vehicle or to put the fear of God in Iraqis. Fleming was one of those Marines, so he spent the day sleeping. Most Marines did, because the heat index soared with the sun to around 140 degrees.

"Ramadi," Fleming said. "I've only been asleep two hours, I don't know if I could—"

Prockop cut him off. "Sounds great, Fleming. I knew you'd be up for it."

Prockop turned and looked at me, smirk on his face.

"I'm volunteering," I said. "I want to take Schleur's place."

"Who the fuck do you think you are?" Prockop said.

I stood stunned. I hadn't expected any resistance. I chided myself for forgetting about Prockop's twisted leadership style, if it could be called leadership.

"Schleur thinks he can get out of this?" Prockop said. "Fuck no. If I have to go get blown up on some fucked up mission, he does too."

"Should I get geared up? When are we rolling out?"

"Why do you want to go? You realize this is a bullshit mission, right?" Prockop said.

"I want to see Ramadi," I said. "This will be my only chance."

"So, you want to have another little war story to tell the girls back home," Prockop said. "Not a fucking chance. You aren't going. Fuck you. But, Fleming, you are for sure going, so get the fuck out of the rack."

"Roger that, Sergeant," Fleming said. He sounded like Eeyore from Winnie-the-Pooh.

Prockop tried to walk past me but I blocked his way.

"You won't let me go because I want to?"

"Yes," Prockop said, then laughed.

"That's fucking stupid," I said.

"Excuse me?" Prockop said. "Are you questioning my leadership?"

"You fucking heard me," I said. "And you don't know shit about leadership. You can run and tell the Captain I said that."

Prockop didn't seem to know what to say, so he just stared at me. His constant boot licking of our Staff Sergeant and Captain had alienated him from the squad, to the point where no one had his back anymore, if anyone ever did. I grudgingly stepped aside as he walked by, making a hasty retreat from the squad bay.

"Did I just hear that right?" Hawkins said.

He hopped down off his top bunk.

"Fucking Prockop," I said. "I should have killed him back in Saq when I had the chance."

Hawkins held my gaze, spit chew into an empty bottle, and nodded. The night we colluded to murder Prockop if his negligence got any of us killed seemed like years ago, although it had only been six months. Whether we could have gotten away with it we'll never know, but I'd agreed to be the triggerman if the time ever came. I tried not to be angry, tried not to think that maybe it would have been better to do the unthinkable, but the more I tried to push the thoughts away the more they seemed to propel my mind into a dark pit. It wasn't fair to not allow me to go on a run to Ramadi simply because I wanted to go and what kind of person used such logic to run a squad of Marines? Anger made my vision twist. I started to feel dizzy. Lights flashed in front of my eyes. I wiped beaded sweat from my forehead and gripped a nearby bunk to steady myself.

"Are you all right, Big Head?"

I clenched my jaw and waited for my head to clear.

"This place is making me sick," I said. "Fuck Prockop and his bullshit attitude."

Hawkins nodded.

I paced back and forth in the squad bay as the five-vehicle convoy got ready to leave the wire. There wasn't a mission briefing and I realized it had been many months since Weapons Platoon had any kind of mission brief or debrief. Being a QRF meant that we generally didn't have time for them, but when I thought back to our time at Riviera, I knew that the briefs had stopped back then, in what now seemed like another world. I missed the FOB and the town of Saqlawiyah. Back then when we left the wire, I'd felt free, away from the confines of the small FOB's razor wire perimeter. Now when QRF left the wire, instead of feeling free I felt chained to my turret as if stuck in a grotesque ride at Disneyland. The more I thought about feeling trapped in Hob compared to Saq, the more anger spiraled through me, until my hands trembled. I watched Marines don gear from my squad bay door. Schleur looked over and saw how angry I was to be left behind.

"Don't be mad, Big Head," Schleur said. "Just another story I'll have over you."

He laughed. But I didn't return the laughter. I looked at him like I smelled dog shit as he left.

Suddenly, the anger in me snapped taut as a cord and I had an idea. I knew how to get back at Schleur in a way that would really get under his skin. Something inside of me wanted to wipe the smile off his face. I went outside. When I rounded the back of the Humvee, I found Schleur standing outside of the driver's door, donning his helmet.

"Hey, Schleur," I said. "This is the patrol when a mortar hits your Humvee. This is it. You're done for."

Schleur looked over at me, his mouth open and eyes big.

"How the fuck could you say that?" he said.

I threw my head back and laughed, big guffaws racking my body.

"Dead man walkin'!" I shouted and pointed at him.

Schleur took his Kevlar helmet and slammed it hard against the Humvee door's ballistic glass window.

"What the fuck?!" he bellowed.

Schleur started pacing frantically back and forth, his long legs almost going akimbo as he pivoted hard to turn around and go back the other direction. I knew I'd got him right where it hurt most, in the superstitious spot every Marine had. Mortars squad feared all the old taboos—they didn't eat the Charm candies in MREs, didn't ever ask if it was going to rain, and most certainly didn't joke about Marines getting killed—but MachineGuns didn't hold the same beliefs. The only thing we held sacred were the guns and sometimes not even those. I smiled wide at Schleur before walking away from him, his face contorted in anger and frustration. Before I walked back into the barracks, I turned and jeered at him one more time.

"You're a fucking dead man, do you hear me?" I said. "Flip upside down and burn to death, good to go?"

"It's so fucked up you would say that..." Schleur's voice faded into nothing as I walked away.

I sat on my rack and seethed until I heard the trucks' diesel engines start up and rumble away toward the front of the base. I didn't really want Schleur to die, nor did I think a mortar or IED would actually hit him. Death didn't come to us that easy. Not like how it came to my grandmother a few months before when the cancer in her liver finally overwhelmed her. She'd had years to prepare, a full life behind her, children who would outlive her, and a family by her bedside even though I'd been stuck here in Iraq. She went in her sleep, between two cool sheets, beneath an IV drip of painkillers. It wasn't like that for us here. We didn't go quietly; none of us ever would. A lot of guys still had one bullet tucked away, just for them, in case of imminent capture after all other rounds were expended. But most Marines had slid that single round into a magazine long ago, after hearing from the other FOBs how the suicide bombers rushed the gate with no regard for their own life. Death wasn't going to slip through the night into our squad bays and silently slit our throats.

Death came to us through the snaps of sniper fire and thunderous roll of high explosives going off, making the air ruckle and break. Dying on some bullshit run to Ramadi was something that would have happened right at the start, maybe even in the middle, but now

I just couldn't see it happening. Sure, it had all the tragic irony to make Schleur wary a dark omen would turn into self-fulfilling prophecy. Maybe if he had been good-looking or charming, but Schleur was ugly and brutish like the rest of us. Being a working-class guy who still believed in much of the political ideology that sent him over here, I figured that Schleur had many years of pain left in front of him.

Thinking of my grandmother made me wish for home. Returning seemed more like a myth than a reality. People kept telling each other that we'd all go home in just a few weeks, but there was a big part of me that was sure it was just wishful thinking. In the middle of the deployment there had been talk that maybe we would get extended, but I'd heard our return home, as scheduled, was date-time group locked-in on command's calendars. That time was soon approaching, but nothing was guaranteed. The Marines replacing us had already lost a man to vehicle rollover when a driver thought he saw an IED on the side of the road and tried driving an up-armored Humvee like he'd seen in the movies. That was their beginning, a man dead for no reason before they officially had their AO turned over to them. Our ending as Battalion QRF had been extremely stressful, causing the tenuous relationships in the squad to come near breaking point in the last few months, but we could be thankful that we made it and had been spared having to kill anyone.

A voice pulled me out of my reverie as my thoughts became fuzzy. Rose was trying to tell me something. My hearing wasn't as good as it used to be, the loud trucks and guns having deafened me over the course of the tour.

"Big Head, did you hear what Staff Sergeant said to the LT of the unit that's replacing us?" Rose had a lopsided grin on his face, the kind that he got whenever he passed gouge he knew would get a reaction from those around him.

Our Staff Sergeant was known to be a real buddy fucker, going out of his way to whisper in officers' ears that we didn't need downtime or that we could stand to miss a few meals. While both of those things were true since we'd rotated to Hob, it didn't make any sense to make the war harder on grunts than it already was and whenever the Marines of Weapons Platoon got wind of the Staff Sergeant being a sycophant instead of sticking up for us, we became furious.

"He told the LT to tell his platoon not to buy our televisions from us, because we can't take them back," Rose said. "So basically, he just fucked everybody for no reason."

Anger rippled through the Marines in the squad bay. For about a week, everyone had been trying to sell the televisions they'd bought to the Marines replacing us. For this reason, I'd never bought a television. Some Marines had been lucky to purchase their television secondhand from the Marines we replaced at FOB Riviera, but most had ended up blowing around three hundred dollars on a brand new one from the big PX across the MSR at Taq. Marines murmured about how asking fifty dollars for a three-hundred-dollar television was more than reasonable. It was Lowery who finally spoke aloud what everyone was thinking.

"Fuck that. I'll break mine before I leave it for a bunch of stingy assholes," he said.

"Let's take them all out and break them right now," Rose said. "Before Staff Sergeant gets back from the chow hall with the other unit's LT and tells us we can't."

A frantic energy filled the air as every Marine who had a television they were trying to sell hastily un-plugged it from the wall and lugged it to the side of the barracks. A few Marines brought cabinets they'd been trying to sell. For a moment, I wondered if this was a wise move, considering that no one had even tried ne-gotiating with the other Company's Marines, but then I thought, *Why the hell not?* I was in a foul mood and breaking things would cheer me up. Mundell appeared with an axe from somewhere just as a few stragglers arrived with chairs and a small table.

"Holy shit," Rose said. "Look at all this stuff!"

All the televisions were lined up, their screens gleam-ing in the sunlight. There had to be a couple thousand dollars in electronics waiting to meet the axe's steel, along with couple hundred worth of furniture. What the Marines in the Company replacing us didn't understand was that it wasn't the cost of the items we were selling that was the real burden, it was convincing higher-ups to let you carry leisure items with you on convoys back from the PX in Taq. The war didn't afford many oppor-tunities for a Marine to go to Taq, buy a TV, and then have room aboard an MRAP to make sure it got back in one piece.

But the Marines replacing us didn't understand a lot of things. Right after they showed up, steps on the shower trailer had been broken. Shortly after that a pair of boxer briefs was found by a toilet; the underwear had been soiled and a small mural had been finger-painted with shit on the side of the bathroom stall above where they lay. Not to mention how the shitter trailer always smelled like piss now, because the new Marines didn't bother to aim. They were like children.

They didn't understand how hard to come by material things were in Iraq, how they needed to be cherished as precious, not treated as if a replacement was standing by. We all hated them, the fools that had already gotten one of their own killed, and they knew it. While standing post one night, I took a *Playboy* and went through, page by page, and drew dicks on every single woman—hairy dicks, long dicks, short dicks, dicks with warts, dicks that had loops like roller coasters. When my shift ended, I brought it over to the new Marines' barracks and handed it to a PFC walking in. I told him to take it to his squad leader and tell him it was a gift from Echo. After that they all stayed away from us, wouldn't even talk to us in the chow hall line. They knew how we felt about them, but evidently they doubted our resolve.

We took turns smashing the televisions. I don't remember who went first. I went third or fourth. I'd handled an axe before in my childhood, chopping wood for the furnace. Fine white cracks ran away from the blow I shattered into the black glass. I smiled real big. I looked around at the rest of the squad and they were smiling too. The second blow sundered the television in half, causing it to gape open like jagged teeth. People laughed and milled about, some taking pictures and others filming. Someone showed up with two other televisions when we were about to move on to the furniture. By the time we'd had our fill, everything lay in pieces. Just as the dust settled, I looked away to see our Staff

Sergeant and the other unit's LT walk into the barracks.

"I wonder what Staff Sergeant thought of that?" Rose asked. He laughed.

"He did *not* look happy," Lowery said.

"Who gives a fuck," Mundell said.

Hawkins strode over from the other side of the shattered glass and splintered wood. "Did you guys see that?" Hawkins said. "The LT was looking at Staff Sergeant like, *Are you going to stop this?* and he wouldn't look back at him, just kept his eyes locked straight ahead as they walked by."

"What were they doing walking by?" I asked.

"Coming back from chow," Lowery said, then chuckled.

"We probably should have picked a better spot than right by the barracks," Mundell said. "I bet he bitches to Prockop about this."

Rose told some of the junior Marines to throw away the broken pieces and sweep up the glass and we all headed back inside. Just as I laid down on my rack, I heard the element that went to Ramadi rumble back into the patch of desert that we called our parking lot, nestled between bombed-out buildings. I found myself indifferent to the idea of Prockop being upset with me. If Prockop got mad, what could he do? Maybe a group punishment or maybe haze a few of the senior Marines. It wouldn't matter to me either way. Marines had wanted help breaking their expensive electronics with an axe and I had been happy to oblige them. If that somehow didn't fall in line with the Staff Sergeant's plans to see the platoon's spoils of war be left behind and stolen by jackals, good. I hoped the Staff Sergeant had made a fool of himself telling the

LT how we would leave behind our things, so there was no need for anyone to pay us the small amount of money asked. I hoped as soon as Prockop walked back in from going to Ramadi that the Staff Sergeant filled his ear with bellyaching about how MachineGuns were a bunch of animals and he needed to get a muzzle on us. It was the end of the line, what the fuck were they going to do? We were going home in a matter of weeks.

After the Marines from the convoy unloaded the trucks and dropped gear, the door to our squad bay opened, slapping the wall behind it.

"What the fuck happened while we were gone?"

It was Schleur. He wasn't mad anymore. From the smile on his face I knew he'd already heard but wanted me to tell him anyway.

"Staff Sergeant told the LT not to let his guys buy our stuff because we can't take it with us or ship it home," I said. "So, we broke everything."

Schleur let out a laugh that sounded like gravel in a blender.

"What did Staff Sergeant say?" he asked.

The door slapped the wall again as McShane stuck his head in the room.

"Hey, Schleur," McShane said. "Everyone from Mortars and Assault are hauling their shit outside to smash it. It's gonna be awesome!"

"What? Who said?" Schleur asked.

"Kistler and Crawford say it's good to go," McShane said. "They heard what Staff Sergeant said and everyone is freaking out."

The two Mortarmen left in a hurry. A few minutes later, Prockop came in and stared at me while I lay in my rack, hands behind my head and boots up, crossed on the footboard. He told me how Staff Sergeant was furious at me. I told him it didn't make any sense for Staff Sergeant to be angry at me, because I didn't have a say in whether or not everyone wanted to break their televisions. Prockop tried giving me a stern talk, but I couldn't help but laugh when we heard glass being smashed right outside the squad bay windows. Prockop left, fuming, but I didn't give it any thought. It was somehow appropriate, him deciding at the end of his second deployment that the time to rein it in was when we wanted to smash televisions. Everything else we'd done, well, that was good to go as far as he was concerned. The drugs, the drinking, the violence. All of it.

As the destruction outside died down, I started drifting off to sleep. I wasn't on QRF that day, or was I? It didn't matter anymore. I hoped when I woke up I'd be back home, far away from this place.

SICK IN THE GULLIVER

THE WAR FOLLOWED US HOME. OR, WE BROUGHT it back with us. Echo Company formed ranks on Al Taqaddum Air Base and filed onto planes that would take us back around the world to California, where we spent a month demobilizing before going home. The demob, as we called it, was filled with classes that Rose handily summarized as, "Don't kill yourself or beat your wife." I sat with my squad as someone talked to us about anger management or how to handle depression. I had the same attitude as most Marines: the classes were bullshit and I was fine. I didn't understand and, like when I'd first gone over, the veterans didn't warn me. I think they knew, though. I think they'd been through it before, at the bottom of bottles or staring down the barrels of guns held by their own hands.

Echo got off the plane in Iowa and rode buses to Fort Des Moines. Families waited in the wet grass outside of the drill center on a blustery night as Echo Company, deployment 8-2, had its last formation of the tour. Girlfriends, wives, and parents strained their eyes in earnest, to make out the faces of loved ones standing rank and file; children called out to their fathers and grandparents huddled together under the harsh lights of the parking lot. Military bearing wavered under the emotional strain, marking some Marines' faces with a latticework of tears. When we were dismissed, it signaled the end of that version of Echo; our Major would be changed out of his position as CO with another Major and the men who had volunteered from other units in the Corps would go back to them. He gave a last rousing speech, about how we had braved the dangers of snipers, IEDs, sickness, and other hazards of war. He wanted us to understand that we were heroes. But I didn't feel like a hero. Even though I was back home, I felt like I'd just stepped out of Iraq, like any moment I'd wake up to Sergeant Prockop throwing open the door of my room at FOB Riviera, screaming about how we needed to be out front in battledress ASAP.

As Marine Corps Reservists, we would be the most prone to veteran suicide in the coming years. As the formation broke and Marines rushed to the waiting arms of their families, they entered a kill zone from which there was no route of egress, no enemy to return fire on. Back home was a new kind of killing field.

Some Marines adjusted well to being back. A few of the old timers took it in stride with such grace they made it look easy. Schleur moved in with his girlfriend and started going to college while managing a large gas station. Kistler started a marketing business that made signs. Riggan broke up with his fiancée and moved in with Low. Not everyone adjusted so well though, and the ones that did never seemed to be Machine Gunners. Our twenty-five-person-strong section could only serve as bad examples, in lectures that other platoons' leaders would give to their Marines. We never connected the dots from our behavior to consequences; sometimes, terrible things happened to us, of absolutely no fault of our own. Most fell back on the old idiom Sergeant Prockop had often said in Iraq: "It's the nature of the beast."

Everyone was drinking heavily. Just as when we were in Iraq, some of our problems were so universal there was no use trying to talk to each other about them. If any one of us had the answer, we surely would have applied it to our own life. Lowery found out his wife had been cheating on him all deployment while systematically draining his bank account. He ended up left with nothing but a divorce for his work overseas and a sob story as old as soldiering. Hawkins ended his engagement with his long-time girlfriend and hit the bottle. Ulrich broke up with his girlfriend, then they got back together, then broke up again—I lost track after a while.

We had ample opportunity to observe each other's lives and compare them to our own because young Marines tended to stick together post deployment. Dark days were upon us, this much was certain, and I couldn't figure out why. I lived in a college town where I was enrolled at the local university as an English major. Hawkins lived in the same city, went to the same college, and often we found solace at the bar together.

I didn't know why my girlfriend had left me again—never considering the thirty pounds I'd put on from drinking constantly or my ill temper—and was trying to figure it out one night as I drank whiskey to make it all go away. It never occurred to me that maybe it wasn't fair to expect a twenty-one-year-old to be faithful for my thirteen-month deployment—three months mobilizing, nine in country, one month demobilizing. It must not have occurred to Brandon or Hawkins, either, as we drank. But Brandon seemed to know more than he was telling us. I grew aware of it slowly at first as I sat beside him at the bar in a stupor. Brandon was Hawkins' friend from way back, a pudgy farm kid with a blond buzz cut and an easy smile. Hawkins and I had started going out and meeting up with others—sometimes men we'd served with, sometimes not. As I talked about my heartbreak I could feel Brandon wanting to say something, so I just asked him if he knew anything, because he'd been friends with my ex.

"I think she cheated on you with that one Bosnian guy that's in my grade," Brandon said. "What's his name? I forget now."

Blurry-eyed, I looked at him. "With who?"

"I never knew she cheated with that guy," Hawkins said. "I've hung out with that motherfucker since we've been back. I always liked him."

"Yeah, I know who you're talking about," I said. "I've always liked him too." The guy I was thinking of had been nice to me ever since I got back, but maybe it was because he'd been fucking my girlfriend and felt bad.

"She said they pretty much had sex," Brandon said. "I mean, did everything but sex, but might as well have."

"What the fuck," I said.

"You never told me that," Hawkins said, then looked at me. "I didn't know, man."

"That fucking bitch!" I yelled, throwing the tumbler in my hand against the wall. The sound of glass breaking made me smile, reminding me I was still strong.

The bartender wasn't too happy about me breaking a glass in the bar, but I told him to shut up and pour me another, and he did. I think the bartender had seen us around before, knew we were veterans and heard us talking. He tried being nice.

"What are you boys doing tonight?" the bartender asked.

Hawkins downed his shot and looked up at him with the dead, glassy eyes. "What the fuck does it matter?" he said, slamming down the shot glass so hard it broke.

"You guys gotta get outta here," the barkeep said. "I don't want any trouble, but you guys gotta leave."

We staggered out onto the street in a pack that spread out to take up the sidewalk and part of the road. A few more veterans had come to join us drinking, showing up just as we got kicked out. I recognized one of them, Allen, by his military haircut and posture. He'd done a couple of tours of Iraq. I liked Allen because Allen knew the score, just like me and Hawkins did. The kids that surrounded us in the crowded bar district of this college town had never earned their way. Most of them still lived off mommy and daddy's money. They didn't know a goddamn thing about war and didn't care to. They were gutless pukes who didn't know to show us respect because we'd done something with ourselves and made sacrifices for our country, for them. The more I thought about it as I staggered down the street, the angrier I became. Not just about the college kids or some guy cheating with my ex while I was gone, but the way civilians acted like the ramifications were all part of the job.

"What the fuck do these motherfuckers know, huh?" I asked no one in particular. I couldn't walk straight and didn't try to.

"Not a goddamn thing, Big Head," Hawkins said. "That's for sure." It sounded like he'd said, "mush fur shurr," at the end. I knew what he meant though.

Hawkins took the lead and walked our group into a bar a few blocks away from the one we'd just gotten kicked out of. I was the last one in the group through the door or would have been if there hadn't been a girl with high cheekbones and delicate features standing outside, smoking a cigarette. She reminded me of every other woman who'd ever cheated. She kept talking to a guy in Timberland boots and a hip-hop snap-back cap. I stopped and stared at her for a second.

"Shut up, slut," I said.

"What did you just call me," she said, recoiling.

"You fucking heard me, bitch," I said.

She looked from me, to the man standing by her, then back to me. It must have become obvious the man she had been talking to wasn't going to stand up to the drunken brute swaying in the breeze who'd just confronted her, so she spoke again.

"I'm going to go in there and get my boyfriend and tell him you said that," she said. "He'll beat you up."

"Listen," I said. "You go in there and get your boyfriend and you bring him out here. I'll kick his fucking ass."

The girl turned and stormed inside. I looked at the man she'd been talking to and he nervously smiled in return.

"Fucking slut," I said again, then lit a cigarette.

The man nodded, laughing a small laugh as he took a few steps away from me.

I flicked the cigarette at his feet and walked into the bar, so drunk I completely forgot I'd just called a girl a slut and offered to kick her boyfriend's ass. As I walked over to the bar and ordered a beer, I noticed a girl who looked vaguely familiar flitting from boy to boy, hurriedly whispering what sounded like an angry plea in their ears. There was a brief stir amongst a group and finally Hawkins was approached at the bar by one of them.

"Did you call that girl names?" the college kid asked, five of his friends standing behind him.

Hawkins turned from the bar, his over-six-foot linebacker frame towering above the people around him. He took a second before he answered, smiled real big.

"Yeah, I did," Hawkins said. "Want to go outside and fight?"

The boy nodded. Hawkins looked at me and I knew all I needed to. We were going outside. After filing out of the bar, I turned to face the kid who'd confronted Hawkins, not realizing one of his friends had waited a second to follow the two groups out; I was blindsided by a punch to the ear. Brandon and Allen let their fists fly. Hawkins picked someone up by the throat and threw him against the wall where he crumpled like a rag doll. The air whirred with knuckles and popped when the blows connected with eyes, teeth, and heads.

The next thing I knew, Hawkins was on top of the guy who'd hit me and I stood behind him. White stars trailed through my vision from the punch to my ear. Every time Hawkins' piston of an arm drew back, I'd lean over him and punch the kid in the face—the kid's head kept hitting the concrete in a *knock-knock, knock-knock* rhythm. We moved with the unison of men who'd trained to fight together, fluid and harmonious. After a few seconds of this, the kid's left eye had already swollen into a thick knot and his lips looked like chicken liver. To my right, someone was yelling. I hit the kid one more time, hard, then looked toward the voice.

"Stop! You've got to stop!" a young man was yelling.

Out of the corner of my eye, I barely caught his slim build swimming in a hooded sweatshirt, glasses reflecting the streetlights.

"What the fuck did you just say to me, motherfu—" I started to ask, but trailed off as I turned to look at him. The man had a huge pit bull with him that was straining against its collar, snarling.

"I called the cops," the man said. "If you don't leave him alone, I'm letting the dog go."

I straightened up and surveyed the situation. Brandon and Allen were standing there watching Hawkins punch the kid in the face, over and over. The college kids who first accosted us had fled into the night. The man with the big, snarling dog stood looking at me with a fear in his eyes I hadn't seen since Iraq. I didn't blame him one bit; watching two men work as one to demolish a kid's face was something he'd probably only seen in movies.

"Hawkins," I said.

He didn't listen the first time, so I yelled his name again and he finally looked up at me. He was covered with blood. It was all over him, staining his shirt and speckling his face. His fists looked like he'd been smashing grapes.

"We've got to get out of here," I said, panic creeping into my voice. "The cops are coming."

We ran and no one tried to stop us. But we couldn't outrun the war. I followed Hawkins as he weaved through back alleys all the way to Brandon's house, where we cleaned up the best we could. I borrowed one of Brandon's shirts and threw mine away for the drive home. We stood in a small circle and talked about what had happened. No one said it was my fault; they just didn't care. It hadn't entered anyone's mind to assign blame. This was just another accident that managed to happen to us, like a car crash or lightning striking.

* * *

BUT LIGHTNING KEPT striking. The next week it was a different bar and a different fight. This time some guy was pretending to be in the Air Force, either to impress us or to pick up women, and Allen couldn't abide. Hawkins and I tried everything to quiet the situation. Well, that is to say we tried everything we were willing, which amounted to buying everyone a car bomb. I figured that a pint of Guinness with a shot of my favorite Irish whiskey and some chocolate liqueur for flavor would make everyone see that it wasn't worth fighting over. I didn't want to get kicked out of the bar so early in the night and we were running out of places to drink. But after taking down the concoction, Allen wanted to fight even more.

"He doesn't have the right security clearance," Allen said.

"What?" I said. I had no idea what he was talking about.

"That lying cocksuck doesn't know what the fuck he's talking about—he doesn't have the security clearance right. I asked him what kind he had and he got it wrong," Allen said.

Hawkins saw us talking and made his way over from the bar. We stopped talking to wait for him and Allen took the opportunity to make scary faces at the offending fraud and his friends.

"Big Head," Hawkins said. "That guy has it all wrong. Don't you see? His facts aren't straight. It's like how a Marine would never get his MOS wrong. This clown is just running around lying to everyone. What would we do if he was lying about being a Marine?"

I nodded. I wasn't sure what I was agreeing with, but I nodded anyway because whatever they did I would go along with it. If one of us fought, we all fought. I knew damn well we'd mop the floor with them.

Hawkins and Allen walked over to the faux airman and his group of three friends. I didn't follow though; I'd agreed to fight but didn't want to help start it. I was drunk and things weren't adding up. What if Allen had heard wrong? What if the faker was just too embarrassed to say he was in ROTC? I couldn't hear what was said, but saw Hawkins duck his head down to ask the offender a question. Then I heard Allen.

"You're a liar," he said. "You aren't in the Air Force."

The faker was built like a small wrestler and he didn't seem scared of Allen or Hawkins. I couldn't hear what was said next but he must have swung on Allen, or at least it was easier to think that, because a fight erupted right there at the bar. Allen fell to the ground holding someone while Hawkins' arm worked its piston motion into faces. The fight spilled out onto the street with the fraudulent airman and his friends fleeing and us in pursuit. Hawkins led the charge after them down the sidewalk and briefly we caught up. In those last few moments, Allen slammed a head into a parking meter and Hawkins swung wildly, denting in an SUV's quarter panel. The thick of Hawkins' forearm connected with the lying braggart's face and sent him flying, the torn-off front of Hawkins' shirt in his clawing hand.

I'd gotten turned around just before the clash, taking a right around a car when I should have taken a left, losing just enough time to watch helplessly. The fray gave me great anxiety for the safety of my friends, but at the same time I felt relieved to sit this one out—relief followed by shame for being on the sideline. When I closed the short distance, the boys we were fighting turned and ran, this time with urgency.

"Fucking cowards," Hawkins said, then he screamed it as loud as he could. "You fucking cowards!"

Allen was panting and leaning up against a trash bin. He looked like he'd caught a couple of shots to the face but would be all right. Hawkins had blood on him again.

"Are you all right?" I asked him.

"Of course," Hawkins said like I was being silly. He looked at me, a giant grin spread across his face.

"Kind of like being back in the shit, isn't it?" he asked me.

I threw my head back and let out laughter that boomed down the street, then doubled over with my hands on my knees. The anxiety I'd felt rushed out, mixed with the relief and the shame. I laughed because it felt good, just like during some of the worst times in

Iraq. It was the same feeling of release. When I finally stood erect again, I wiped tears from my eyes.

"Maybe a little bit," I said. "Back in the shit."

After we left to avoid talking to the police, I wondered aloud to both Allen and Hawkins how long we could keep going like this. They just looked at me strangely like I'd had too much to drink and was being emotional.

"Are you all right?" asked Allen.

"Yeah, he's fine," Hawkins answered for me. "You don't have to worry about us."

* * *

THE NEXT WEEKEND, Hawkins put someone in the hospital. He told me the day after it happened. He'd been over at a friend's place and one of his buddies had run out of beer, so Hawkins took one out of a stranger's six-pack while looking him dead in the face.

"The guy started to say something and I told him we should go outside," Hawkins told me. His voice sounded scared over the phone.

"So, what happened?" I asked.

"I was so mad," Hawkins said. "I got on top of him and just kept hitting him in the face, over and over. When I stopped, he was just lying there in his own blood ..."

Hawkins voice cracked.

"Did you kill him?" I asked.

"He'll live," Hawkins said. "But I fucked his face up pretty good. I would have gone to jail, but my dad knew some of the cops. The guy could still press charges, though."

An ambulance had come. Hawkins took a picture of the guy whose face he'd just pounded in as paramedics loaded him into the back of the vehicle and posted the picture to social media. I'm not sure why, maybe as a cry for help. Hawkins disappeared for a while after that. Something he'd seen that night had scared him; maybe it was the kid's face he'd tenderized or maybe it was the look in everyone else's eyes as he walked back into the party. Whatever it was, he got back together with his ex-fiancée and stopped going out.

* * *

I DIDN'T STOP though. Hawkins' situation had nothing to do with me, of that much I was certain. Somehow, I separated Hawkins' problem with violence from my own. Within a month, I was completely shit-faced again, meeting another Marine, Sergeant Helm, for a drink at one of the bars where all the college kids drank. I'd shaved my hair into a mohawk and wore cut-off digital camo shorts and a tie-dye shirt.

"I can't believe you did that to your head," Helm said. "I don't even want to be seen with you right now."

I liked the mohawk. Having a fin on my head kept people away.

"Fuck off," I said. "Who gives a fuck? Let's drink."

After a half-dozen whiskey drinks, Helm and I decided to go to another bar. We walked down the street past the local Irish pub, just in time to see a curvy bartender I knew push some little guy out the door and scream at him.

"You're kicked out!" she yelled.

"Why?" the little guy asked with a weird smile on his face.

"Stop being a fucking faggot," she said before disappearing back into the bar.

Helm and I had stopped to watch this unfold and now the little guy, about a head shorter than me and two shorter than Helm, turned to us. He still had that stupid smile on his face. It made me so mad. It reminded me of Smith's smile, back at Hob. I just wanted to break it.

"Fuck you," I said to him.

"How was I being a faggot?" the little guy asked me.

He walked with Helm and I down the block and I told him what I thought. I told him that anyone who is creepy to a woman was a shitbag and that he was stupid, ugly, small, weak, and that I hated his creepy smile. The kid stopped walking.

"Oh yeah," he said. "Well then why don't you fight me?"

"Fuck off," I said.

"Why are you walking away if I'm such a faggot?" he asked.

My pulse spiked, making my vision twist for a second. I lifted my arm and stopped Helm dead in his tracks beside me.

"Why are we walking away?" I asked Helm.

"I don't know," Helm answered. "That's a good question."

When I turned around the boy was already in a fighting stance with his right leg back and his shoulders squared on me, fists balled in front of him.

I approached him with a smile on my face. He lashed out with a jab and quick right to my temple, but I was too drunk to feel them. The little guy reset his stance and braced, ready for my advance. I grabbed him by the neck and cocked my arm back to hammer his face until he died. But I couldn't do it. For a second I blacked out and it was like I was back in Iraq, standing at the traffic circle by FOB Riviera with my rifle to a driver's head, whispering *forward* as I flipped the safety off.

The little guy hit me twice, quick with two hard rights, and I was back. I grabbed him and threw him on the curb as hard as I could, hoping to break his ribs. He got up, unfazed, and I backpedaled into the street. The little guy followed, swinging and missing. I grabbed him and threw him down on the ground shoulder first—hard. Cars backed up quickly; it was a busy Friday night on a college main street. Letting him start the fight paid off, as people got out of their vehicles to run to my aid.

"Someone hold him," I said. "Or I'll kill him. I swear it."

A man who'd exited a red Ford F-150 grabbed hold of the little guy, who tried wrenching away, only to have other sets of hands laid on him.

He screamed a question again and again.

"Am I a fucking faggot now?"

The last I saw of him, a group of people were holding him as he struggled, their forms lit by the Ford's head-lights. Helm and I melted into the crowd of onlookers and beat a hasty retreat into another bar, where we holed up until I insulted the manager and got kicked out. We walked home in good spirits.

"Hell of a night," Helm said.

"It's like the war is following us," I said.

"What?" Helm said, looking at me sharply.

"Doesn't it seem that way to you?" I asked. "Like it's stalking us. Through streets, bars, restaurants. In our dreams?"

Helm didn't have an answer. He just stared ahead. Helm's way of dealing with things had been to stockpile ammunition, in preparation for a distant doomsday. He firmly believed that every Marine was fine, that there was no way any of us had PTSD. He didn't see the irony when he talked about building defensive positions on his family's farm.

We weren't the only ones. Swede, a Machine Gunner, had gone out drinking hard in Omaha and had a flashback in front of a crowd. He was waiting in line at a food stand after the bar closed when he lost it.

"Bring me some chai!" Swede demanded of the man running the food stand.

"I don't have any chai," the man said. "This is a gyro stand."

"Get me some chai right fucking now, haji!" Swede said.

"I'm not even Arabic," the man said. "I'm Greek."

The man pointed to the sign above the stand that noted GREEK GYROS. A crowd was gathering around them. The bar closing had created a potential flashpoint with the sudden influx of drunk pedestrians.

"Fuck you!" Swede screamed. "Your name is Muhammad! Now get me some fucking chai!"

Someone out of the crowd handed Swede their Starbucks latte, hoping it would calm him down. Swede didn't want to calm down, though. Some friends of Swede's, a few Marines, appeared out of the throng of people to drag him away.

A less amusing and much darker episode happened to Swede after the Marine Corps Ball celebration. Swede's date decided to clean his clock in public and to his credit he didn't lose his mind, but he did throw her against a wall; from what I understood from those Marines who counted Swede a close friend, this wasn't the first time she'd been abusive. I'd never been able to pry the details out of him. Comments I made like "Golden Gloves Champ!" and "Mortal Kombat!" created a rift between Swede and me, especially when instead of recanting I stepped up my attack. There was little else to do at the monthly drills we had to attend while coasting out of our military contracts, so we occupied ourselves with tormenting each other. The MachineGuns squad bay—a small room packed with lockers and a single, dingy sofa—became known to the rest of the platoons as a place of open hostility. Most Marines avoided talking to any of us at drill; when we were all together it was especially bad.

With over twenty Machine Gunners in the section, there were new stories at every drill about brawls, bar girls, heartache, bad dreams, and drinking. Even the quiet Marines got in fights. Larkin laid out his mom's boyfriend and Smith settled a dispute concerning the validity of his service by punching a redneck in the face.

It was a different kind of war now, one without Final Lines of Departure or mission briefings. The squad was largely leaderless after Prockop transferred units, not that leadership at drill would have helped us in our day-to-day lives. The unit lost Marines to jail as people picked up drug habits or became criminals. It didn't register with any of us that we could just as easily go to jail from fighting as from stealing a car for drugs. Some Marines were broken from deployment and started to process out of the Corps—I was one of them. The weight of ammunition, weapons, and body armor had compacted some of the discs in my back, making it difficult to do the strenuous hikes the Corps required. It was strange to see my Marine brothers going off to ranges on weekend drills while I stayed behind with a dozen other walking wounded, and stranger still when unit leadership acted angry with us for being injured, as though we had any control over it. They believed the bullshit about Marines being tougher than pain, that we couldn't wear down to nubs of who we'd been.

The bonds of war loosened the longer we were stateside. The once-a-month drills came to seem a contrivance to get together and "remember when." But the Marines of MachineGuns either didn't want to talk about the deployment or thought it was a complete waste of time that had cost the Battalion lives and America countless billions. What bound us together was misery and fear. We collectively hated Echo now and loathed the staff. Most of the officers had moved on after deployment, either dispersing to different reserve units or going back to the fleet. The fighting force of active-duty troops seemed so removed from us now after deployment, like we had been left behind at some shit post in the middle of nowhere and they didn't care what happened to any of us.

The staff stayed, however. We hated them and they hated us. The once-shared burden of war removed, the staff became like fat old men ordering us around.

Gunny Vance started implying that, at one point, he'd been a part of a Marine Recon unit, the absolute elite of the Marine Corps world. He only ever did this with Marines that were new joins or junior enough that the shiny gold scuba bubble and flashing jump wings filled them with awe. Rose and I were shocked that one of the senior enlisted cadre would falsify his service. We decided to ask Riggan and Low about it, in a garage of Fort Des Moines that had been designated the smoke pit.

"Do you guys ever remember Gunny Vance telling Special Forces stories before?" I asked them both.

"Vance is telling people he was in Recon?" Riggan asked.

"What a fucking boot," Low said, using the pejorative term for new joins. Boots would lie about their experiences to impress you, try to make you think they had seen some shit.

Rose and I stood silent for a few seconds, puffing on our cigarettes, looking back and forth from Low to Riggan.

"So, was he ever in Recon or what?" I asked.

"Fuck no," Riggan said. "He went to jump school and whatever diving school."

"Maybe he went through some kind of training or something," Low said.

"Big Head is the one that heard him talking," Rose said.

"He said something about taking a beach," I told them. "With Recon."

"You have got to be fucking kidding me," Low said.

Riggan shook his head in disgust.

"Funny how this hasn't come up before now in the entire six and a half years I've worked with Gunny Vance and two tours of Iraq together," Riggan said. "Never once have I heard this."

Vance making up war stories reminded me of Prockop's unprofessional conduct in Iraq, but in a different way. Prockop was long gone by then, having fled to our sister unit in Omaha to escape the scorn of a squad who'd deemed his leadership lacking. A few days of drill wasn't long enough to punish any of us when we ignored or disrespected him. He stuck it out for a few drills, but that was it. In the absence of NCOs, Marines were promoted.

Riggan and Low were both now NCOs of the United States Marine Corps, the backbone of America's greatest fighting force. Low was a Sergeant and Riggan was a Corporal. Someone from their squad had told me they'd moved in together after Riggan broke it off with his fiancée and they were partying like old times again. The only past faux pas of newly-appointed NCOs I brought up was McShane and Andreason shooting cows from Post Two, back at FOB Riviera. At first, they both denied it, but then McShane broke down laughing. He thought it was hilarious that they'd been killing the local Iraqi's livestock while bored on post.

"Big Head, I used to laugh so hard when you would call in shots fired from Post Four and the COC wouldn't believe you!" McShane said.

"You motherfucker," I said. "That's some sick shit, killing those people's livestock. You ruined lives because you were bored and you think it's funny."

"Oh yeah?" McShane said. "I don't remember ever putting a gun to a kid's head like you did."

During a supply run to an Iraqi Police station, a young, mentally challenged Iraqi child of seven or eight had stood screaming at my turret gunner from the middle of the street. I told him to stop, but when he didn't I stormed out of the driver's seat and leveled my pistol at his head. It was the kind of story that made new joins and civilians look at me like a monster.

"Whoa now," Mundell said, interrupting our exchange as he ripped gear out of his locker.

McShane got the same shit-eating grin he always got on his face and laughed his booming, deep laugh.

"Big Head getting screamed at for calling in shots fired and the COC chewing his ass when he wouldn't back down after we said there wasn't any is one of my favorite memories of Iraq," McShane said.

Only the veterans in my squad called me by my call sign anymore. Little things like this were the relics of our former brotherhood. Non-veterans could call me Big Head but their tongues would never suss out its intimacy like the Marines who had been ready to die for me by the Euphrates. For a while, when Echo first got back, everyone lost their thousand-yard vacant stare. But then the newness of everything wore off and we found that our memories of home didn't match up with the reality we had returned to, while at the same time Iraq and everything about it became a memory so sharp it cut into our dreams. I felt like the Marine I'd left behind in Iraq was more real than the civilian I was supposed to come back and become.

But then I got medically separated from the Corps and lost the thing that connected my past to my present, an existential crisis to add to a litany: recurring dreams and night terrors, mood swings, lots of anger, a general distrust of others, hypervigilance, and the idea that the government was watching my every move, cataloging everything. I couldn't relate anymore to sports, television, radio, bars, or materialism. When I returned, I'd felt detached from the culture around me and there was no reintegration in a larger sense. I didn't believe anymore—in any of it. I didn't believe in my people's government or their God or any of the petty things they seemed to cling to for dear life every day.

I pursued education, taking refuge in books, and wondered even more why people couldn't see what was happening around them, how the blinders were on so tight all they could manage was a blank stare at flashing screens. That's when I noticed the stare on them, but it was different than it had been on the faces of Marines in war-torn Iraq. Stateside, the look didn't manifest outward, but inward. I couldn't make them believe that Iraq was real—not really. The disconnect in them was the opposite that it was for me; they'd never lost the belief in country and still believed all their bourgeois problems were real. As much as I tried, I couldn't convince them we should bring the troops home and as much as some people tried to convince me everything was all right I wouldn't be swayed either. I stayed the course of reason when examining the actions of my nation and countrymen. I took a personal inventory of what I believed to be true and I gave the best account I could.

SOLDIER'S HEART

THE DREAMS CONTINUED AFTER I ROTATED BACK home to Des Moines, Iowa, in August 2008. Long after I was done fighting the war in Iraq, it continued to rage on in my head. But it wasn't until mid 2012 that I couldn't take it anymore. I thought back over the last four years of my life, carefully counting them out on fingers. I wondered if the VA would lock me up. I tried to sound stoic when I called them for help. Right away, the operator asked if I was having any suicidal thoughts, *suicidal ideations*. I said, "No."

I said no because I'd asked around before I called the VA. Older veterans had told me that there were two questions I'd be asked: "Are you going to harm yourself?" and "Are you going to harm anyone else?" The answer to both questions, those older vets informed me, had better be a definitive "no."

That day, I didn't mention the piece I'd written for the literary magazine at my university. It was about a veteran named Frank who struggled with suicidal ideation. He'd planned it out in his head, laid out the tools, but then the urge ebbed into his unconscious. I'd explained to the magazine's editor, a professor at the university, that the piece was creative non-fiction. I was Frank. Still, I didn't want my school's counselors calling me. I saw them as people that had gone straight from high school to college and then right on to their careers—riding desks. I didn't want them trying to coach me through the aftermath of war. I didn't want to have to explain episodes of utter despair or how a depression so complete would drive me to seek solace in sleep, only to find my nightmares waiting.

"We'll get you help, son," the operator said.

No one from the VA ever called me back. I waited a few weeks and called again, this time insisting on setting up an appointment with someone in the mental health department. When I eventually made it to a mental health evaluation, an intake person asked if I felt like I'd blocked out any of my experiences in Iraq. I sat stunned for a few seconds. No one had ever asked me that before. The idea had never crossed my mind. What if my unconscious mind had kept things from me? I considered this possibility for a few minutes and my gut told me the answer was "yes." I thought about it in the days following, not obsessively, but my mind kept wandering back to the question.

NO MARINE EVER thinks he's going to be the one who's fucked up—and that's exactly how I thought about it too, that there would be maybe one or two people that came back and had problems readjusting. No Marine ever thinks most of his squad isn't going to be able to sleep because of severe insomnia. No one thinks they'll have flashbacks or nightmares that continue in a loop forever. Now, our backs are bent from the war. Now, there are whispered conversations on the phone late at night.

"Are you having visions?"

"Do the nightmares follow you?"

"What is happening to us?"

We speak about the men we were, then of regrets. Eventually, the conversation turns to the VA hospitals and how the scandals on the news show veterans' healthcare is as fucked up as the military. I already feel the real Iraq slipping back into people the same way insurgents ducked down side streets and faded into crowds when they saw us patrolling, all armor-plated and machine gun wielding. In memory, Iraq has transformed into the Pirates of the Caribbean ride at Disneyland—no fear, all spectacle.

AN OLD-TIMER SAT in the waiting room. He gibbered to himself, white froth and spittle at the corner of his mouth. Then he started whining in a high pitch that reminded me of the dogs in Iraq. He rocked back and forth while he gnawed on his arm. I turned to the guy sitting next to me and gave him a look like, *What the fuck?* No answer. This guy was a million miles away, retreated into himself, all the switches for emotions shut off and held down. The only other person in the lobby was some retired Army brass, who had finally convinced his grandson to talk to a professional. I listened to them as I watched the gibbering man convulse as he rocked, chewing on the top of his wrist, hyperventilating.

"I want to get my old uniform out with all the ribbons," the young man said. "I haven't worn it in forever."

The grandson talked like he was just going to wear it around for no reason, like it was normal to wear a military dress uniform to the bar in the middle of Iowa. The granddad didn't seem to want to encourage dress up.

"Last night, when you called and told me you were ready to get some help, I was glad," the old man said. "I knew you needed to talk to someone for a while now, but a man has to be ready. You can't force it." I looked from the older man to the grandson and imagined how grueling a wait it had been for each of them.

❋   ❋   ❋

AT FIRST, THE broken images that emerged held no relation to the idea that I might be blocking out a memory from Iraq. But one night, shortly after I'd called the VA, I woke up in a cold sweat with the image of an Iraqi child stumbling away from me and I knew something had changed. It felt like an accusation had been leveled at me. What had I done? I couldn't remember. But as I lay shivering in soaked sheets from the night terror, I knew I wouldn't have to wait long—my sins would find me out. The children started weighing heavily on my mind.

The Iraqi children would run out from the shacks, huts, and houses to ask the Marines, patrolling on foot or in vehicles, if they had any chocolate. The children would scream the word over and over in an accent that made the word end in "lot" instead of "lit." Sometimes they'd throw in the word "football" in case we'd brought along any of the soccer balls shipped to us by people back home. At first Marines—myself included—had been friendly with the children, handing out soccer balls and chocolate when they asked.

Sometimes, I'd even give children lit cigarettes to finish for me. Iraqi children started smoking around the age of three or four. They often had tough calluses on their feet instead of shoes and those deft feet bore them over streams of raw sewage and filth. They moved in packs; sometimes a larger child would lead the pack. They fought over candy like it was the only food they'd get to eat, like they were starving in the streets. Their clothing was almost always threadbare, but sometimes bore the logos of American pop culture—50 Cent, Pepsi, the L.A. Lakers, and others. The children seemed like miniature adults to me, full of guile and malice, rather than vessels of innocence and naiveté. They'd swarm us, asking for food, trying to tear the gear off our body and pick our pockets.

When I remembered how the children swarmed us, I knew with a sickening certainty I'd been blocking out the image of someone striking a child. The idea that I'd seen Marines striking children surfaced in fragments at first, as if through a thick haze. But *who* had I seen strike a child? There'd been one patrol when we'd gone static and we'd been swarmed by dozens of children. No one discharged a weapon to scare them off. We didn't want to give away our location to every insurgent in the vicinity.

We were in Azurdia, once a lush suburb of Fallujah, where rich men built enormous houses between the Euphrates and Fallujah's power plant and train station. I remembered how I had pulled my pistol and waved it at the kids' faces around me, scattering them. And I remembered seeing Marines punch children in the head.

Opaline blue eyes turn resolute as nail heads. Doc Bance rears his arm back and smashes it down on the skull of any child who tries to get into his pockets. The thump of the hard-plastic knuckles of his gloves, knocking down kids, is vivid in my memory; then I'm back there, standing outer security during the halt. My right hand hangs at my side, pistol pointing at the ground as I watch Bance lash out again and again. A few other Marines start doing the same. The children flee; their shrieks and yelps remind me of dogs.

After this recollection, my heart grew heavier. How many other memories was I suppressing? The fragmented images swirled through my dreams—a war-torn street, streams of raw sewage, Iraqi children, Marines patrolling, trash everywhere. A child falls to the ground—but now I distrusted that initial recollection.

It had not been Bance; inexplicably, I knew this. So, who had been the *first* person I'd seen striking a child? Awake late at night, unable to sleep after dreams had awakened me, I'd rest my head in my hands and think. I examined the fragments one by one.

Early in the deployment, my unit had favored foot patrols over vehicle-mounted patrols, so that gave me a rough time and place for the event. I needed to remember where and when I'd seen that first child struck. We would have been on foot then. This is what

I remembered of those early foot patrols: the school and hospital riddled with fist-sized holes. These institutions bore the heaviest scars while most of the other buildings bore only pocks, left from smaller rounds. The mansion by the Euphrates belonging to one of Saddam's sons had been torn open by several tons of guided munitions. Iraqis had cowered as we raised our hands to them in salutation. The unit before us had lost men to insurgent machine guns and our Marines responded—indiscriminately slaying Iraqis on the street—but never found the culprits or their guns. In my memory, I imagine that unit left a heavy mark on the minds of the Iraqis that survived the onslaught.

I tried to relive the scene. I sensed it was important. I needed to know when the first blow had been directed at a child and who'd thrown it. *Not Bance, not Bance,* I thought as I massaged my temples.

Fremil. I saw Fremil pull out a police baton and swing it at a child's head, but he missed, too slow in all his gear to touch the lithe child. Trash. Marines patrolling, children swarming them. Fremil raised the baton, the child screamed. But Fremil wasn't the first to strike a child.

I lifted my head from my hands and started to pace a well-worn trail through my apartment. I needed to know. The fragments wouldn't come together and I couldn't make them. Marines patrolling, plastic bags snapping in the wind, children swarming, one falls. Not knowing was making me sick. I couldn't remember.

I began to wonder why I couldn't remember this one incident. I had plenty of other memories of Marines acting out in Iraq—doing drugs, group masturbating, drinking, fighting, setting farmers' fields ablaze, shooting cows and dogs. Why was this one buried so deep in my subconscious?

The street, where had it been? The trash—everywhere—provided no clues; garbage coated every Iraqi urban area like a film. But it wouldn't have been likely we'd walked the streets of Fallujah or Habbaniyah; there, many streets were turned into aqueducts and used by rural communities to water their fields of wheat and alfalfa. That narrowed it down to Saqlawiyah, a town hit hard by the war, nestled into a bend in the Euphrates about fifteen kilometers west of Fallujah.

Exhausted and sheened in sweat, I made a stiff drink before slipping back into bed. I drifted off. Finally, the fragments came together.

✳ ✳ ✳

I'M IN SHADYVILLE, a borough of Saqlawiyah, with its bustling market and ditches swollen with sewage, dog carcasses floating atop. I walk down the garbage-covered street. In front of me, Mundell and Ulrich's heads move as if on swivels. Children, mostly barefoot with distended bellies, run out from the neighborhood across from the market, near the minaret. I ignore their cries, try to look everywhere at once while I cling to my rifle. Many residents of Shadyville are marked with deep scars from bullets and shrapnel, webs crisscrossing their necks and faces. The kids, ages maybe four to seven, run up to Mundell's lanky figure and start yanking on his gear, trying to tear off pouches or his gas mask satchel.

Mundell swats at them lazily, kicks dirt after them when they skitter away. The children do the same to Ulrich and he just laughs and keeps walking.

My anger grows as I watch the pack of children harass Ulrich and Mundell. I want the children to fear me. I want them to respect and venerate me. Two of them turn from Ulrich and rush at me. I yell at one and he jumps away. The other holds firm though, looks up at me; his eyes fill with defiance. I snarl at the street urchin who thinks he can defy me. He holds his ground and I know he won't step aside, that I'll have to move him. My grip on my weapon tightens and my rifle barrel strikes across his face, sending the child stumbling. The child catches himself before he falls and comes at me, fists raised.

Are his balled hands raised in aggression or defense?

The rifle barrel hits the child on the side of his head, raising a deep purple welt on his cheek that looks like it might split open. The child drops to his knees, bawling, begging for me to stop. I shift my weight to my front foot, ready to deliver a kick to his jaw when a voice stops me.

"Big Head," Mundell shouts my call sign. "What are you doing?"

I look at the rifle barrel that had struck the child, follow the barrel up to my hands. I'd just hit a kid as hard as I could. I'd hit him in the head with the steel of my gun. I feel cold in the blazing kiln of the desert. I shiver. The boy I'd beaten staggers away, only with help from the other. I squeeze my eyes shut and see images like photo negatives—a street in Shadyville, pools of raw sewage, Iraqi children, rotting dog carcasses that burst open and writhe with maggots, Marines patrolling, trash everywhere. The child staggers—and when I open my eyes, I see Ulrich swat an eight-year-old to the ground.

* * *

I PUSHED FORWARD and pushed everything that had just happened deep inside me somewhere else. I didn't think of that scene again until five years later when I woke up from a dream, shivering in my own sweat, wondering what kind of monster would beat a starving child, a child begging for food. If I'd done this, other Marines had certainly done worse. What kind of nightmares visited them in the night?

I used to think it shameful for a person to end his own life. I thought that before I had my first flashback; I was driving home from the East Coast in the summer of 2012. I'd driven westbound from Vermont until turnpikes became highways, through late night into the pitch of early morning—zero dark thirty. The moon waxed in the sky, its stains showing dark against pale white. The road stretched out before me; I had hours to go. But suddenly, I was driving east. Puzzled, I searched for a road to turn around on and wondered how I'd managed to flip my trajectory across America's rust belt, to invert the simple course I'd set out on. I searched for a cigarette in the center console and when I looked up I was back in Iraq.

The ditches next to me deepened from gently sloping basins for excess rain into canals that plunged twenty feet with quick moving water at the bottom. Cattails and reeds grew tall, fed by the water, the tops waving outside my windows. The road in front of me, no longer paved with a yellow stripe down the center, transformed into a narrow, muddy road with deep ruts. Off to my left, I saw tracers twinkling in the night sky as they arced up and away from a machine gun in an errant burst. With the sound of gunfire far enough in the distance that it didn't worry me, I slowed down to try to get my bearings.

Was I still driving backward? Backward, instead of back east? Instead of turning around, I'd somehow been flipped. The ditch to my right moved out in front of me on the road; the road gave way and fell into the canal. I swerved sharply into the left lane, looking up at the last moment to see I was heading into oncoming traffic before I weaved back over into my lane. I took my foot off the gas pedal but I didn't hit the brake. Rain spattered against my windshield. I flicked on my wipers only to hear them grate across dry glass. I glanced down at my phone, cigarette dangling from my dry lips. I realized there was no one I could call for help. The car rolled to a stop. I told myself it would be safer to sit idle on a deserted country highway until I figured out what was going on.

This is it, I thought. I lit my cigarette. I told myself I needed to get out of the vehicle.

The compulsion to exit my car came from somewhere deep inside me, born in a time years past, back in Iraq when we'd exit the vics to face the unknown that lay outside the Humvee's armor plates. I took a long drag of my cigarette. Its cherry blazed a dull red that lit the two rectangles of my glasses. I wished my old team leader was with me—he'd know what to do—or my squad; with them, I could fight the world. My hand groped at my thigh. For a second, I thought I'd closed my fingers around the grip of my old service pistol, but my hand came up empty. I'd never been unarmed in Iraq before and I was scared.

I swung the door wide open, then yanked my hand back as the rain poured from the sky. The drops felt icy, but when I looked at my arm it was dry. The mud outside my door was Iraqi soil, churned up into sludge. I was in Iraq. I'd never been surer of anything in my life. I looked at the horizon and saw only a few tracers arc through the sky, the staccato report of the machine gun muffled. I wondered if the locals would remember my face, if the children had grown old enough to yearn for revenge. I stepped out into the puddle of mud.

But when I looked up, the horizon belonged to the American Midwest. I peered up at the sky and found the constellations familiar instead of strange. The road was solid and paved, the rain gone, the skyline clear of clouds and dark as the depths of the sea without a glimmer of tracers' flight. I let out a long sigh of relief.

I was back home.

Iraq, ten klicks west of Fallujah, sweeping the canal roads at night during a winter storm. I'd hated those patrols more than anything else, even more than the sewage and the rats. The dread that built up all day, knowing my squad was slated to leave the wire that night to patrol the network of narrow access roads flanked by irrigation canals and, finally, loading the trucks—everyone grim.

All the old feelings rolled through me, one by one, rocking me back and forth as I sat on the hood of my car, smoking.

❋ ❋ ❋

FINALLY, I WALKED with my shrink toward his office. "There's an individual in the waiting room," I said, choosing my words carefully. "He seems to be in great distress. I think he might require immediate attention."

"What's he doing?" my doctor asked.

"Acting like he's back on a battlefield somewhere and trying not to scream."

My doctor opened his office door. "Well, then he's in the right place." He looked at me with a grim smile as I took a seat in the familiar chair.

For the rest of the day all I thought about was that guy in the waiting room. I saw him staring into the past—blank expression masking his face while he cried. I'd forgotten what it looked like to see a man break. I wanted to go back for that guy, to join him on whatever battlefield he couldn't leave behind and fight to the end. But I couldn't help him now. Maybe no one could. Most important, I still had my own fight.

I REMEMBER MY dad taking our dog out behind the barn, after it got bit by a rabid raccoon and started acting strange. I'd protested. Couldn't something else be done? Couldn't we take our dog to the veterinarian or just let it run free in the woods? Maybe it would die on its own somewhere. Peaceful. Alone.

But my father persisted in his stoic logic. "What do you do with a rabid dog?" he asked.

When I didn't reply, he answered for me.

"You put it down."

But when he'd given me my first pellet gun it was with strict instructions to never shoot a songbird. He emphasized this, refusing to hand me the firearm until I promised. When I'd asked why, he told me it was for the same reason I should never chop down a tree that bore fruit unless I had to; these living things made the world a better place.

I am sick, but I sing. If not me, who else will remember dogs shrieking in the night, a pack turned in on itself like a writhing snake? Maybe if I share these nightmares, someone with similar dreams will take solace. Maybe that person will feel less alone. We are more than rabid dogs. Even in those pits of great distress and existential crisis, we are more than monsters. When I ask someone to envision me striking their child with a rifle barrel and they look at me like the harbinger of death, I know that, though my song sounds more like a piercing howl than something melodious, it needs to be heard. I hope that others hear before it is too late. But if they do cross over, I want them to know that I understand.

PUBLICATION ACKNOWLEDGMENTS

Every Man a Fortress—*Lunch Ticket*
Between the West Bank and the Sea—*Atticus Review*
Iron Heart—*The Rumpus*
Post Four—*Pithead Chapel*
River City—*Indianola Review*
White Whale—*Iowa Review, Jeff Sharlet Memorial Award for Veterans runner up*
Operation Iraqi Freedom—*Narrative, Sketch*
Accessory to Genocide—*Brevity*
Fear City—*Phoebe, Best American Essays shortlist 2016*
A Bridge to Nowhere—*War Lit & the Arts*
Two Shallow Graves—*The Florida Review, Best American Essays 2017*
Double Entendres—*Gulf Coast*
Short Timers—*Duende*
Soldier's Heart—selections from this chapter first appeared in *Chataqua* and *Burrow Press*

THIS BOOK IS ONE OF THE
MANY AVAILABLE FROM
UNIVERSITY OF HELL PRESS.
DO YOU HAVE THEM ALL?

by **Tyler Atwood**
an electric sheep jumps to greener pasture

by **John W Barrios**
Here Comes the New Joy

by **Eirean Bradley**
the I in team
the little BIG book of go kill yourself

by **Suzanne Burns**
Boys

by **Calvero**
someday i'm going to marry Katy Perry
i want love so great it makes Nicholas Sparks cream in his
pants

by **Nikia Chaney**
us mouth

by **Leah Noble Davidson**
Poetic Scientifica
DOOR

by **Rory Douglas**
The Most Fun You'll Have at a Cage Fight

by **Brian S. Ellis**
American Dust Revisited
Often Go Awry

by **Greg Gerding**
The Burning Album of Lame
Venue Voyeurisms: Bars of San Diego
Loser Makes Good: Selected Poems 1994
Piss Artist: Selected Poems 1995-1999
The Idiot Parade: Selected Poems 2000-2005

by **Lauren Gilmore**
Outdancing the Universe

by **Rob Gray**
The Immaculate Collection/The Rhododendron and Camellia Year Book (1966)

by **Joseph Edwin Haeger**
Learn to Swim

by **Lindsey Kugler**
HERE.

by **Wryly T. McCutchen**
My Ugly & Other Love Snarls

by **Michael McLaughlin**
Countless Cinemas

2/20

CPSIA information can be obtained
at www.ICGtesting.com
Printed in the USA
FSHW02n0257190918
52272FS

9 781938 753305